TRANSREALIST FICTION

**Recent Titles in Contributions to the
Study of Science Fiction and Fantasy**

TRANSREALIST FICTION

Writing in the Slipstream of Science

Damien Broderick

Contributions to the Study of Science Fiction and Fantasy,
Number 90

GREENWOOD PRESS
Westport, Connecticut • London

Library of Congress Cataloging-in-Publication Data

Broderick, Damien.
    Transrealist fiction : writing in the slipstream of science / by Damien Broderick.
        p.   cm.—(Contributions to the study of science fiction and fantasy, ISSN 0193–6875 ;
    no. 90)
    Includes bibliographical references and index.
    ISBN 0–313–31121–8 (alk. paper)
    1. Science fiction—History and criticism—Theory, etc.   2. Science fiction—
Authorship.   3. Fantastic, The, in literature.   4. Realism in literature.   5. Reality in
literature.   I. Title.   II. Series.
PN3433.5.B76   2000
809.3'8762—dc21   99–049691

British Library Cataloguing in Publication Data is available.

Library of Congress Catalog Card Number: 99–049691
ISBN: 0–313–31121–8
ISSN: 0193–6875

First published in 2000

Greenwood Press, 88 Post Road West, Westport, CT 06881
An imprint of Greenwood Publishing Group, Inc.
www.greenwood.com

Printed in the United States of America

The paper used in this book complies with the
Permanent Paper Standard issued by the National
Information Standards Organization (Z39.48–1984).

10 9 8 7 6 5 4 3 2 1

Copyright Acknowledgments

Grateful acknowledgment is given to the following sources for permission to quote material previously published or taken from the Internet: Nathan Bruso-vani; Mark E. Crosby, "A Protestation of Faith"; C. Mitch Hagmaier; Sylvia Kelso; Eugene Leitl; Susan Matthews; Amy Stout; Jo Walton; interviews with Rudy Rucker. Some parts of this book have appeared in somewhat different form in *Science Fiction Commentary* and *The New York Review of Science Fiction*.

Every reasonable effort has been made to trace the owners of copyright materials in this book, but in some instances this has proven impossible. The author and publisher will be glad to receive information leading to more complete acknowledgments in subsequent printings of the book and in the meantime extend their apologies for any omissions.

For John Clute

the world's finest science fiction critic

Contents

Introduction: Beyond Imagination

Eventually an imaginary world is entirely without interest.
—Wallace Stevens, *Opus Posthumous* (p. 175)

Transrealism means writing about your immediate perceptions in a fantastic way. The characters in a transreal book should be based on actual people [and hence] richer and more interesting. . . . My transreal novels aren't exactly autobiographical: I have never really left my body, climbed an infinite mountain, met a sphere from the fourth dimension, infected television with an intelligent virus, etc. But they are autobiographical in that many of the characters are modeled on family and friends—the main person of course being modeled on me. The science fictional ideas in my transreal fiction have a special role. They stand in for essential psychic events.
—Rudy Rucker, Interview with John Shirley,
"Introduction," *White Light*

In the mannered, funny tragicomic screenplay *Six Degrees of Separation*, John Guare's self-deluding scamster Paul (played by Will Smith) takes almost exactly the opposite tack from the transrealist prescription sketched above by its originator, writer and mathematician Rudy Rucker. Paul captivates his upper-middle-class victims, after feeding them an excellent pasta, with this coolly impassioned sermon, its text *The Catcher in the Rye*:

The imagination has been so debased that imagination—*being imaginative*—rather than being the lynch pin of our existence now stands as a synonym for something outside ourselves like Science fiction or some new use for tangerine slices on raw pork chops—what an imaginative summer recipe—and *Star Wars!* So *imaginative* and *Star Trek*—so imaginative! And *Lord of the Rings*—all those dwarves—so imaginative.[1]

Paul's own lurching impersonation—he passes himself off as the son of Sidney Poitier, who also famously and discomfitingly came to dinner—is, in its way, an impressive self-fashioning. "The imagination," he tells the Kittredges, whose home he has invaded, "has moved out of the realm of being our link, our most personal link, with our inner lives and the world outside that world—this world we share ... I believe that the imagination is the passport we create to take us into the real world" Guare, *Six Degrees of Separation*, (p. 41).

Unmasked as a fraud and impostor, Paul admits that this stirring Jungian outburst was filched from the "Graduation speech at Groton[2] two years ago" (p. 128). His own imaginative duplicity cannot hold up as a passport into that privileged corner of the real world he would like to enter. How much less effective, then, must be the nakedly spurious or ersatz kind of imagination that his borrowed speech scolds. *Science fiction, minimal culinary daring, hobbits*—these, Guare insinuates (with a suitable measure of unreliability and ambiguity) are more correctly seen as ways to avoid the self, the real. "To face ourselves," Paul tells his hosts, while doing nothing of the sort and therefore, in his inevitable fall, pointing the validity of his moral, "[t]hat's the hard thing. The imagination. That's God's gift to make the act of self-examination bearable" (p. 41).

We may find this persuasive, in its way, and yet—science fiction, *un*imaginative? How absurd! Perhaps not. In *The Statesman's Manual* (1816), Samuel Taylor Coleridge characterized imagination as "that reconciling and mediatory power, which incorporating the reason in images of the sense, and organising (as it were) the flux of the senses by the permanence and self-circling energies of the reason, gives birth to a system of symbols, harmonious in themselves, and consubstantial with the truths of which they are the conductors." This high-flown apotheosis might seem, to the convinced aficionado of sf (the mode's accepted friendly shorthand for science fiction, speculative fiction or science fantasy), a rather apt description of science fiction at its best—but Coleridge would not have thought so. Famously, he distinguished (in *Biographia Literaria* [1817] chapter IV) between *imagination* of this Miltonic order and a distinct faculty that he dubbed mere *fancy*.[3] Science fiction's invented worlds and characters, on this account, would be fanciful rather than truly imaginative.

Suppose that it is so. What solutions might an ambitious genre writer or reader find to remedy this deficit? (It might not, of course, be a deficit, but rather just a variant, or even a distinctive feature—as it is, perhaps, in the explicitly allegorical.) One broad class of answers seems to be emerging out of the often lazy or clichéd textual practices of "imaginative writing" in the sense Guare's Paul deplores. That answer, I will argue, comprises an inventive way of blending with science fiction's unprecedented possibilities other ways of telling stories, both traditional and innovative, that link "our inner lives and the world outside that world."

Following sf writer Rudy Rucker, I call this way of doing things with words, images and ideas *transrealism*, although I extend his original coinage. Not only is transrealism writing about immediate reality—or your idiosyncratic perceptions of it—in a fantastic way, it is also a way of writing the fantastic from the standpoint of your richly personalized reality.[4] To the extent that Guare's implied critique is justified, a new creative intervention of both kinds is urgently needed. Perhaps something of this gesture is registered in Arthur Rimbaud's words, in August 1873:

Sometimes in the sky I see endless sandy shores.... A great golden ship, above me, flutters many-colored pennants in the morning breeze. I was the creator of every feast, every triumph, every drama. I tried to invent new flowers, new planets, new flesh, new languages. I thought I had acquired supernatural powers. Ha! I have had to bury my imagination and my memories! What an end to a splendid career as an artist and storyteller! ... I called myself a magician, an angel, free from all moral constraint ... I am sent back to the soil to seek some obligation, to wrap gnarled reality in my arms.[5]

As it happens, more than a century later, quite a few writers in and out of science fiction have been eddying in the slipstream of science toward a gnarly attractor in narrative space (as a physicist might put it), a way of combining wild ideas, subversion and criticism of the supposedly inviolate Real, together with realistic thickening of the supposedly airy fantastic, all bound together in a passionate, noncompliant act of self-examination.

This book is an invitation to refigure parts of that textual site currently labelled "science fiction" bringing it into registration (perhaps surprisingly) with other textual sites often regarded as widely separated. In extending this invitation, more is required than a simple analytical anatomy or parade of instances of transrealist writings. We will find it necessary to explore various sectors of the established landscape, spend time in subfields where quite disparate mechanisms are at work centrally, where apparently dissonant tunes are being played on a shared ensemble of instruments. We shall look as well, therefore, at brilliantly conceived alternatives to the transreal option: fictions that plunge away from any direct or even indirect appeal to the human heart in favor of constructing imaginary posthuman worlds (I am thinking especially of the important new work of Greg Egan, who stands narratively almost as the polar contrary to Rucker while sharing many of his mathematical interests). We need to reconsider, as well, some of the classic moves made inside the evolving games of science fiction and fantasy—those moves, and their histories, which both reader and writer must learn in a (usually youthful) apprenticeship, via drenching exposure to the semiotic environment and set of tools I elsewhere analyze as the sf megatext.[6]

DEALING WITH DEATH

Human life seems to be made up of endless attempts upon the impossible or at least the out-of-reach. That's true for most of us about many aspects of life and for all of us about some of them. Consider, for example, the big truth we divert our gaze from much of the time, even when we watch actors pretending to blow apart the guts and brains of other actors, on the screen, for our enjoyment: the truth that we all dry up and die, sooner or later. Death is a bad thing and so far impossible to avoid. So too are excessive suffering and loneliness and the other miseries afflicting us clever animals. Fantasy allows us to resolve some of these fears and hungers in prompted imagination, which has its good side and its bad. It is a happy discovery that we can evade the cruelties of *what is given* by freeing our dreams and taking solace there.

A side benefit is that by dreaming "magical" solutions to our woes and limitations, sometimes we work out how to fix them in reality. For hundreds of thousands of years humans looked wistfully at the birds. Now we can fly among them, indeed far higher. It is even conceivable, hard though it seems to swallow, that medical and other technologies might combine, perhaps as early as the 2030s or 2050s, to end the inevitability of senescence and routine death.[7] Fantasy's downside is precisely its flight from reality, from engagement with what ails us and what gives us joy. But the hazards of science fiction are much overrated.

In 1969, the excellent sf writer and commentator Algis Budrys distilled what every one of his peers hoped to achieve in this distinctive, disturbing mode of writing. His apothegm neatly welds together head and heart, giving neither of them priority while scanting neither. "I don't see how a science-fiction writer can do more than wring your heart," he wrote, "while explaining how it works."[8]

Certainly that is what I try to do in my own science fiction, when I am not trying to be funny instead and sometimes then as well. Of course I often fail and cannot make any claim to considerable achievement. Still, when I reread those words by Budrys recently, I felt an odd chill of recognition, recalling a pivotal moment near the close of my novel *The Dreaming Dragons* (1980). The eponymous dragons are those unconscious forces epitomized in the late Carl Sagan's book about the evolution of the human brain, *The Dragons of Eden*, and more than that, as well: the descendants of a dinosaur lineage from an alternative history in which mammals never quite surpassed their great predecessors, who persisted to evolve intelligence and wisdom. The novel's climax carries several characters into a kind of technological atrium of the collective unconscious, figured as an ancient machine within which all our minds are routinely echoed and archived: backed-up, one might say, against the decay and death of our bodies. My protagonist, a middle-aged scientist with a penchant for the paranormal and mystical, nears the moment of rapturous reunion, deep beneath a sacred mountain in central Australia, with this source of all being, human and draconic alike. Out of the body (or so it seems to him), he visits his sleeping family halfway around the world to make his sorrowing farewells:

Like an arrow of pale fire he passed to their home, to the crumpled bed where Selma lay sleeping. The digital clock showed that by her time it lacked a quarter hour of midnight. Without stirring, she knew his presence. Willy, she told him, you should have phoned ahead. I'd have—Oh. He took her hand and she came out of her body into his arms, pressing her face against his chest. He told her: This will be a dream to comfort you. . . .

   Hovering, he considered his pulsing heart, atria and ventricles, relaxing in diastole, contracting fiercely in systole, the striated muscles of interdigitated actin and myosin filaments, the resting membrane potential at 84 millivolts and its reverse potential convulsion at 103 millivolts. He observed the twin syncytiums, and the impulses surging across the A-V bundle. He waited for the depolarisation plateau, watched the calcium ions diffusing inward through the cardiac membrane, its permeability to potassium ions falling. The depleted tissues outside the membrane sucked hungrily at the calcium suspended in the enclosed extracellular fluids. He reached down calmly, then, and shooed the ions away. Potassium conductance plummeted. The dynamic of his heart sagged, faltered, ceased. He died.[9]

THE VOICES OF SPACETIME

   Science fiction is no unitary whole, of course; that is half its point. Its tools and perspective shifts, its adapted or invented tropes, have been turned to new ways for imposing old restrictions, as well as new ways to open nailed-up doors, not to mention new ways of breaking new ground. And however much canons are exposed, ridiculed, subverted and declared redundant, they persist or reemerge. In this ceaseless whirl of adaptation and novelty, inevitably conducted under circumstances imposed and constrained from outside sf's own internal dynamics (it is above all a form of commercial entertainment), this most recent of emergent literary and paraliterary modes struggles between temptations.

One of these, we now begin to see, is the invitation to a transrealist writing, imaginative writing that is not satisfied with the purely imaginary. It can only be understood—and either resisted or accepted—in view of those alternative gestures: at worst, to complacent narratives of comfort and convenience; or, by contrast, to unsettling postmodernist ontological disruption; or, finally, to explorations of a condition beyond even the transreal. One might call it, perhaps, the hyperreal, if the term had not already been frittered away. So this book can provide no single, univocal argument. It is, inevitably, a braided text, enacting in its comings and goings just that fractured realm with which it engages; or, to use a slightly different metaphor, tossed and turned in the turbulence of writing's endlessly chaotic slipstream.

TRUTH IN ADVERTISING

Finally, before we begin properly: Criticism has its quandaries. Who are we critics doing this for? How much are we suppressing, anyway, in this supposition that we are indeed "we," with some joint stock of common truths, perceptions, positions, cultural capital? Is art or literary criticism *sub specie aeternitatis*, as it often comically pretends, or *du jour*? Who is sitting here in judgment of someone's months or years of effort, who is this arrogant character asserting with a straight face that for the duration (75,000 or so words) "Science fiction, c'est moi?"

Just now it's me—and to the extent that you, the reader, are criticizing me, it's you. So be reassured that the argument in this book does not suppose itself to be the word of God, even when the shape of critical language makes it sound as if that is what I am trying to marionette.

NOTES

1. John Guare, *Six Degrees of Separation*. Xeroxed filmscript, copyright 1989.
2. A famous preparatory school near Boston.
3. The salient passages from Coleridge are conveniently gathered in Walter Jackson Bate, ed., *Criticism: The Major Texts* (New York: Harcourt, Brace and World, 1952), pp. 386–87.
4. The term had already been used, in a somewhat similar way, before Rucker published his manifesto. It is the term adopted by two artistic brothers. The elder, Yuri Brusovani, a painter, "is the founder of transrealism, a new artistic method." The younger, Nathan Brusovani, is a photographer and a digital designer. See their own manifesto, and examples of their work, at their web sites: http://best-place.net/best/Brusovani/nathan_brusovani.htmandhttp://www.geocities.com/~brusovani/statement/statement1_index.htm

The former site declares:

Starting from 1978 the artist works on the concept of transrealism, combining modern acrylic technical methods with artistic manners of the old masters. The "trans" prefix meaning "above", "through", "beyond" actually marks this term as belonging to a way of depicting space and time which is different from that of the known ecto-realism (outer, external). Due to acrylic paints and the latest artifices in painting the artist is able to create multi-layer, multi-dimensional spaces on canvas where realistic, sensual images become metaphoric. The transparent watery colors allow, unlike the oil, to give a feeling of transparent reality, in the space of which comprehension the voices interweave and material objects become transparent to a multitude of meanings and senses. Polyphony is the principal method of transrealism, whose goal it is to recreate a concept for new comprehension of reality, not a plain one, based on individualism, i.e. the dictatorship of a single voice, but multilayered where every voice is independent and is looking for a dialogue with others.

(Cited with permission of the Brusovani brothers.) The overlap here with Rucker's program is only partial, since his strategy depends powerfully on just the individual and idiosyncratic perspective that the Brusovani brothers reject.

5. Arthur Rimbaud, *Complete Works*, trans. Paul Schmidt (New York: HarperColophon, 1976), p. 213.

6. See my *Reading by Starlight: Postmodern Science Fiction*, especially chapter 4. In the present investigation, I have chosen to keep theoretical and scholarly apparatus to a minimum, although everything here is plainly inscribed against the background of Western literary theory's ongoing search for adequate means of analysis and synthesis. Any reader seized by the need to pursue my theoretical presuppositions might turn to the text just mentioned, as well as to *The Architecture of Babel*, which deals with the distinctive yet overlapping semiotic systems at work in the humanities and the sciences, and *Theory and Its Discontents*, which tries to deconstruct some of the more disturbing moves frequently played in the theory game, and to reconstruct relations between the so-called Two Cultures on a new (if highly speculative) historical matrix.

7. This apparently outlandish prospect is discussed in my popular science book *The Last Mortal Generation* (1999).

8. Algis Budrys, from his review "Galaxy Bookshelf," in *Galaxy*, 27, no. 6 (January 1969) of Samuel R. Delany's novel *Nova*. I am grateful to Mr. Budrys for e-mailing me the exact form of this quotation, which I recalled vividly after nearly three decades.

9. Damien Broderick, *The Dreaming Dragons: A Time Opera* (Melbourne: Norstrilia Press, 1980), pp. 220–21.

1

Signs Fiction

[F]iction—that clacking, crudely carpentered old roller coaster, every up and down mocked by the triviality, when all is said and done, of human experience, its Sisyphean repetitiveness . . .
                                    —John Updike, *Toward the End of Time* (p. 277)

The battleground on which I have fought is not merely the divide between fiction and SF, between human and animal. It is also across another—perhaps equally fictitious—divide, that between creation and criticism.

   Our characters have to encompass struggles with conflicting kinds of belief. Mary Shelley's father, William Godwin, is generally seen as a cold, unloving father. So he was. But he had a miserable childhood . . . was often whipped, and was brought up in a strict Calvinist faith. . . . Doubt entered when he read a French book of the Enlightenment. Those two warring systems of thought, based on faith and reason, also penetrated the sad heart of his daughter Mary and, *mutatis mutandis*, still bedevil us today.

   Do you imagine that space travel will resolve the struggle?
                                    —Brian W. Aldiss, *Bury My Heart at W. H. Smith's A Writing Life* (pp. 145–46)

Binary oppositions, la la. Yet they once had brave days,[1] and still lurk in the basement of our thinking, critical or otherwise, especially when we approach hybrid or hyphenated or zeugmatic forms of writing.

A *zeugma* is the rhetorical yoking, apparently unnatural or at least against the grain, of two quite different terms into one condensed and startling figuration. In this book I mean to consider—to tease into parts, then to recombine those severed parts, not once but several times, not in one way but by various paths—a popular but still despised zeugma: sf or "science fiction." We shall find that it now has two doubled neologistic twins: slipstream and transrealism. Or perhaps the latter is just richly imaginative fiction itself, caught in the slipstream of science. The former, *slipstream sf*, is defined somewhat sarcastically by John Clute, in the *Encyclopedia of Science Fiction*: "stories which make use of sf devices but which are not GENRE SF. The image is either nautical or aeronautical: a ship or an airplane ... can create a slipstream which may be strong enough to give non-paying passengers ... a ride."[2] The instance Clute offers is the near-sf novel *O-Zone*, by Paul Theroux, set in the future but constructed so clumsily (or so it is widely agreed by sf insiders such as writer and critic Thomas M. Disch)[3] that its author reveals how comprehensively and datedly he has rediscovered the wheel.

However, Clute adds, although *slipstream* is apt as a description of "commercial piggybacking," to apply it to the whole range of non–genre sf[4] is inappropriate, since "the term—which implies a relationship of dependency—can seem derogatory." Oddly enough, the term's originator, sf writer Bruce Sterling, did not intend to give offense, or at any rate not in that way. To the contrary. Cyberpunk's sometime PR agent (and fine writer in and out of that branch of the sf business), Bruce Sterling coined "slipstream fiction" as the *mot juste*, proposing it in 1989 as a telling metaphor not without its freight of resentment.[5] According to a meditation he cited, by another ambitious sf writer, Carter Scholz, science fiction in the 1960s and 1970s "had a chance to become a worthy literature; now that chance has passed. Why?" Sterling asked. "Because other writers have now learned to adapt SF's best techniques to their own ends." Since those "other writers" had already in their grasp a whole armamentarium of skills and techniques usually ignored by traditional sf creators, this left the old guard high and dry, by-passed, sluggish textual dinosaurs outpaced by small quick mammals.

If so, what of *transrealism*? Rudy Rucker, who coined the literary use of the term in 1983 (in "A Transrealist Manifesto," published in the *Bulletin* of the Science Fiction Writers of America), meant something like the innovative sf of Philip K. Dick, justly accounted by John Clute "one of the two or three most important figures in 20th century US sf and an author of general significance" (Clute "Dick, Philip K." p. 328). In his most rewarding fiction, Dick used what anthropologist Clifford Geertz (1983) has called *thick description*, detailed rich observation of consensus reality serving to anchor the weirdness of sf's disruptive tropes. Of course, "consensus reality" is itself, in some degree at least and perhaps in very large measure, always-already an epistemological construct. It blends a mix of what we learn from the dominant culture as it shapes our upbringing directly and what we negotiate in our passage through a complex, many-dimensioned and conflicted world.

Certainly not *everything* is a social construct, despite the tendency in current thought to read all the world as contrived text. The underlying architecture of constructed reality—if a materialist reading of science is correct—is a preexistent spacetime physics, patterns of quantum logic and relativistic causality beyond our command. Empirical enquiry does tell us a great deal about that impermeable level of reality, even if perhaps its substrates will forever evade our deepest understanding (but then again, perhaps a genuine Theory of Everything is waiting in the wings).[6] It is also increasingly evident that the evolutionary history of *Homo sapiens sapiens* has forged some measure of species-wide "human nature" common to us all, as the structuralists once taught.[7] Atop these givens, however, are those many contingent, somewhat or even extremely arbitrary, mutable cultural and ideological frames within which we live and love and have our social and individual being. These elusive schemata are what make some of us Western readers of sf, others !Kung San hunter-gatherers, others again fierce Taliban warriors, Buddhist mystics, Indonesian astrologers—or Western readers of almost anything *except* science fiction!

In a coarse-grained demarcation, then, transrealism denotes *sf with heart*, portraying against its fantastic and disruptive invented settings naturalistic characters (some of them robots or aliens) with complex inner lives and personal histories somewhat resembling the density of recognizable or real people.

That distinction itself, admittedly, requires a lot of flexible negotiation. Consider the following typical exchange between two articulate sf readers, neither a professional critic nor theorist, in a discussion thread on an Internet newsgroup.[8] At issue was the comparative fidelity to the Real in two famous sf novels set in drastically anarchic futures—Ursula K. Le Guin's solemn *The Dispossessed: An Ambiguous Utopia* (1974) and Neal Stephenson's gonzo *Snow Crash* (1992), its main character brazenly named Hiro Protagonist. Jo Walton observed that both books

question what "realistic" means. *Snow Crash* is far more "realistic" than *The Dispossessed*, in that it is set in a recognisable future United States. . . . Pizza, the Mafia, skateboards and nuclear weapons appear in roles clearly derived from those they enjoy today. [. . . It] is easy to see how that world—which is of course exaggerated somewhat for satiric purposes—could come into existence. Yet in every other way *The Dispossessed* is more realistic—it is psychologically realistic,

the characters are . . . rounded and act as one would expect real complex characters to act. In *Snow Crash* the characters act like people in a cartoon—of course,
this is part of the fun of the book.

This seems a sensible and plausible assessment. Equally telling,
though, is C. Mitch Hagmaier's retort:

an interesting assumption: that naturalist "psychological" interpretations of character motivation is actually more realistic than off-the-cuff postmodern silly-walk
character motivation. [. . . T]he character interaction in *Snow Crash* resembled
what I've seen of the real world much more closely than the stiffarsed mannerism
in Le Guin's work. Le Guin's style fits in with the whole socialist/modernist
insistence on fully articulated, unified personalities, people that seem to know
their own minds. One of the things that struck me about *The Brothers Karamazov*
. . . was just how science-fictional the character portraits seemed to be. [Their]
personalities were in flux—not stable, set types that act as simple I/O [comput-
erized In/Out] devices, but rather semi-predictable mysteries.[9]

Le Guin herself faces this issue in the introduction to her late collection
A Fisherman of the Inland Sea (1994):

The cardboard-character syndrome was largely true of early science fiction, but
for decades writers have been using the form to explore character and human
relationships. I'm one of them. An imagined setting may be the most appropriate
in which to work out certain traits and destinies. But it's also true that a great
deal of contemporary fiction isn't a fiction of character. This end of the century
isn't an age of individuality as the Elizabethan and Victorian ages were. Our
stories, realistic or otherwise, with their unreliable narrators, dissolving points
of view, multiple perceptions and perspectives, often don't have depth of character as their central value. Science fiction, with its tremendous freedom of metaphor, has sent many writers far ahead in this exploration beyond the confines of
individuality—Sherpas on the slopes of the postmodern. (Pp. 3–4)

What, then, of the suggested contrast between the anarchist sf novels of
Le Guin and Stephenson? Might science fiction, after all, yet find some
escape from both these kinds of genre cardboard cages—the mannered
and the cartooned—while retaining the benefits of both old and new
ways of writing it? Transrealism is a narrative strategy meant to do just
that. (One narrative strategy among many, of course; it need have no
imperial designs!)

What Rucker called for was an internal renovation of sf's peculiar
mode of writing, a mode so often spurned by the literary for its failure
of imagination. As we've seen, that paradoxical and haughty appraisal,
or rebuff, is perhaps justifiable in Coleridgean terms. So the transrealist
way of writing sf might itself be viewed as a slipstream, one that is
dragging writers in a direction counter to slipstream proper, yet merging

with it in the downstream delta: tugging at those writers attracted in the first instance to the genres of the fantastical, writers with some measure of insiderly expertise in its characteristic and unusual skills.

Transrealists find themselves drawn back into the refreshing stream of (for want of a better term) literary or canonical writing as it is commonly understood and embraced by "mainstream" readers—that is, readers most at home in the genre so rarely acknowledged as such: traditional "literature" with its freight, as Belsey (1980) notes, of "classic realism."

Simultaneously, such transrealist writers are plunged into the slipstream of science, an immense and consequential torrent of public, validated knowledge of the universe. Science is a body of communal understanding that is growing exponentially (in every culture that has adopted its practice and learning since the Renaissance) while deepening into theories of profound subtlety and generality. And here again, Le Guin's own recent reflections on her art remind us to retain a suitable generosity toward the many ways a story can be told, the many kinds of stories that involve us diverse human readers. Her great early novel *The Left Hand of Darkness* (1969), with its androgyne characters in a frozen world, differs from a "realistic novel" such as *Pride and Prejudice* just by asking us to accept, for the moment, those minimal variations in "narrative reality:" "The description in science fiction is likely to be somewhat 'thicker', to use Clifford Geertz's term, than in realistic fiction, which calls on an assumed common experience. But the difficulty of understanding it is no greater than the difficulty of following any complex fiction. . . . All fiction offers us a world we cannot otherwise reach"—(Le Guin, *Fisherman*, pp. 2–3).

THE REAL THING

An immense philosophical and critical literature stands behind these shirtsleeve distinctions. If realism nowadays sounds like a gesture at unproblematic imitation of a stable world simply observed by the senses, ironically it came from Aristotelian discourse as a signifier of metaphysically independent Universals (by contrast with *nominalism*, which held that categories in perception and thought were just tokens of instances in their general class). Twelfth-century philosophers spilled a lot of ink on disputes between what the victors came to call Exaggerated or Ultra-Realism (the *antiqua doctrina*) versus Moderate Realism (the reckless *moderni* of Abelard).[10] Luckily, we can ignore most of this hairsplitting. Realism in the literary sense, as a post-Revolutionary, post-Romantic movement in France in the middle of the nineteenth century, was a kind of adamant empiricism: unmannered and perhaps unmannerly, focused on social diversity rather than on the privileged and exalted, open to variety instead of imposed and traditional values, a literature suited to a time convulsed by modernizing change—in a word, a more democratic writing.

Plainly, the tendency of such fiction must be to avoid and even execrate romance, consolatory illusion, free invention: *imagination*. The freethinker Ernest Renan, age 25 in the middle of the nineteenth century, wrote programmatically in *The Future of Science* that "The real world that science reveals to us is by far superior to the fantastic world created by the imagination."[11] Emile Zola declared of Balzac, Stendhal, the Goncourts that "their talent does not depend on their imagination, but on the fact that they render nature with intensity" (Grant, *Realism*, p. 30). Fidelity to the observable facts was crucial.

Prominent in naturalism's line of literary development (although preceded several decades earlier by Stendhal and Balzac), Zola asserted that art should not just imitate but *duplicate* reality. Against the Romantics, he urged a literary form that approached world and society as a scientist approached experimental phenomena; his manifesto essays were explicitly titled *The Experimental Novel* (1880). Plot and imagination were superfluous. A story would unfold in the very notation of the real. It was an absurd prescription, even if it had a kind of revival in the *nouveau roman*, that arduously metaphor-free "anti-novel" of Alain Robbe-Grillet (*For a New Novel*), three generations later than Zola (and such moods and modes do seem to roll around cyclically).

Arguably, realism in art was the counterpart of Comte's positivism in philosophy (Grant, *Realism*, p. 35)[12]—the very contrary of its traditional Aristotelian affinity. This was indeed fiction in the service, if not the slipstream, of emergent science, with a vengeance. More than a century later, the transrealist prescription arises in a climate almost indescribably otherwise, one in which the romantic, the illusory, the fantastic, suffuse everyday life in a miasma of film, television, music, advertising, tourism, computer recreations, the very fashioning of the quotidian itself. A return to the gnarly texture of things is no naive embrace of an inappropriately reductive or positivistic "clear window pane" theory of representation. It is a hand outstretched for an oxygen mask in a billowing, choking haze of intoxicating perfumes. At the same time, a ruthless pragmatism, a corrosive institutional reality principle, threatens to devour us even as we are seduced by the smoke and mirrors. The heartbreaking realities of living in a machine world call for a redemptive infusion of the genuinely fantastic, illumination of the kind that the modernists and surrealists sought as they attempted their own escape from a pendulum swung once more, and too bitterly, into Gradgrind sterility:

"You are to be in all things regulated and governed," said the gentleman, "by fact. We hope to have, before long, a board of fact, composed of commissioners of fact, who will force the people to be a people of fact, and of nothing but fact. You must discard the word Fancy altogether. . . ."

He had been put through an immense variety of paces, and had answered volumes of head-breaking questions. Orthography, etymology, syntax, and prosody, biography, astronomy [etc., etc.] were all at the ends of his ten chilled fingers. . . . If only he had learned a little less, how infinitely better he might have taught much more! [13]

This is Charles Dickens's Victorian caricature of Philistinism writ large, in his 1854 novel *Hard Times*, but one not without its own taint of anti-intellectualism. For some of us, "head-breaking questions" are the best kind to ask and the most satisfying to answer. Science fiction has always made sport of just such topics and fields of expertise, rejoicing in a playful way that the human mind and heart can both describe and reconstruct the universe in part exactly by *discovering and knowing facts*. What *is* truly death to the spirit, what Dickens excoriated, is that typical industrial betrayal of imagination—and even of Fancy—for without them, an array of *soi-distant* brute facts is nothing but a look-up table to be consulted mechanically by a robot.

When the repressed imagination struck back, it took a variety of paths to the light, most notably surrealism and other varieties of modernism. Not all of these methods repudiated science, hypothesis, experiment, theory. The Australian critic Russell Blackford remarks the simultaneous and superficially paradoxical advent of William Morris's *The Wood Beyond the World* (1894) and *The Well at the World's End* (1896), pastoral dreams that simply deny the brutal actuality of his century's technological revolution, and H. G. Wells's *The Time Machine* (1895), *The Island of Dr. Moreau* (1896) and *The War of the Worlds* (1898), in which imagination blossomed in a wholly fresh way out of science rather than blindly against it (even when Wells's imagination sought to critique the scientific abuses he foresaw). [14]

A century later, each of these lines of literary developments had become immense marketing juggernauts, although usually in debased forms: commercial fantasy, from Morris via Tolkien, and commercial science fiction, from Verne and Wells via (in one direction, which might loosely be called "realist") Heinlein, Asimov, Clarke and the rest of the *Astounding Science Fiction* lineage, and (in another, or "romance" line) Hollywood, where the two subtraditions of fanciful invention fused once more, to the clatter of cash registers and the despair of many aficionados. Meanwhile, literature as constructed by its canon-makers largely ignored these mutants, while secretly borrowing back some of their more minor and tractable techniques.

COPPING THE SATIRE PLEA

Not that sf has lacked defense for its social utility. Kingsley Amis, famously, made the case for sf as satire in his 1959 lectures at Princeton

University, published in the United States the following year as *New Maps of Hell*:

With the "fiction" part we are on reasonably secure ground; the "science" part raises several kinds of difficulty, one of which is that science fiction is not necessarily fiction about science or scientists, nor is science necessarily important in it. . . . Science fiction is that class of prose narrative treating of a situation that could not arise in the world we know, but which is hypothesised on the basis of some innovation in science or technology, whether human or extra-terrestrial in origin.
    [. . . S]cience fiction presents with verisimilitude the human effects of spectacular changes in our environment, changes either deliberately willed or involuntarily suffered.[15]

This surely is a *kind* of realism, although it might sound like a recipe for complacent disaster tales of the John Wyndham *Day of the Triffids* variety.[16] In fact, for Amis, the most valuable manifestation of sf was the stinging jest. His most detailed accounts were reserved for the works of the accomplished and imaginative satirist Frederik Pohl. Amis scandalized and affronted most sf readers of the time, who fancied that sf was a frightfully serious if highly adventurous business, by blithely declaring Pohl "the most consistently able writer science fiction, in the modern sense, has yet produced. . . . His mode is typically the satirical utopia, with comic-inferno elements rarely absent; his method is selective exaggeration of observable features of our society."[17]
    In her 1960 *Fifth Annual* volume of *The Year's Best S-F*, the eclectic and perhaps influential anthologist Judith Merril frothed and seethed at the opinions of this "British humorist with pretensions to critical judgment of science fiction."[18] In one respect, though, Merril found herself in agreement with Amis. *Science fiction*, both commentators felt, was no longer an appropriate name for this kind of writing. Walter M. Miller's admirable post–nuclear holocaust novel *A Canticle for Leibowitz*, Merril noted, had escaped dismissal at the hands of influential reviewers by the simple expedient of not being labeled as sf. "Thus freed of the Curse of the Tag, an excellent novel became eligible for consideration on the level on which it was written." In her jovial, elbow-nudgingly relaxed way, Merril concluded: "Well, if this is what it takes to persuade 'literary' folk to read a good book and enjoy it—down with 'science fiction', sez I. Let's have a new label. Or none at all" (p. 313). A little later Merril did what she could to replace "science fiction" by a term Robert Heinlein suggested: "speculative fiction." That tag in turn, according to some, swiftly took on the odium of snobbishness, pretentious imposture and overreaching and hence has tended to languish outside of some quarters of academic criticism. (In the greater world, the journalistic term "sci fi," a 1950s pun

on a now-expired glamor term, "hi fi," has gained almost overwhelming currency—there is a Sci-Fi TV channel, and video stores rack their sf under that heading—although most older practitioners and readers eschew it rather angrily.)

Even as it continued to be ignored or despised by the mainstream establishment Merril wished to colonize, sf held an important brief as marginal social criticism. Most commentators make an obligatory nod to its role during the McCarthy persecutions of liberals and leftists during the American fifties. It is doubtful, though, if reading most sf as satire does more than attenuate (and, for middle-class liberals like Amis, domesticate) its genuinely disturbing and effective alienation effects.

In the decades that followed *New Maps of Hell*, several "waves" passed over the surface of sf, including the New Wave propagandized by Merril herself and despised by Amis, culminating (if we somewhat quixotically neglect the impact of mass-media colonization) in current slipstream and transrealist work that blurs at several of its boundaries into magic realism, metafiction and other transgressive writing/reading ecologies cultivating literary and paraliterary byways well beyond the trim pathways of nineteenth-century realism. "What one really wants to see," Amis claimed in 1960, "is not merely a process of self-reform on the part of existing science-fiction authors, but an irruption into the field of a new sort of talent: young writers equally at home in this and in ordinary fiction."[19] When it happened, Amis loathed the result.[20] Of course, and crucially, in the meantime "ordinary fiction" had shifted ground as well. "There is in fact," according to Christine Brooke-Rose, "remarkably little thematic or formal difference between Pynchon and Samuel R. Delaney [sic] (*Triton, Dahlgren* [sic]), a Science Fiction writer turned 'experimental' and treated seriously as 'New' SF by postmodernist critics (but not by SF critics who find these self-indulgent, in sex and violence as well as in prolixity and preciousness."[21]

In broader terms than his perhaps playful or self-serving stress upon the goading and satirical (he had made his own name, after all, with *Lucky Jim*), Amis confessed himself "grateful that we have a form of writing which is interested in the future, which is ready . . . to treat as variables what are usually taken to be constants, which is set on tackling those large, general, speculative questions that ordinary fiction so often avoids."[22] Decades later, some commentators agreed in principle with this assessment. "Science fiction's two major claims to originality have been its presentation of new metaphors for the human condition, drawing them from practical science and theoretical extrapolation, and its ability to evoke reaction by delineating the normal with 'one small change' that results in a new perspective," the nonacademic critic and prize-winning sf writer George Turner claimed.[23] Turner called for sf to "get back into the prediction business. . . . We need a new breed of sci-

ence fiction and a new breed of historically and socially educated writer
to drag the genre screaming into contact with the facts of life."[24] Which
fetches us back to the ancient and continuing arguments over the status
of the Real and its representation in avowedly realist fiction.

STORIES: JUST SO

Is language best modeled as *representation* or *construction*, or some
blend of the two, or something else altogether? Literary theory usually
approaches the topic via the long debate, immensely sophisticated (and
often, ironically, barely intelligible or at any rate hardly credible), over
representation. How do words relate to our inward understanding of the
world and to the outer world itself? Can we think without words (uttered or otherwise)? Is it misleading to posit an external reality independent of text? Haven't Heidegger and Jacques Derrida long since
proved that re-presentation is a notion based on the exploded metaphysical myth of prior presence, a laughably inadequate account of a
process that can have no terminus, only indefinite deferral of reference?[25]
One finds tortured declarations on "imitation versus reference, corre-
spondence, adequation, standing for," such as this from narratologist
Shlomith Rimmon-Kenan:

Grave doubts have been cast [by Heidegger, Wittgenstein, Derrida and Lacan]
on the capacity of language to reach—let alone represent—the world. The pre-
sumption of the existence of a reality prior to the act of representation has also
come under fire. . . . Instead of a thing-in-itself, reality is now considered an absence, and language replaces, rather than reflecting or even conveying, this absent reality.[26]

The ways contemporary theory denies *any* secure access to an external,
nonintentional reality are often baroque and gratuitous to the point of
self-parody, as critics such as Paul Gross and Norman Levitt,[27] and Alan
Sokal and Jean Bricmont,[28] have made painfully clear. Rimmon-Kenan's
solution is a third path, *access*, which has the merit of admitting the
obvious distinction between "absence to consciousness (epistemological
absence) and absence *tout court* (ontological absence)" (Rimmon-Kenan,
A Glance, p. 10).

For the moment, avoiding these turbulent shallows, let's try to concoct
an account of how the brain must represent the world, and its own experience, and how it can communicate that knowledge and experience
(however partially). Luckily, we can base our discussion on the findings
of contemporary neuroscience.

Start with this fairly plausible sketch: When you are awake and paying
attention, your brain (and to a lesser extent the rest of your body) is

flickering from one complex and composite state of activation to another. Brains are in some measure partitioned—localized stroke damage interrupts only some functions, paralyses just one part of the body—but also globally cross-wired. What strikes us as seamless experience is always a composition. Consider the way we hear by *watching* as well as by listening: when "pa" is played on a tape machine while you watch lips mouth the syllable "ka," you will hear the constructed compromise "ta"—even if you know what trick is being played on you. That is because your brain combines conclusions or guesses it reached in two distinct modules on opposite sides of the head.[29]

For you to think (and perhaps utter the word) "dog," parts of your brain must enter a quite specific state. The detailed description of that state is still unknown, although brain scanning methods are getting more precise each year, but it seems likely that at least *some* consistent neural activation takes place each time you think of a dog.

Perhaps that sounds like a shockingly reductionist claim, impossible to test. Not so. In 1998, it was reported that when electrical (EEG) and magnetic recordings were taken while two subjects listened repeatedly to twelve different Subject-Verb-Object sentences, characteristic traces corresponding to both the sentences and individual words could be obtained from each subject by averaging the repeated measurements, Fourier-transforming and filtering the signals, and so forth. These averaged trace profiles could be matched correctly with the right sentence about half the time rather than the chance frequency of one time in twelve. (Of course each subject had a distinct pattern for a given sentence, since each brain processed the input idiosyncratically.) So when a subject heard "Bill loves Susan," even with this crude system the subject's associated brain-wave trace could be distinguished about half the time from those correlated with "Mary sees John" or the ten other alternatives. Something detectably regular was going on inside those heads when a given sentence passed from their ears to the acoustic processing modules of their left hemispheres.[30] Despite Derrida's opinion to the contrary, it seems likely that their brains were forming recurrent representations of the words, representations that correlate with mental mappings and the experience of recognizing and understanding the sentences. But even if the coarse EEG and magnetic traces were picking up nothing more than a particular neural response to a given *sound sequence*, that still shows all we need for this argument.

Meanwhile, as you decode sentences to make sense of them, other parts of your brain are doing their own housekeeping chores, or mulching "in the background" on bigger problems, or maintaining your balance and orientation in the world, and controlling your blood pressure and digestion and levels of circulating hormones. One pedagogical reason this account might still seem unobvious even to people who have studied the relevant disciplines has been pointed out by linguist and cognitive scientist Steven Pinker: "I believe that with the exception of Perception and, of course, Language, not a single curriculum unit in psychology corresponds to a cohesive chunk of the mind.... It is like explaining how a car works by first discussing the steel parts, then the aluminum parts, then the red parts, and so on, instead of the electrical system, the transmission, the fuel system, and so on."[31] Worse yet, the chunks that many literary analysts have worked so hard with during the last two decades bear such names as "desire," "absence" and "the body." Those terms have their uses, of course, even if it is arguable that they are employed so broadly and compulsively, often after the fashion of a catechism, that they now resemble earlier explanatory or discursive items once prominent such as "phlogiston," "aether" and "the soul."

A MATTER OF TASTE

Theory—or metatheory—is a strange and wonderful concept. For twenty or thirty years it has been central to sophisticated cultural analysis, but people still get stirred up about its pretensions. (I am one—my *Theory and Its Discontents*, grounded in both poststructuralist deconstruction *and* the sciences of the insistently empirical, is explicitly ambivalent about the claims and posturing of high critical theory.)

It used to be supposed that the world is just out there, on the other side of a clear sensory window pane. Hence Hemingway might write (in an apparently unsentimental "transparent" style later parodied unmercifully): "The next year there were many victories. The mountain that was beyond the valley and the hillside where the chestnut forest grew was captured and there were victories beyond the plain on the plateau to the south and we crossed the river in August and lived in a house in Gorizia that had a fountain and many thick shady trees in a walled garden and a wistaria vine purple on the side of the house."[32]

Now we're sure that the experienced world is itself a construct, a somewhat unstable patchwork of mental models driven partly by what is outside, partly by genetically ordained internal grammars, partly by the local, contingent cultural templates that shape us from infancy on (including, especially, the language we use to categorize and communicate our grasp of the world). It is naive to suppose that culture and language can ever capture or portray "just how things are"—and hence no less naive, and unjust, to fear and hate anyone whose inner maps conflict with our own—but still it takes quite an effort to see that our worlds are built-up in accord with these internal maps or theories. Education helps; it is easier to reach such counter intuitive insights with the aid of difficult books and dialogue with other people who have been down the same path.

Science fiction often does this unsettling job just because its imaginative specialty (as well as its fanciful technological and social changes) is to slam comfortable expectations upside down. Sf can destabilize our prejudices, and do so without preaching, for fun. All too often, of course, it more subtly *confirms* our local comfort zones, and we go on just as smugly as before, having "experienced" the Truths of our prejudices enacted in the thirtieth century. But the option for genuine cognitive and moral shock is available in sf in a drastic way that conventional fiction can't readily achieve—for evidence of this, look at Joanna Russ's wonderful, scorching feminist novel, *The Female Man*. Here the narrative voice splinters into four versions of "Joanna," each the representative of a drastically different culture, each with her own distinctive response to both gender and sex. For this reason it is clearly possible to read *The Female Man* as transrealist, but perhaps that element is overshadowed—as it tends to be in all Russ's fiction and nonfiction, even the most searingly personal—by its ideological designs on us.

THE THEORY OF THEORY

Is this kind of analysis alien to the pleasure principle that impels ordinary readers and viewers to seek out sf? I do not believe so. Many accessible and entertaining guides to theory are available, such as Terry Eagleton's *Literary Theory: An Introduction* (1983): tough-minded, funny and exhilarating, and after some twenty years still highly relevant. Most literary critical books today assume that readers are familiar with at least this level of argument, and with the basic technical terms that postmodernists and poststructuralists have coined to think anew with: signifier and signified (roughly, word or image, versus concept), referent (the thing or state toward which signs point), metaphor and metonymy (signifiers replacing each other according to, respectively, similarity—*food for thought*—or association—*turf* instead of *horse-racing*), paradigm and syntagm (lists of available word choices or synonyms, versus the syntactic "string" or sentence that the selected words are linked into). While this jargon is momentarily alarming, it soon becomes second nature, and is immensely convenient as a concise tool for thinking through the deep issues raised in contemporary discourse. Certainly it has helped me clarify my own understanding of science fiction, which I regard as a distinctive kind of story-telling using *metonymic* (or syntagmatic) *tactics* to achieve *metaphoric strategies*: crudely, "realistic" prose driven by "poetic" imagination.

Does such theory allow us any longer the traditional access to acts of judgment and discernment—of the simple ranking of better and worse examples of the mode of writing we are investigating? If all reading and writing is relative to contingent cultural values, can one sf novel or story be preferred on principled grounds over another? If not, what is the point of urging the adoption of the transrealist program or any other candidate?

It is true that a typical, indeed predominant, poststructuralist move is to "interrogate hierarchies" and swiftly show that subordinate or despised categories are really *required* in the very creation of the locally favored ones. This can be both an important critical gesture, and also a refreshing party trick, as well as a tired shibboleth imbibed and applied mechanically, usually in the direst jargon, in graduate school. Employed appropriately, it usefully provides a formal account of why, say, "woman" has been the "marked" or suspect category when placed in binary opposition to "man," the unmarked or default case. Using this gambit, paraliteratures such as sf, "kiddie lit" and pornography have been clawed back from the critical abyss. I insist, though, that any situated judgment is going to discriminate between good and ill instances of these recovered texts. To make that claim is not an exploded error of smug, repudiated critical methods; it is a necessity, given the way the human brain organizes and processes information about the world. Let us pause for a moment's reflection on how we know this to be so.

If you point to a running rabbit and say to a Martian lexicographer, "rabbit," ve knows that rabbit probably means something that just happened. This assumes that ve grasps (a metaphor) the notion of "pointing" as indexical or deictic (another metaphor). Maybe the utterance stands for—is a verbal token of—a small grey streak, or something edible, or a patch of ground across which something with eyes has scampered, or four legs, or a hot day, or a good joke. As it happens, human beings mostly do not have this problem, because we use, or are, brains sculpted by evolution to thrive in a prechunked universe of local "natural kinds." Tiny babies gaze unerringly at faces in preference to anything else, even pictures of faces, and go straight for the eyes. It is obviously a built-in behavior, underwritten by a brain that is coded for by the relevant set of selected genes, common to the species. Ostensive definitions, of the kind we employ teach a Martian to speak a human language, are working with, constructed on top of, a complex prepared semiotic mechanism.[33]

The way this machinery works, according to current experimental and observational cognitive science, is not by reference to Set theory, or arrays of necessary and sufficient conditions, or anything like a formal definition. We use "good examples" of things and work outward and inward from such exemplars.[34] A magpie or a robin is chosen by your culture as a "typical" bird, a *best instance*. From that starting point, you and your culture elaborate into subordinate and superordinate categories, inward to scientific subdetails, and outward into all sorts of other flying critters (is a bat a bird?), or critters with feathers (is a dinosaur a bird?), although boundaries remain a matter of convenience and negotiation.

LEARNING HOW TO SEE

It is the same with genres and modes, including sf. I am shown a typical instance (James Blish's *Cities in Flight*, say, or Arthur C. Clarke's *The City and the Stars*) and work in and out from that. If you start instead by using *Star Wars* and *Star Trek* as the canonical exemplars, let alone *The Blob*, you are probably ostending a different category (call it "sci fi"), although many or at least some of its instances will overlap with mine. Reader-response and Reception theory accounts claim that everything is in the tasting, in the use—it's a decision by the audience. Damon Knight famously offered the wry ostensive definition: "Like 'The Saturday Evening Post', [science fiction] means what we point to when we say it."[35] He and his fellow tasters know it when they taste it, more or less. They agree on the exemplars (are enculturated to agree, through their early exposure or priming to agreed "best case" exemplars of the mode or genre), and from there it's just a matter of fine-tuning.

So, no longer demanding *haute cuisine* at every meal, snobs may admit that fish and chips or McDonald's burgers can be eaten without shame—but for all that, nobody doubts that a day-old battered saveloy dropped into dirty used oil, or limp lettuce, soggy tomato, recycled gizzards and stale buns, make for unappetizing take-out. I can tell the difference between Piers Anthony and Patricia Anthony, between Jack Chalker and Daniel Keyes, let alone between pulp-meister "Vargo Statten" and industrial magical realist David Ireland; my nose and taste buds are still working.

Every text is a tool (a Swiss army knife, to borrow an analogy from cognitive philosophy) shaped to work a variety of effects on different components of a human nervous system. Genres are a sort of contract between writer and reader, laying down what to expect in a given text, how the bundles of words are best—most richly—unpacked, opened, used, setting up the reading protocols we bring to the page (or screen, etc.). However various they are, crime novels form a (fuzzily) bounded genre. So do war stories. Cooking books with recipes. Psychiatric reports. Local council documents. Gothic romances with embossed covers, smoldering heroes and low-bodiced beauties. Sf's textuality, though, operates at a higher level of generality than this: modal, rather than simply generic. I am persuaded that sf (despite *its* embossed titles and stock robots or spaceships on the gaudy covers) bursts such boundaries, sucks genre techniques into its vortex. So we can have sf love stories, sf crime thrillers, sf historicals (often set in histories that never happened). These days, interesting sf tends to be generically hybrid, which doubles the zeugmatic feature we have seen as typical of the mode itself.

A DOG IN MIND

Here is an analogy that helps us think through some of the presuppositions behind any debate on "representations of the real."

Let us stipulate that some reliable, standardized state of your brain, in the midst of its internal pandemonium, is probably switching on when the word or concept or image "dog" flits across your mind. Is what goes on "inside your head" anything like what goes on inside mine? Even if we inhabit much the same universe, and have access to it by much the same sensory apparatus, and build up our implicit theories of its shape and dynamics atop inherited templates derived from both genes and local culture, how can we tell whether we experience the same "reality," let alone adequately "represent" it when we communicate? Well, suppose we humans communicated directly, mind to mind, by "telepathy" (whatever that might be), instead of by such indirect methods as speech, gestures, odors, postures and so on. How could it work? What would it feel like?

How would telepathy convey that same mental content into someone else's head? Presumably by activating their equivalent neural circuits. But it is very unlikely that precisely the same parts of Bob's brain that code neurally for "dog," the same web of synapses, serve that purpose in Alice's. Both sets of neural wiring will almost certainly be in the same general region of the brain (perhaps Broca's area, which handles speech production, or Wernicke's, specializing in comprehension), but although we grow our brains on the basis of common genetic recipes, they develop somewhat chaotically—and indeed change over time in slightly or grossly unpredictable ways.

So you can't have a telepathic channel that works just by echoing the current description of Alice's linguistic brain modules into Bob's. It would be like plugging a Mac motherboard into an IBM computer (although both computers are built of chips), only a trillion times more incompatible. Yet computers *can* be set up to communicate data between each other, however various their operating systems happen to be. That is the basis of the Internet. They do it by establishing and restricting themselves to common protocols—for example HTTP used on the World Wide Web, Hypertext Transport Protocol—which support (uh-oh) "languages": for example, HTML, also used on the World Wide Web, is the Hypertext Mark-up Language. Computer software is programmed in languages, somewhere between formal logical systems like mathematics and hybrid pidgins that resemble human speech just enough for our specialized brains to work efficiently with machines.

Even telepathy—machine-assisted, perhaps, since the real world does not seem to provide much evidence of effective natural mind-to-mind communication—would need a language of some kind to port information on brain states from one head to another. That is, it would need a complex internal mapping device that uses agreed conventions enabling some part of what Alice understands by "dog" to trigger some part of what Bob means by "dog."

Given the huge number of idiosyncratic associations and cross-connections each of us builds up over a lifetime, the compatibility between the two brains is not going to be very great. It might be that Alice is a dog-breeder with a tremendous quantity of fine-grained and emotionally laden knowledge ramifying outward through her brain and body from the central attractor that stores her concept of dog. Meanwhile, Bob has never seen one of these animals and only knows them from books and movies. Still, an adequate interface language will surely impart to Bob *some* of this penumbra of cognitive and affective links, contextual density, when the telepathy process tries to echo Alice's mental state into his head. What would it feel like? Perhaps somewhere between "having someone else's thoughts," "my mind has been invaded!" and a dreamy, imaginative reverie. Maybe even an auditory hallucination, speaking fragments of sentences in a voice plucked from Bob's memories.

TEXT AS PSEUDOTELEPATHY

My analogy cashes out (at last!) like this: It should be obvious that our thought experiment rather closely resembles a description of how we already communicate our inner states by using elaborate semiotic systems of signification—notably, natural languages.

Because our brains are partitioned into hierarchies of modules, not all of them directly aware of each other, it is likely that languages of some sort also serve to keep them in touch, building up that complex dance called a *self* or *subject*. Perhaps these are specific "mentalese" dialects or codes simpler still, but for some higher-level purposes perhaps the brain just conscripts a version of our native tongue, as when we prevocally mutter to ourselves while musing or problem-solving.[36] Does this imply that humans or animals lacking learned language are not selves or persons? Perhaps. Individuals who have *never* developed full grammatical competence—wolf children, deaf people denied access to formal Sign during the critical period—are arguably *not* persons or selves with intentional projects, with a coherent inner conviction of continuing identity and comprehension of an external reality that is amenable to symbolic reference. Oliver Sacks describes such a boy who saw, categorized, distinguished elements of his world, but "could not, it seemed, go much beyond this, hold abstract ideas in mind, reflect, play, plan. He seemed completely literal—unable to juggle images or hypotheses or possibilities, unable to enter an imaginative or figurative realm."[37] Without words or grammar, you *can't hear yourself think*; conceivably there is no you to hear.

Communication, written or spoken, is an extension of such normal inner dialogues (as perhaps consciousness, in turn, is an extension of the symbolizing process enabled or at least enhanced by grammar and lexicon). When we write down what we mean to convey in a linear string of words, or speak it—a process that inevitably either distorts or clarifies what we thought we meant—we are creating a kind of mind virus.[38] It will enter another person's head (quite literally, via their eyes or ears) and try to switch on a series of inner states that are the closest feasible transform of the (partial) states that we encoded in words.

It often doesn't work very well because so much is lost, inevitably, in translation and compression; sometimes you cannot even recover much from a passage you wrote yourself in a markedly different state of mind. Obviously the simplest, most emotionally charged cues are going to be the most effective in eliciting some kind of reliable reactivation of your brain/body state—but then they are bound to lack specificity and nuance. Sentimental movies string together basic narrative moves that work instantly on almost everyone primed or schooled to their reception, restricting their coding to emotionally loaded semiotic elements common to most humans.

If the human brain receiving and trying to process this sort of coded barrage doesn't know the mediating language, the process more or less grinds to a halt. But there are degrees of ignorance. Bob might think he recognizes most of the lexigrams in a printed text, might even employ more or less the same grammar in construing what he supposes must be their meaning, but he is bound to be mistaken at least in part. Alas, the more ingenious his own inner decoder protocols, the more devious his interpretative system, the less likely he is to realize the magnitude of his misconceptions. And such errors can cascade, can multiply by what mathematicians call "combinatorial explosions": a few errors at the root of the tree grow into vastly more errors further up the trunk—until some basic semantic incongruity slams an interpretation to a bruising halt. Then Bob shakes his head and either concludes that Alice is a complete fool or is taking him for one—or, in the best and perhaps rarest of all possible worlds, goes back in embarrassment to track down his misunderstanding.

All fiction, we might say, consists of a web of such signs—but in "realist," especially "naturalistic," fiction, the signs do their fallible best to point to what seems secure, empirical, the Real. Science fiction, by contrast, is a *fiction lacking key real-world referents*. It uses novel signifiers to activate signifieds (conceptual records, maps or vectors) without any counterparts in the outside world—or not as yet, at any rate. Yet those fanciful signifieds are not meant to be taken as metaphors, tropes, diversions, metaphysical attempts upon the otherwise unsayable. It is, rather, a mode of resourceful writing in which the imagined signs have to do all the work, without any backup beyond their inscribed context and their history of use in the sf megatext. This is what Derrida and Lacan would have us believe is the case with *all* textuality, in which signifiers allegedly point only to other signifiers or signifieds—and never to referents—in an endless paper chase. Whether or not this is so, it is *emphatically* the case with science fiction. Sf is a mode, more than any other apart from theology, built crucially and ontologically from signs. Science fiction (forgive the pun) is indeed a kind of Signs Fiction.

NOTES

1. I am troping here on Hugh Kenner's striking opening passage in "Notes Toward an Anatomy of 'Modernism,' " in *A Starchamber Quiry: A James Joyce Centennial Volume 1882–1982*, ed. E. L. Epstein (New York and London: Methuen, 1982), p. 3.

2. John Clute, "Slipstream SF," in *The Encyclopedia of Science Fiction*, ed. John Clute and Peter Nicholls (London: Orbit, 1993), pp. 1116–17.

3. Thomas M. Disch, letter to in *SF Commentary* 67 (January 1989): 10–11.

4. Which he and his co-editor Peter Nicholls prefer to designate *fabulation*, in the *Encyclopedia* entry so titled (see n. 2 above).

5. Bruce Sterling, "Catscan 5," *Science Fiction Eye* 1, no. 5 (July 1989): 77–78. My citations are drawn from a literary shareware form of the text, on computer disk, generously provided by Mr. Sterling.

6. For an admirable and up-to-date account of such ambitious approaches, especially the currently popular M-Theory, see Brian Greene, *The Elegant Universe* (London: Jonathan Cape, 1999).

7. See, for example, Donald E. Brown, *Human Universals* (New York: McGraw-Hill, 1991), and Jerome H. Barkow, Leda Cosmides and John Tooby, eds., *The Adapted Mind: Evolutionary Psychology and the Generation of Culture* (New York: Oxford University Press, 1992).

8. Citations from the discussion are reprinted with permission of the two commentators.

9. Exchange posted on rec.arts.sf.written, 15 July 1997.

10. See, for example, Frederick Copleston, SJ, "The Problem of Universals," in *The History of Philosophy, Vol. 2: Mediaeval Philosophy, Part I* (New York: Image, 1962).

11. Cited in, and translated by, Damian Grant, *Realism* (London: Methuen, 1970), p. 34. Renan delayed publication until 1890, however, at which point he was a convert to Idealism, and in revisionary mood announced that "one doctrine

alone is true, the transcendental doctrine according to which the goal of humanity is the establishment of a higher consciousness" (p. 49). Oddly, this shift somewhat prefigures the way much science fiction manages to combine an apparent respect for scientific findings together with copious use of such fantastic narrative tropes as direct, unmediated psychic mastery of the empirical world, telepathic or machine-augmented union of separate individuals, even an Eschaton toward which history is seen to be converging (such as the universal mentalities at the end of time in, e.g., Stapledon's *Star Maker* and my own *The Judas Mandala*, and in allegedly *non*fiction such as Frank Tipler's *The Physics of Immorality*, and its adaptation in many recent sf novels).

12. Citing Ferdinand Brunetière in *Le Roman Naturaliste* (1883).

13. Charles Dickens, "Murdering the Innocents," *Hard Times* (Harmondsworth: Penguin, 1969), pp. 52–53. The Penguin edition's notes by David Craig note: "this . . . might read like the broadest caricature of heavy-handed literal-mindedness but is again a copy from life. In the aftermath of the Great Exhibition, of 1851, a Department of Practical Art had been set up to promote industrial design" (p. 319).

14. Private conversation, 1999.

15. Kingsley Amis, *New Maps of Hell* (1961; London: Four Square, 1963), pp. 14, 20.

16. For many years, the elegant "world disaster" novels by this British author were synonymous with sf among nonspecialist readers in his country, and some were placed on high school syllabuses; the most famous is *The Day of the Triffids* (1951). John Wyndham shared with the early J. G. Ballard a proclivity for tales that catastrophically disrupted the social order; unlike Ballard's, his works recovered that order in a soothing rebirth of tough-minded middle-class decency.

17. Amis, *New Maps of Hell*, p. 102.

18. Judith Merril, *The Year's Best S-F: Fifth Annual Edition* (New York: Dell, 1960), p. 14.

19. Ibid., p. 130.

20. As indicated in Amis's introductory remarks to the anthology, *The Golden Age of Science Fiction* (London: Gollancz, 1981).

21. Christine Brooke-Rose, *A Rhetoric of the Unreal* (Cambridge: Cambridge University Press, 1981), pp. 415–16. The parenthesis is left open. It is a matter for conjecture whether this, along with the spelling errors, is indicative of Brooke-Rose's attention to detail. An impassioned assault on her methods, especially as applied to Tolkien, is Professor Norman Talbot's "The Maltreatment of Fantasy," *Australian Science Fiction Review* (March 1988): 6–16; he berates her "insulting carelessness," and is scathing in general about poststructural essays at sf criticism, rebuking "Todorov's neurotically cramped definition of 'The Fantastic' " (p. 9).

22. Amis, *New Maps of Hell*, p. 134.

23. George Turner, *In the Heart or in the Head* (Melbourne: Norstrilia, 1984), p. 205.

24. Ibid. That this tack pays dividends is seen in the success of Turner's novel about the Greenhouse effect, *The Sea and Summer* (London: Faber, 1987), winner of the Arthur C. Clarke Award, and runner-up for the 1988 Commonwealth Prize and the John W. Campbell Memorial Prize. Interestingly, though, it is arguable

that the novel's true force lies in its dense evocation of character—an aspect, doubtless, of "the facts of life."

25. Jacques Derrida, *Of Grammatology*, trans. Gayatri Spivak (Baltimore: Johns Hopkins University Press, 1974).

26. Shlomith Rimmon-Kenan, *A Glance Beyond Doubt: Narration, Representation, Subjectivity* (Columbus: Ohio State University Press, 1996), pp. 8–9.

27. Paul Gross and Norman Levitt, *Higher Superstitions: The Academic Left and its Quarrels with Science* (Baltimore: Johns Hopkins University Press, 1994). My approval of their unmasking of certain fashionable nonsense does not extend to their apparent political agenda. As Alan Sokal has noted: "On the substantive issues they address, I agree with them about 75% of the time. On the other hand, the TONE of their book is very arrogant, which I find irritating and which many readers will undoubtedly find infuriating. Despite this, it seems to me that sophisticated intellectuals ought to be capable of separating a book's content from its tone, and of rationally judging the book's arguments without regard for its tone or for the psychological qualities of the authors" (23/27 July 1998, e-mail replies to Hal Tasaki, posted at http://www.gakushuin.ac.jp/~881791/Alan. html).

28. Alan Sokal and Jean Bricmont, *Intellectual Impostures: Postmodern Philosophers' Abuse of Science* (London: Profile Books, 1998) [a revised translation of the 1997 French edition].

29. See the lucid popular account in Rita Carter, *Mapping the Mind* (London: Weidenfeld & Nicolson, 1998), p. 144. This sort of simplified but up-to-date account should be required reading for literary theorists or philosophers unfamiliar with the startling information on brain and mind function now available from scanning technologies. Another useful source, invoked below in discussing Philip K. Dick's fiction, is V. S. Ramachandran and Sally Blakeslee's *Phantoms in the Brain* (London: Fourth Estate, 1998).

30. P. Suppes, B. Han and Z. L. Lu, "Brain-wave Recognition of Sentences," *Proceedings of the National Academy of Sciences* 95, no. 26 (22 December 1998): 15861–66. I am grateful to Anders Sandberg, in Sweden, for drawing this report to my attention.

31. Steven Pinker, *The Language Instinct* (London: Allen Lane, 1994), p. 421.

32. Ernest Hemingway, *A Farewell to Arms* (1929; Harmondsworth: Penguin, 1974), p. 8.

33. See the excellent, lucid and up-to-date popular discussion in Pinker's *The Language Instinct* and idem, *How the Mind Works* (London: Allen Lane, 1997).

34. I discuss this model, associated with Berlin and Kay, and Eleanor Rosch, in *The Architecture of Babel* (Melbourne: Melbourne University Press, 1994), pp. 57–59.

35. Damon Knight, *In Search of Wonder* (Chicago: Advent, 1967), p. 1.

36. Nicholas Humphrey's *A History of the Mind* (London: Chatto & Windus, 1992) argues that consciousness is sensation—not "perceptions, images, thoughts, beliefs"—become self-aware in feedback loops inside the brain. Feelings are *"activities* that we ourselves engender and participate in—activities that loop back on themselves to create the thick moment of the subjective present" (p. 207). Such reverberant feedback loops somewhat resemble the reentrant mapping loops cen-

tral to Nobelist Gerald Edelman's model of mind in *Bright Air, Brilliant Fire: On the Matter of Mind* (London: Allen Lane, 1992). In neither case is natural language part of the account, but higher levels of consciousness certainly seem to require feedback loops that manipulate mental representations.

37. Oliver Sacks, *Seeing Voices* (London: Picador, 1991), p. 40.

38. A recent attempt to put this perspective on a scientific footing, at least in broad terms, is psychologist Susan Blackmore's rather too-crudely titled *The Meme Machine* (London: Oxford University Press, 1999).

2

Realism and Reality

[Philip K.] Dick engaged the mutant logic of late capitalism and the technological simulacrum before Baudrillard knew a megabyte from a baguette, coming to the conclusion that only an antagonistic relationship with reality—even to the point of madness—is sane. In a world of crystal-clear transmission, Dick turned up the static between channels, turned up the volume, and listened for hidden messages. His skepticism constituted an increasingly fervent metaphysics. He was obsessed with the Gnostic concept of a demiurge, a false god who obscured the true world with illusory time and space. Part of the authorial fragmentation that pervades Dick's work arises because, though he clearly identified with his flailing characters and their metaphysical morality plays, he remained the demiurge of his own narratives.

—Erik Davis, "Technomancer" (p. 17)

Mid-twentieth-century valorization of realism (replete with arduously detailed "effects of the real" embedded in a closely observed social context) found its *locus classicus* in Erich Auerbach's ambitious 1946 study *Mimesis: The Representation of Reality in Western Literature* (translated 1953).[1] For Auerbach, "In so far as the serious realism of modern times cannot represent man otherwise than as embedded in a total reality, political, social, and economic, which is concrete and constantly evolving ... Stendhal is its founder" (p. 408). That theme is elaborated in the Marxist theories of Georg Lukács (*Studies in European Realism*, 1950),

Pierre Marcherey (*A Theory of Literary Production*, 1978), and Fredric Jameson (*The Political Unconscious*, 1981), although Jameson was later to emerge as the premier theorist of the postmodern (*Postmodernism, or The Cultural Logic of Late Capitalism*, 1991). While such adversaries of the dominant social order agree in praising verisimilitude, they all insist that we ought do more than acquiesce in the simple gratifications of (re)evoking a detailed world someone has envisaged on our behalf, for our consumer pleasure. They demand a critical reading that penetrates behind the credible impersonations of naturalistic novels or dramas, a wily reading that detects the *ideologemes*—those concise narrative units that figure the transactions of entire social classes—at work behind the plausible masks.

Nowadays we routinely expand this sort of "interrogation" (as it is rather creepily termed; I have noted elsewhere that interrogation is usually the privilege of terrorist regimes) in quest of the hegemonic skeleton and musculature beneath the text's seductive face. We are right to do so, but we need to remember that such interrogation can be (perhaps must be) conducted along many different axes, not just those that chance to be fashionable. Buried in any entertaining text are suppressed ideological dimensions of power, knowledge, gender and sex, economic and social class, race, religion or its lack, ethnic difference; contrasts of center/margin, rich/poor, colonizer/oppressed, established/marginal, able/impaired, schooled/uneducated, beautiful/plain, sturdy/enfeebled, young/old, tall/short, plus a host of other parameters already well diagnosed and described and a further host as yet opaque to analysts. The task of unpicking these constellations of privilege, delusion and contestation is ceaseless, fortunately for departments of cultural studies.

To catch the flavor of this way of reading, consider Catherine Belsey's pungent summary of what her Marxist analysis regarded, more than two decades ago, as realism's chief role and limitation:

Classic realism, still the dominant popular mode in literature, film and television drama, roughly coincides chronologically with the epoch of industrial capitalism. It performs . . . the work of ideology, not only in its representation of a world of consistent subjects who are the origin of meaning, knowledge and action, but also in offering the reader . . . the position of subject as the origin of both understanding and of action. . . . The reader is invited to perceive and judge the "truth" of the text, the coherent, non-contradictory interpretation of the world as it is perceived by an author whose autonomy is the source and evidence of the truth of the interpretation. (Belsey, *Critical Practice*, pp. 67–69)

Yet this diagnosis, too, is patently reductive, even as it tries to critique what it discerns (or, by its own self-reflexive account, "constructs") as the self-satisfied univocal reductionism enacted, in accordance with its unstated ideological charter, by bourgeois naturalism. A sinuous perspective more sophisticated than Belsey's is mapped by Jameson in a discussion of "Magical Narratives":

Let Scott, Balzac and Dreiser serve as the non-chronological markers of the emergence of realism in its modern form; these first great realists are characterized by a fundamental and exhilarating heterogeneity in their raw materials and by a corresponding versatility in their narrative apparatus. In such moments, a generic confinement to the existent has a paradoxically liberating effect on the registers of the text, and releases a set of heterogeneous historical perspectives . . . normally felt to be inconsistent with focus on the historical present. Indeed, this multiple temporality tends to be sealed off and reconstrained again in "high" realism and naturalism, where a perfected narrative apparatus (in particular the threefold imperatives of authorial depersonalization, unity of point of view, and restriction to scenic representation) begins to confer on the "realistic" option the appearance of an asphyxiating, self-imposed penance. (Jameson, *The Political Unconscious*, p. 104)

In short, any revived or imported "realism" toward which *trans*realism may aspire is always itself endlessly problematic. Let us, however, at this point, stipulate the general force of these claims and cautions as a given, and move on. The curious feature of today's standpoint is that romance and arcane game-playing (not to mention arcade game-playing) rather than stark realism are frequently in the ascendant, even in what remains of "high" literature outside the abiding language explorations of poetry. Think of the continuing taste for Latin American and derivative magical realisms and for intrusions of sheer and sometimes extreme invention into the basic narrative fabric of novelists such as Martin Amis, Antonia Byatt, Don DeLillo, Margaret Atwood, Ian McEwan, Toni Morrison, a hundred others.

Yet despite all the foregoing concessions, none of us has any difficulty, I feel certain, in distinguishing quite different degrees of realism in Tim Burton's Gothic, histrionic and very enjoyable film *Batman: The Movie* (1989) or Kevin Reynold's *Robin Hood: Prince of Thieves* (1991) with Alan Rickman's deliciously pantomimed wicked Sheriff of Nottingham, and, say, Anne Tyler's odd but psychologically probing novel of a dysfunctional family, *The Accidental Tourist* (1985) or Robertson Davies's magical, Jung-drenched *Deptford Trilogy* (1987). However much each of these texts is a contrivance, an artifact of both fancy and imagination, it is beyond question, I think, that the latter are more "realistic" than the former, however much (not all that much, perhaps) the cartoons slyly serve to deconstruct their viewers' cosy ideological assumptions.

SCIENCE AND/OR FICTION

On the face of it, though, looked at through traditional prejudice, it's hard to find a pair of zeugmatic concepts more estranged than *science* and *fiction*.[2] Each seems to square off against the other, key instances of the celebrated split between the Two Cultures, artistic humanities versus natural sciences. Recall a roster of the mythology of their oppositions:

Science, we suppose, is the disciplined quest for absolute, fundamental truth. All art, by contrast (to bend Walter Pater's famous dictum) aspires to the conditional.

Fiction's home is the heart, while science dwells in the head.

Science seeks to condense the empirical into broad generalizations, compress the thousand things into naked equations: the *objective*. Fiction strives to render or construct the contingent, the particular, the fleeting and ambiguous: the *subjective*.

Fiction burrows inward, science soars outward.

Science simplifies into stark graphs valid for all times and places. Fiction complexifies into nuance, joy, heartbreak, the uncanny, the sublime, the provisional, the extraordinary within the ordinary.

Such divisions into contrasted categories swiftly fall apart, however. Is it fiction or science that is holistic rather than reductive? Science, we guess at first, is surely the very paradigm of the reductive, stripping the meat and fat from the bone, boiling down the flensed carcass into a skeletal substrate, all sumptuous life reduced to numbers. But that's true also of the mechanics of fiction, as narratologists show us: every imagined action, in folk story and Tolstoy alike, derives from a handful or two of types, functions, actants, deployed in words built from an equally small number of distinguishable acoustic or graphic segments. Meanwhile, even the most austere and limited science cannot (or should not) escape the context of its whole surround, as the nonlocal connections of quantum theory prove, the vast geometries of Relativity's inertial frames, the dense ecological webs of the life sciences, the no-less-dense economic and psychological webs of culture. Fiction's mythemes, science's vectors and tensors, serve alike to direct us in (re) constructing stories adequate, in some appropriate and contextually satisfying fashion, to the unspeakable plenitude of the world.

So the unpromising zeugma *science fiction* is not so anomalous after all, perhaps. Science and fiction alike are attempts on an imaginative embrace of the world we move through, the world within which we have our being as striving, suffering, malicious and loving human beings. That world extends, we now know, from elementary strings or membranes in eleven dimensions supporting the quantum, all the way out to the unbounded boundaries of a cosmos tens of billions of light-years in extent, 13 billion years old.

To sit beside a spark-spitting, hand-warming fire in the dark of the night and tell stories beneath the stars is to find yourself poised between infinitesimal and infinite, speaking (even in the tongues of angels, even with charity) in a language always inadequate to the world's capture. And even granting those limits, so much of the world is now known best by the several sciences that it would be absurd and self-mutilating for a storyteller to ignore that rich, dense and exfoliating wisdom, just as a scientist lacking utterance, argument, engagement, contest, narrative is not merely mute but entirely ineffectual *qua* scientist, let alone as a fellow denizen of the human community.

We humans love stories. All of us love hearing them, or watching them enacted, and most of us love telling them to each other. A few even make a living out of it. Surely it is one of the strangest appetites any animal has ever contrived.

The appetite is protean in form, and there is famously no disputing with varieties of taste. Some of us dote on spectacle, the uncanny, the sublime, or the melting, anguished romance of humans besotted with each other but baffled by fate, or imagined danger and its escape or endurance, or the solitary voice speaking its singular yet weirdly recognizable experience, or the nuanced annotation of those subtle protocols and gavottes that constitute civilized life. We love stories mazed with difficulties, sorrow, tragedy, for in the narrative space of fiction the tragedy always falls upon somebody else even while we gaze at its nemesis through the victim's borrowed eyes.

Do we tire of stories, even when they repeat themselves, as they must? Only when and if we tire, fatally, of life itself. It is easier, though, oddly enough, to grow weary of imagined pleasure and repletion than of pain, trouble and arduously attained solution or its poignant thwarting. We hunger for obstacle. All happy stories are alike but an unhappy story is unhappy after its own fashion. Call that perverse appetite for story, which has no formal name, *Scheherazadenfreude*.

What's its spring? That matrix of language competences built by certain genes into modules in our human brains, no doubt, and its rich, exfoliated, ribald expansion in shared cultural memory, and in the sluggish or swift chemistry of our emotional bodies, poised to bound into one prepared state or another at the merest hint of a script, a stage direction, the fall of light on a flushed cheek or averted eye. Perhaps deepest source of all is the endlessly forgotten cycle of dream, when our disconnected brains go off-line and cavort amid scraps of recollection, cutting and pasting preposterous collages of fanciful incident, churning this garbled narrative through filters meant for the arbitration of the real world's rude empirical constraints. Little wonder that Tolstoy's great romance *Anna Karenin*[3] begins not just with an unhappy family unhappy after its own fashion (for our delectation) but with Prince Stepan Arkadyevich Oblonsky's recollected, fading *dream*:

"Yes, but the dream Darmstadt was in America. That's it—Alabin was giving a dinner on glass tables—and the tables were singing *Il mio tesoro*. No, not *Il mio tesoro*, something better; and there were some little decanters who were women. . . . Yes, it was a nice dream—very nice indeed. There was a lot that was capital but not to be expressed in words or even thought about clearly now that I am awake." (P. 14)

Oblonsky's domestic crime, for which he has been exiled from the matrimonial bed, is precisely to have treated women as decanters, even as he decanted his own self-satisfied yet uncertain ego into them. Count Tolstoy wrote, of course, before Freud delivered his own diagnosis of dreams, but he knew perfectly well that the phantasmagoric pleasures of that supine, barely twitching state were not to be expressed in words. And yet the efforts of his own artistic life would produce vast, overflowing oceans of words meant to capture and impress the clear ideas of waking thought even as they worked on his readers by putting them, at best, into a suggestible state of receptivity and prompted imagination not altogether unlike dream (at the risk, it must be admitted, in the lugubrious case of many, of literally sending them to sleep).

TRANSREALISM

Somewhere between dream and domestic fiction, cast like a strange shadow on the pages of story by the brilliant illumination of science, is the transreal, something new in the world. *Transreality* and *transrealism* are not yet terms in current circulation, not even within high literary and cultural discourse theory. I shall argue their usefulness. If language is the map we use to negotiate the human universe, it's also the machine we employ to extend our living quarters. Inevitably, it generates new nouns and verbs as deftly as rabbits generate rabbits. In the case of transreality and transrealism, the new words are needed to allow us to describe new textual practices—new ways of writing and reading, fresh methods for constructing and construing the world we inhabit.

Transrealism, as noted earlier, is a term invented in 1983 by sciencefabulist Rudy von Bitter Rucker, a professor of mathematics, enthusiast for higher dimensional analysis and computer specialist in simulation (he worked as Mathenaut in the Advanced Technology Division of the software company Autodesk). His own indicative transrealist fiction includes *White Light, or What is Cantor's Continuum Problem* (1980), the short stories in *The 57th Franz Kafka* (1983), *The Sex Sphere* (1983), whose protagonist has delirious sex with the pheromone-reeking extrusion of an *n*-dimensional being from Hilbert space, and *Saucer Wisdom* (1999), a *non*fiction fiction. Not all his writing is strictly transrealist and ranges from the protocyberpunk *Software* (1982), for which he received the inaugural Philip K. Dick Memorial Award, its sequels, *Wetware* (1988), *Freeware* (1997) and *Realware* (2000) plus a near-future extrapolation of genetic algorithms and artificial life, *The Hacker and the Ants* (1994), to a chimerical meditation on Edgar Allan Poe's mythos, *The Hollow Earth* (1990). But in Rucker's most innovative fiction, as John Clute astutely notes, "his protagonists—even the sexually ravaged first-person narrators of several texts, sometimes named Bitter, who must in part be autobiographical—are beguilingly raunchy, vigorous and zany" (Clute, "Rucker, Rudy," p. 1033).

In the 1980s the term *transrealism* was, however, an instrument whose time had not yet quite come, and it sank without trace. Even when Rucker collected his 1983 transrealist manifesto and an assortment of strange transgressive fictions into a book shamelessly titled *Transreal!* (1991), that too failed to capture critical attention. One British reviewer, Simon Ings, dismissed the program scornfully, calling it "an embarrassing farrago of things our first creative writing teachers taught us ('Although reading is linear, writing is not') dressed up in cyberpunkoid rhetoric. Transrealism ain't nothing but fiction sold short, and too cheap a statement of intent from a writer whose European influence has been oft (over?)-stressed."[4] To the contrary—the notion usefully coordinates our understanding of this new kind of writing invented as recently as the second half of the twentieth century. The extension of the device into full-blown "transreality"—an ontological condition rather than a form of textual construction—is, however, my own tentative coinage and by no means to Rucker's taste.

Transrealism, on this account, is a key to one of the next fictions after science fiction: a blend of speculative fantasy and bitter psychological truth-telling, a mode devised and explored in various measure by such innovative writers as Philip K. Dick, "James Tiptree Jr." (Alice Sheldon), J. G. Ballard, Joanna Russ, James Morrow, Karen Joy Fowler, Jonathan Carroll, Lisa Goldstein, John Calvin Batchelor, Rucker himself, and more literary names such as Thomas Pynchon, John Barth, Iain Banks, Martin Amis, Margaret Atwood. To date we seem to find more men than women attracted to the strategy, although as Rucker observes: "this style . . . might in fact be very congenial for [women writers], given the fact that women's fiction tends (I think) to contain more detailed and close observation of the world."[5]

PUNK AND CIRCUMSTANCE

"The Transrealist," declared Rucker at the outset, "writes about immediate perception in a fantastic way" (*Transreal!* p. 435). It is equally true that a transrealist writes about the fantastic, the invented, the inverted, the dementedly shocking, via well-known literary techniques developed to capture and notate the world of immediate perception.

After two centuries of opulent, realist fictions, narratives in which the meaning of each sentence hinges upon our acceptance of its closely observed and reported world, we now find literatures denuded of realism "weak and enervated," Rucker tells us (p. 435). For all that, there is also a widespread sentiment that strict realism itself has lost its edge. To reflect back the given world faithfully, and nothing more, is arguably to compromise with everything tawdry, corrupt and manipulative in the world—a world that *is*, alas, *the case*. "The tools of fantasy and SF [that is, science fiction or speculative fiction]," notes Rucker, "offer a means to thicken and intensify realistic fiction" (p. 435). Yet "a valid work of art should deal with the world the way it actually is" (p. 435). In consequence, "Transrealism tries to treat not only immediate reality, but also the higher reality in which life is embedded" (p. 435).

It is the grittiness, the circumstantial *density* and chaotic unpredictability of lived reality that's absent in most speculative fiction, science fiction, magical fantasy, even some magical realism. Granted, to insist upon representations of "the world the way it actually is" reopens instantly the immense debate on the shaping power of ideologies, discursive formations, Foucauldian tussles over power and knowledge, Derridean disruptions of all and any texts. I mean to bracket off such critical-theoretical concerns, since they tend either to paralyze discussion or send it veering off into uncontrolled dissemination. There is a text in this class, and that text is Rucker's oeuvre and his theory of writing sf.[6]

Through historical accident, most of today's fantastic fictions are written and received within an intertextual surround of decidedly generic, formulaic works and the tired paraliterary conventions they embody. They are obviously packaged and sold that way. Jonathan Lethem, a successful newcomer straddling the sf-slipstream divide, is uncompromising: "Among the factors arrayed against acceptance of sf as serious writing, none is more plain than this: the books are so fucking ugly. Worse, they're all ugly in the same way, so you can't distinguish those meant for grown-ups from those meant for twelve-years olds."[7] One finds the characters and settings of most sf and fantasy cardboard (think of *Star Trek* or any megaselling fantasy trilogy on the supermarket bookshelves) because they are templates put into creaking, predictable action—even though part of the genre writer's craft is to disguise or superficially refresh this tired pattern of narrative action. In part, this is understandable, even forgivable, for the figures and behavior of fanciful fiction are unavoidably, to some large extent, allegorical. However vivid, each represents or dramatizes only a handful of aspects of individual psychology or cultural dynamics. That is, genre characters are not intended as rounded or verisimilar portraits of humans in a richly known world. They tend by design and inadvertence toward the archetypal, the schematic, the iconic.

There is a way to leap over these generic temptations and limits, although until now few writers of the fantastic have made use of it. Oddly enough, it is the method employed by traditional fiction writers. One simply (simply!) draws upon the internalized understanding—the cognitive and emotional models within one's head and heart—of people one knows best:

In real life, the people you meet almost never say what you want or expect them to. From long and bruising contact, you carry simulations of your acquaintances around in your head. These simulations *are imposed on you from without*; they do not react to imagined situations as you might desire. By letting these simulations run your characters, you can avoid turning out mechanical wish-fulfilments. It is essential that the characters be in some sense out of control, as are real people—for what can anyone ever learn by reading about made-up people? (Rucker, "A Transrealist Manifesto," pp. 7–8).

Of course, we do not live in a truly random world, a world of other people "out of control." However much we relish the unexpected, too much novelty drives people into anxiety and illness. Rucker's distinction is perhaps a shading on previous analytics rather than a total revision. What's more, one finds a kind of dialectical relationship between the generic and the artistic, not simply a gulf between the small and the great, the fatuous and the true, the tawdry and the beautiful (or terrifyingly sublime). Brian Stableford has drawn attention to this complex transaction:

It is worth noting . . . that novelty can only arise against a background of the expected, and that there could not be such a thing as a sense of irony or . . . tragedy if certain expectations were not in place to be violated. For instance, Shakespeare's tragedies would not qualify as such were we not programmed to think that in some ideal sense Romeo and Juliet "ought" to live happily ever after in domestic harmony and that Othello's misunderstanding . . . "ought" to be cleared up. (Stableford, "How Should a Science Fiction Story End?" p. 8)

What distinguishes consumer tripe from literary canon, on this account, is the degree to which the former merely consoles readers with a fairy tale world of justice and happy outcomes, while the latter draws a more scorching and clear-eyed portrait of life in a heedless reality. (Is it fruitful to make such discriminations, as if matters of taste were anything better than subjective, or, worse, ideological impostures and impositions? We'll return to this enduring objection in a moment.) Stableford adds:

Formularization and an editorial insistence on "happy endings" are widely-recognized hallmarks of the kinds of fiction that are damned as products of "mass culture". It is worth reiterating, though, that the "realism" and "originality" of great literature are obtained by the refusal or variance of something preexistent, and could not have the effect they do were the expectations appropriate to popular fiction not already in place. Thus, for instance, *Middlemarch* has the reputation of being the first novel written for grown-ups because it flatly refuses to regard getting married and coming into an inheritance as automatic solutions to all the problems of existence in the way that earlier novels had tended to do. (Pp. 1, 8)

The crucial postulate of postmodernism is that our certainties—artistic, and in ordinary daily life as well—have been steadily and progressively undermined, especially since, say, the 1950s. Relentless change affects everything. Virtual replaces "real." But "real," as we have seen, was *always* at least in part a construct, so this earthquake is more a shift in understanding than a change in the world. If so, we *live* postmodernism. Therefore we always-already have a theory of it, structuring our daily experience, just as your cat has a brain-wired theory of birds as it prowls the garden.

On the other hand, theories running on autopilot deserve mistrust, even if they're zany and pomo. We are well advised to dredge them up into full view, squeeze them through some logical sieves (themselves theories, of course), put their predictions to the test.

INVENTING WORLDS

Construed as a mode, sf's textuality is distinguished from, say, the fantastic (the mode of uncanny realism), the mimetic (the mode of naturalistic realism), surrealism (the mode of the unconscious run riot); feel free to add your own modal groups. Still, it is unlikely that effective sf can be written that leaves behind the known world entire. A truly successful sf novel, by that criterion, might be unintelligible. Stanislaw Lem has tried several times to write about recognizable humans who *encounter* the utterly incomprehensible—and the result is bafflement, a humiliated return to local human concerns. Gregory Benford's Galactic sequence of novels has been set in a far future of chip-implanted and augmented human clans, but the texture of these ambitious books tends to the stolid and lumpy.[8]

On the other hand, we can take educated (or wild) guesses at some of the technologies that will emerge in the next 50 to 200 years and try to imagine life in a world so skewed. You run swiftly into combinatorial explosions of feedback loops. Consider a recent sf fad, molecular nanotechnology: Greg Bear tried bravely in *Queen of Angels*, as did Neal Stephenson in *The Diamond Age* and Linda Nagata in *The Bohr Maker*, but such *mises en scene* tend to go schematic or clotted or turn into a fable very quickly. Can we truly imagine a culture (many cultures) where molecular compilers build any commodity we desire out of gunge for the price of electricity? Where nano surgeons rewire consciousness, or upload it to multiple bot copies, or ensure physical immortality, or rejig DNA so we grow whatever new parts we wish for? Where genuine artificial intelligence (AI) goes hyperintelligent within months or decades of its emergence? Where quantum computers put us in contact with alternative superposed universes (if that means anything)? Where all this is happening at once, and not in A.D. 5001 but to our grandchildren? It does make for wonderful storytelling, just *pour le sport*. The chief metaphoric message is, perforce, the medium: things *change*, including humanity. So old metaphors like the Apocalypse might turn out to be literally instantiated in another current hot meme, the Singularity (tipped to happen around 2050), when all the curves of radical change go asymptotic, straight up. Transhumanity or posthumanity. If so, that's not a metaphor any longer—it's a terrifying, ebullient promise.

We shall return to this extraordinary breach with both reality and transreality in chapter 6. For the moment, let us return to sf textuality proper and to a less apocalyptic topic: the vexed question of sf's own special way with words, the typical way in which it deploys its referentless signs, builds worlds out of words.

NOTES

1. Erich Auerbach, *Mimesis: The Representation of Reality in Western Literature*, trans. William W. Trask (1946; Princeton, NJ: Princeton University Press, 1953).

2. A related rhetorical gadget is *syllepsis*, in which a single word is applied simultaneously to two quite distinct topics; perhaps sf or SF is a form of syllepsis fiction.

3. L. N. Tolstoy, *Anna Karenin*, trans. Rosemary Edmonds (Harmondsworth: Penguin, 1954).

4. Simon Ings review of *Transreal!*, in *Foundation: The Review of Science Fiction* 54 (spring 1992): 99.

5. Rucker, personal communication, 13 June 1999. While of course, I do not wish to *exclude* women from any emerging transrealist canon, I do find more men than women in the sf texts I have read. The critic Sylvia Kelso usefully questions this assertion, mentioning as candidates for the transrealist strategic subcategory "Connie Willis (at least with *Lincoln's Dreams*), well-known one-offs like Emshwiller's *Carmen Dog*, and Dodderidge's *The New Gulliver*, to Shale Aaron's *Virtual Death* and into (commercial) fantasy 'proper', with Sheri Tepper's *Beauty*, Megan Lindholm's *Cloven Hooves* and "The Fifth Squashed Cat,' " and so on. She adds that any apparent *ad hoc* gender exclusion in advance

is actually a gender-related canon-forming strategy, which was isolated by Laurie Langbauer with the formation of the "realist canon" back in the 1800s. They excluded everything that they considered "romance"—but romance was identified with women writers. So? you say. But then Anthea Trodd turns up the romance club of Stevenson, Conrad, Haggard, et al, in the late 1800s–early '90s, promoting romance at the expense of realism, and they figure REALISM as female and ROMANCE as masculine. In other words, "women don't enter this canonical field" is to me a portable set of ideological goalposts. (Personal communication, 15 November 1998)

Such categorial slippage, often in the service of an implicit sexual politics, is always a hazard when discussing a new way of looking at a fuzzy set of texts. I anticipate a lively debate over demarcation if the transrealist strategy catches the interest of other critics and theorists. For the record, I am not certain that some of the texts Kelso cites are properly regarded as transrealist, in the sense defined by Rucker, since they do not feature narrators based directly on the writer's acknowledged experiences. Emshwiller's story, for example, is focalized through a dog, Pooch.

6. I am troping here on Stanley Fish's celebrated punning title in his early reader-response study *Is There a Text in this Class? The Authority of Interpretive Communities* (Cambridge, Mass.: Harvard University Press, 1980).

7. Jonathan Lethem, "Why Can't We All Just Live Together?: A Vision of Genre Paradise Lost," *The New York Review of Science Fiction*, issue 121, vol. 11, no. 1 (September 1998): 8. This is the uncut version of an article first published in the *Village Voice* as "Close Encounters: The Squandered Promise of Science Fiction."

8. These start with *In the Ocean of Night* (1977) and conclude six books later in *Sailing Bright Eternity* (1995).

3

Science Fiction's Crazy Prose

Although entirely derived from books, these codes, by a swivel characteristic of bourgeois ideology, which turns culture into nature, appear to establish reality, "Life." "Life," then, in the classic text,
becomes a nauseating mixture of common opinions, a smothering
layer of received ideas . . . a fatal condition of Replete Literature,
mortally stalked by the army of stereotypes it contains.
                    —Roland Barthes, "The Voice of Science," *S/Z* (p. 206)

In the best of all possible words, prose and ideas would be seamlessly
united. I do not mean that only impeccable thoughts or perceptions
ought be condensed and conveyed by sublimely fitted words. Although
success in that task has its sublime pleasures: consider this sentence from
William Faulkner's *The Sound and the Fury*, matched by few in the science
fiction canon: "I ran down the hill in that vacuum of crickets like breath
travelling across a mirror,"[1] or Vladimir Nabokov's wickedly transgressive luxury in his famous opening lines: "Lo-lee-ta: the tip of the tongue
taking a trip of three steps down the palate to tap, at three, on the teeth."[2]
It might be preferable, though, and often is, for elusive and contrary
ideas to bash their way onto the page and the reader's eye through a
verbal thicket that enacts the difficulty, resistance and pain of experience
and the world's intractability.

"Writers are still asked where they get their crazy ideas from," remarks agile Brian Aldiss, a wizard with words; he means especially sci-

ence fiction writers, professionals in crazy ideas. "They are less often asked where they get their crazy prose from."[3] Let us ask that now.

On the whole, "literary" readers still appear to define the special excellence of their favored texts by implicit reference to verbal texture (apt, oblique, perhaps diffident, worldly, effortlessly musical—where melodies can be, as noted, troublingly harsh or succulent and seductive) as well as serious themes, psychological penetration, the kit and caboodle of traditional fiction's efflorescene. None of this seems automatically to exclude or damn science fiction's crazy prose. For that matter, is it really all that crazy? Aldiss again: "Science fiction writers on the whole present their ideas in the plainest possible terms. Style is clear glass, designed to be seen through uninterruptedly to the meaning. This is preferable if the idea is to disconcert the reader, or to offer something new. Cut glass, stained glass, equally admirable where apposite, is more the manner of a Bradbury, a Sturgeon, a Gene Wolfe, or an Iain Banks" (Aldiss, *"The Atheist's Tragedy* Revisited," pp. 170–71). Or a Brian Aldiss, one must add—nor are these exemplary writers out of the genre, nor would any be known (except perhaps Bradbury, and more recently, in his non-sf recension, Banks)[4] to those with an exclusive taste for Doris Lessing, Beryl Bainbridge, Toni Morrison, Margaret Atwood, Antonia Byatt, Joan Didion, Ian McEwan, Salman Rushdie, Richard Ford, Philip Roth, John Updike, Kazuo Ishiguro.

Oddly, though, during the last couple of decades the prose of eminent literary writers and of ambitious science fiction writers approached each other asymptotically. (That mild borrowing from mathematics—an asymptote is the curve of an equation whose values ever more closely approach some limit without quite reaching it—is perhaps an instance of the language mutation I am invoking.) Still, surely the two are readily distinguished by a sensitive ear. Compare the following passages, one from an ironic literary lion long familiar to subscribers of *The New Yorker,* the other a British sf novelist and scholar who once turned out quickies for what was called the American pulp market:

It was in September 1973, shortly after returning from his honeymoon, that Adam Zimmerman began to read *Sein und Zeit* by Martin Heidegger. Although he was a native New Yorker, he read German fluently; he was the grandson of Austrian Jews who had fled Vienna with his father (then an infant) in 1933, and a perverse estrangement from his parents had made him more enthusiastic to retain his national roots than his religious ones. For this reason he had always remained aloof from *schmaltz* while being self-indulgent in the matter of *angst,* and he was ready-made for that sanctification of self-pity which is the existentialist's red badge of courage.

The mild inwardly directed mockery of a late twentieth-century New York Jewish writer (Woody Allen drifts to mind) plays like a smile at the edges of this opening sally, with its name-droppings and games. This story's title is "And He Not Busy Being Born," from Bob Dylan's song—hence Zimmerman, Dylan's birth name—while Adam is the Ur-name not just of the only man *not* born, earliest of Zimmerman's ancient lineage, but the first also of those busy dying. Cultural specificity is affirmed (Yiddish *schmaltz*, German *angst*) and denied (the happy escape in advance from the death camps, Zimmerman's desire nonetheless to recover those befouled national roots) or confounded (the gesture simultaneously at European postwar modish philosophy, itself entangling collusion with Nazism and brave resistance to its evil, and Stephen Crane's paradigmatic American literary study of Civil War psychic wounding). Ambiguity and layering in every word.

Place this concentrated if arch local realism against a vision of utter alienation from the familiar, the quotidian:

This planet supports but two life-forms—myself, and an immense fungus that has covered all but the stoniest of available land. The brownish, writhing, mounting formations aboveground are but a fraction of its mass, made up of microscopic hyphae that extend their network in all directions, knotting and interweaving into the mycelium that makes up the thallus, or undifferentiated body, of my immense companion in vitality. It does not speak, or visibly move, but it does undergo change, the telltale mark of an organism. . . . Sometimes I find in the convolutions of a folded outcropping some striking anthropomorphic set of ridges and vesicles—another man, about to stand forth!—and sense a joke, a thinking comment, a wry salute from my ubiquitous co-inhabitant.

This passage, too, is drenched in the lexical specificity (the vernacular, as it were) of an exact culture, but it is the culture of scientific botany, making it a jargon, technobabble—rootless, so to speak, as valid on a planet where only a vast fungus shares the whole world with a single human observer as in the laboratory or lecture theatre of a university, or a bustling public botanical garden thronging with urban people who barely know a plant from an animal. This dependency upon specialized jargon and concretized metaphors—for what is the planet, if not a peep inside some psychic scar of the late twentieth century—is surely the fatal error, unforgivable and boring, of science fiction prose.

Perhaps not. The first passage is the opening paragraph of a story published by Brian Stableford in the British sf magazine *Interzone*. The second is from John Updike's recent novel, a lyrical, brutal meditation on death and millennium, *Toward the End of Time*, from which I drew the goadingly disillusioned epigraph opening chapter 1. Surely no writer is more firmly bedded down in the embrace of sophisticated upper middlebrow textuality than Updike. It is doubtful, and regrettable, that as many as one *New Yorker* reader in a hundred will have heard of Stable-ford.[5]

I certainly do not wish to deny that there is something distinctive, special, irritating, exhilarating in science fiction's own characteristic crazy prose. This book will spend quite a lot of effort exploring it. But the very evolution that has permitted the emergence of transrealist fiction, and adjacent mutations, depends on a transition sketched in 1997 by sf new-comer Michaela Roessner:

In the early days, science fiction usually (but not always) tended to revolve around plot and nifty futuristic ideas. Not much else was necessary. The novelty and uniqueness of the genre were sufficient to charm, and the fact that the read-ers tended to be youthful didn't hurt, either . . . [Later, the] craft of writing sci-ence fiction was growing up. Characters in stories had friends, enemies, families, and a personal history. . . . Now we find writing in which fictional characters enjoy relationships and personal histories not simply to make them more engag-ing to the readership but because, just as in "real life," it is exactly those rela-tionships and personal histories that make things happen, that drive the plot.[6]

And that grown-up people wish to read about. Cartoon figures slamming each other in a cartoon landscape, however vivid and concussive, have less and less appeal once the teenaged years are past. The trap for any fiction written in full awareness of scientific and technological change is apparent: The world's stability cannot be assumed, nor can the psychic makeup of its inhabitants. Whether or not we and our children are to be gene-modified and morphed into forms that resemble nothing so much as comic strip figures (and that is surely part of any likely future), we are already subject to massive flux in our daily, ordinary lives. We might not see those changes from month to month or even year to year, yet we register their accumulation at some profound inner level of excite-ment and trepidation.

So for escape, entertainment, diversion, even grownups in their hun-dreds of millions attend cinema showings of vastly expensive cartoons of the future: all the *Star Wars, Aliens, Terminators, Jurassic Parks, Fifth Elements* the studios choose to pump out. And the tragedy, for sf, is that these childishly rudimentary if prodigious compilations of gaudy im-agery, shock, hyped cartoon embodiments of our lusts and fears, become the standard emblem for an entire mode of narrative invention. It is as if—and as bizarre as if—all the world's subtle masterpieces of fiction dealing with human love were absorbed unthinkingly and with a sneer into the category *Mills & Boon* or *Harlequin Romance*.

It requires no complex argument to show that this would be a cardinal error of ignorant reduction, degrading nuance—unread and on the basis of categorial prejudice—into an assumption of stereotype. True, simple routinized template-structured romances have found their recuperation lately in popular culture arguments of some finesse. But such arguments, if they are wise, retain limits to their claims. The latest consolatory Gothic or romance novella at the newsstand is an etiolated parody of Jane Austen, Flaubert, Tolstoy. Impossible, then, to conceive of literary readers confusing the two classes of tales of men and women in love (in whatever combination) and putting aside A. S. Byatt's *Babel Tower* with a sneer on the grounds that it is, after all, of the same species as Danielle Steele's latest blockbuster.

Yet that is how most of the literary readers I encounter respond to science fiction. Who can blame them? When journalism reaches for a catch phrase to anchor the latest astonishing marvel to leap from the laboratory or launch pad, the stock of comparisons is meager: the new ion engine from NASA is "like *Star Trek*" (although ion engines were being built and investigated long before Gene Roddenberry's derivative series was first broadcast in the 1960s), clones are "like *Frankenstein*" (published in 1818), the newest spectacular technology is no longer "mere science fiction," or it is but we are advised to recall, for its fictional equivalent, the stories of Jules Verne and H. G. Wells from a century and more past (or, for the excessively up-to-date, Isaac Asimov, Ray Bradbury or Arthur C. Clarke, writers famous two generations ago).

SOMETHING NEW, SOMETHING OLD

Strikingly, this has been going on for a long time, whether or not sf happened to be passing through high and profitable public acceptance. In 1947, Dr. J. O. Bailey began his important early analytical history of the genre, *Pilgrims Through Space and Time* with a plaint that could have been penned last week: "It is time that this body of literature, often considered a curious and childish by-way, is defined, presented in some historical survey, sampled, and analyzed to see what its major patterns and ideas may be."[7] Alas, sf is still defined either by the lowest denominator of the mass media, or as the dutiful stodge of school reports (Verne's sf having peaked, to stress it again, in the 1860s and 1870s, Wells's in the last decade of the nineteenth century), or, at best, by reference to stories by men—and most of the sf writers *were* men, then— whose best work was complete before the first Sputnik went into orbit in 1957. Astonishing! Meanwhile, much genre science fiction "product" relaxes before this news of its widespread acceptance among the unsophisticated, of whom, inevitably, there are always many more than there are literary readers. Like a self-fulfilling prophecy, the largest proportion of mass-market sf regresses—although hardly ever to the dismal depths of its early pulp years, for even the unsophisticated have moved on—or stands still. Give a dog a bad name.

Yet that is very far from the whole story. Fiction written in the shadow and illumination of advanced science is sometimes obliged, in being true to its own strengths and possibilities, into an oppositional stance that faces off its traditional forebears. Consider, quite explicitly, the mockery of literary pretensions—rather broadly sketched—by the venturesome scientists about to cast themselves, for the knowledge they will gain in the extended instant of their deaths, into a black hole, in Greg Egan's stylized and rebarbative short story "The Planck Dive." A blowhard poet (hapless daughter apparently in tow) arrives to plague the exploratory crew with his sanctimonious epic ambitions:

Prospero began soberly. "For nigh on a thousand years, we . . . have dreamed in vain of a new Odyssey to inspire us, new heroes to stand beside the old, new ways to retell the eternal myths. . . . But I have arrived in time to pluck your tale from the very jaws of gravity!"

Tiet said, "Nothing was at risk of being lost. Information about the Dive is being broadcast to every polis, stored in every library." Tiet's icon was like a supple jewelled statue carved from ebony.

Prospero waved a hand dismissively. "A stream of technical jargon. In Athena, it might as well have been the murmuring of the waves."

Tiet raised an eyebrow. "If your vocabulary is impoverished, augment it—don't expect us to impoverish our own. Would you give an account of classical Greece without mentioning the name of a single city-state?"

"No. But those are universal terms, part of our common heritage—"

"They're terms that have no meaning outside a tiny region of space, and a brief period of time. Unlike the terms needed to describe the Dive, which are applicable to every quartic femtometer of spacetime."

Prospero replied, a little stiffly, "Be that as it may, in Athena we prefer poetry to equations. And I have come to honour your journey in language that will resonate down the corridors of the imagination for millennia."

Sachio said, "So you believe you're better qualified to portray the Dive than the participants?" Sachio appeared as an owl, perched inside the head of a flesher-shaped wrought-iron cage full of starlings.

"I am a narratologist . . . I have come to create enigmas, not explanations. I have come to shape the story of your descent into a form that will live on long after your libraries have turned to dust. . . . To extract the mythic essence, mere detail must become subservient to a deeper truth."[8]

Much later, falling into gravity's inexorable doom and loving every moment of it, Prospero's much put-upon daughter, Cordelia, smiles. "Baudelaire can screw himself. I'm here for the physics" (p. 291). And physics is what Egan provides: scads of physics, physics at the margins of the known and beyond, physics rendered not so much in storytelling's ancient visceral imagination as in a kind of cool, ironic allegory of equations tormented to the limit. This is a very odd textuality indeed, even for hardened sf readers. For literary chauvinists, it is surely as dull as it is abhorrent.

An Australian cultural commentator, Mark Davis, has offered an astute sketch, and criticism, of the literary establishment's rules of engagement in his (and Egan's, and my) country: "Local literary culture, to its detriment, seems obsessed with the business of 'being a writer' rather than with . . . having something to say. This is one of the reasons why the high canon of local fiction often seems so self-conscious and contrived. Younger writers who master the style—a sort of manneredness that labours in the shadow of Patrick White's brilliant metaphors—sometimes find themselves invited to sit at the big table" (Davis, p. 137). Small chance, then that Greg Egan will receive the engraved calling card any time soon. His altogether astonishing and *sui generis* creation are entirely absent from tallies such as the Booker Prize short-list. General readers are simply insufficiently adventurous, open to challenge, eager to stretch their imaginative capacities. They have no appetite for the elation of fresh thoughts superbly deployed, preferring familiar feelings delicately annotated. Much of the imaginative writing conducted within the embrace of the sciences is a closed book to those self-exiled in this fashion.

In a way, that is understandable and even excusable. Each mode of writing generates, and requires familiarity with, its own "megatext"—a specialized set of codes, tropes, constructional conventions, already-writtens, been-there-done-thats. Alas, the megatext maneuvers central to good science fiction are unknown to the bearers of cultural legitimation and often intrinsically offensive to these anointed gatekeepers. To gain anything like the full density from any given late-model science fiction story, novel or film, we must read it through, within and against the colossal megatext of earlier sf. There is nothing lofty or metaphysical in that claim—the megatext is simply (complexly) an intricated network in individual and collective memory, a scaffolding built from the scraps of half-remembered tales, reiterated structural principles, narrative road rules explicit and shadowy. How, then, is the bewildered *habitué* of Malouf or Drabble going to feel when she opens Egan's spectacular novel *Diaspora* and reads this account of "orphanogenesis": "The conceptory was non-sentient software, as ancient as Konishi polis itself. Its main purpose was to enable the citizens of the polis to create offspring: a child of one parent, or two, or twenty—formed partly in their own image, partly according to their wishes, and partly by chance. Sporadically, though, every teratau or so, the conceptory created a citizen with no parents at all" (p. 5). Sf's crazy prose! Conceptory? Teratau? And that is just the first paragraph of the first chapter.

What is the general fiction reader to make of this scene, one I find entirely gorgeous in its rococo *chutzpah*:

Waiting to be cloned one thousand times and scattered across ten million cubic light years, Paolo Venetti relaxed in his favorite ceremonial bathtub: a tiered hexagonal pool set in a courtyard of black marble flecked with gold. Paolo wore full traditional anatomy, uncomfortable garb at first, but the warm currents flowing across his back and shoulders slowly eased him into a pleasant torpor. He could have reached the same state in an instant, by decree, but the occasion seemed to demand the complete ritual of verisimilitude, the ornate curlicued longhand of imitation physical cause and effect. (P. 155)

That final whimsical remark, of course, like the parody of Tennysonian bombast in "The Planck Dive," is surely also an ironic bow toward the canons of taste in the ruling literary community within which Egan dwells as a dispossessed alien artist. If he must, Egan can do the police in different voices (as T. S. Eliot put it in *The Waste Land*), but by and large he chooses more oblique and interesting impersonations.

In *Diaspora* (1997), nothing less is plotted than the next three thousand years of life, mind and their elected varieties in an onion-shell universe vastly larger than anything we currently perceive from the estate of barely modified humanity. In a sensational, concerted and frankly demanding act of reality-creation, Egan finally shifts some of his posthuman characters into a macrosphere (dubbed U*) with more spatial dimensions than ours. Luckily, their minds and bodies can be morphed to deal with the shocks—as our minds are, after a fashion, as we struggle to actualize Egan's textual hints.

Orlando braced himself. "Now show me U-star." His exoself responded to the command, spinning his eyeballs into hyperspheres, rebuilding his retinas as four-dimensional arrays, rewiring his visual cortex, boosting his neural model of the space around him to encompass five dimensions. As the world inside his head expanded, he cried out and closed his eyes, panic-stricken and vertiginous. . . . He glanced down at the bottom of the window. The most trivial details in a 5-scape could still be hypnotic; the tesseract of the window met the tesseract of the floor along, not a line, but a roughly cubical volume. That he could see this entire volume all at once almost made sense when he thought of it as the bottom hyperface of the transparent window, but when he realised that every point was shared by the front hyperface of the opaque floor, any lingering delusions of normality evaporated. (Pp. 231–32)

This must certainly put off most readers, unless they are already at home in the sf megatext's extended universe and know, for instance, that a tesseract is a four-dimensional cube with eight cubic hyperfaces. The language Egan must use is often clinical, flat, replete with mathematical tags and floating bits of biochemistry and astronomy and higher-dimensional analysis. We're not used to this kind of thing, not in a novel, for heaven's sake! Not a-sex characters who refer to each other with odd pronouns like ve and vis, not people created from "a string of bits" whose idea of fun is building testable models of the universe in which particles are the mouths of wormholes, who use megatechnology to chase an alien culture through 267,904,176,383,054 shells of an infinitely embedded cosmos, until at last they discern the sculpted interdimensional shape of what Egan has called "the largest structure in science fiction."

And yet—when Egan's posthumans reach the end of their quest, they are faced, as we are, by the same terrible question: What do you do next? Take your quietus? Return to the Truth Mines, quarrying knowledge? If love and death are to be subject to our precise understanding and control—as, sooner or later, they surely shall—what ancient wisdom will come to our aid? None, alas, for "ancient wisdom" is the distillate of ancient dilemmas and conflicts, and those will be solved and done.

THE MISSING MATTER PROBLEM

Egan's kind of late-generation, highly cerebral science fiction prose is always not easy to read, not transparent. Sometimes it is annoyingly expository, no matter how hard Egan tried to disguise the fact—and after all it can hardly be anything else than a stopgap, the kind of impasse even the brightest among us face when peering into the unimaginable future. But it is an ambitious and *artistic* bid at the impossible. His prose and his ideas are matched, and they extend us as we struggle with their formidable, uncompromising clarity. That is why I regard Egan as now perhaps the most important (although as yet far from the best) sf writer in the world. At various times in sf's fairly brief history, writers as various as Wells, 'Doc' Smith, Heinlein, Ballard, Delany, Le Guin, Russ— even Harlan Ellison and Larry Niven—have been pivotal, breaking trails, showing fresh ways for sf to expand into untouched regions of narrative space. Of those, only Wells, Heinlein, Le Guin and perhaps Delany could rationally be regarded as also the best of their time.

In many respects Egan is still an undeveloped literary artist. Even his finest work totters by comparison with the complex best of, say, John Crowley, James Morrow, Bruce Sterling, Michael Swanwick, Gene Wolfe, Joanna Russ, recent Le Guin. These are writers whose texts do more than deploy with clean, brilliant ingenuity some astonishing or seemingly paradoxical insight from science and philosophy, which is Egan's forté. They engage us more fully in their imaginative embrace (however naive and old-fashioned such a formulation inevitably strikes us, all these decades after the advent of poststructuralism's corrosive analytics). Their characters touch us for weeks or even years, having been rendered out of the clay of our own richest self-understanding—the template tales we each employ to explain self and others—reshaped at the prompting of experts in human sensibility who use all the storyteller's tools, including the heart.

Is Egan (as artist) heartless? Does his work lack heart? It can often seem that way. His stories, gathered in the collections *Axiomatic* (1996) and *Luminous* (1998) are, yes, luminous technical feats in opening out or deconstructing axiomatics, individual and cultural. He is enviably in command (or gives the impression of being so) of the latest neurosciences, molecular biology, advanced computer programming, artificial and natural intelligence, evolutionary theory. His politics is crisp, astute, pitilessly candid, and by and large I am sympathetic to its account of human conduct. If his style is—*level* (let's not say "flat")—that isn't because it exults in deflating pretension, like the inverse snobbery of grunge or any other self-consciously boho posture; rather, he tells his stories by means not alien to the French existentialists of the 1940s and 1950s—Camus among the Galaxies, Robbe-Grillet in the labyrinths of the brain's modules. You can see why Egan prefers this antiheroic, antihumanist locution. It enacts his themata. It is the natural voice for a disillusioned, clear-eyed observer of human sanctimony in the last era when self-deceit remains (barely) possible yet almost everywhere regnant. For all that, his work will surely be improved as he extends his range, as he has begun to do in the near-future novel *Teranesia* (1999).

POLISH NOTATION

The writer one tends to think of while reading Egan's relentless fables is Polish sf polymath Stanislaw Lem (when it's not computer scientist Douglas R. Hofstadter or philosopher Daniel Dennett), probing consciousness and volition until those central conceits blink into dazzling fragments, spin, adhere once more, leaving only the impossible afterimage of black-clad stage handlers shuffling spotlit puppets—except that the handlers *were never there*. Lem has even managed to transform his lectures and subversive reflections into a kind of fiction as remote from the traditional apparatus of transrealist character-driven fiction as one might imagine, using a cunning device: He reviews nonexistent books.

So he can propose outrageous concepts without having to justify the skiddy bits or bother with a distracting adventure story or the deployment of sensitively observed characters, while playing Devil's Advocate to his own effrontery.[9] If the Surrealists rejoiced in the gift of meaningful accident, twenty-first-century's science will retain a taste for the fortuitous, Lem has argued, but dispense with the meaning. "Culture exists and has always existed in order to make every accident, every kind of arbitrariness, appear in a benevolent or at least necessary light."[10] This, evidently, is just too bad. "The laws of Nature act not *in spite* of random events but *through* them. . . . Life is one of the rare winners in this lottery, and intelligence an even rarer . . ." (Lem, *One Human Minute*, pp. 99–100). It is a unendearing philosophy, and only Lem's prodigious inventiveness and wordplay keep it palatable. The first third of *One Human Minute* "reviews" the vast compilation of that name, an imaginary *Guinness Book of Records* that spells out in endless tables of statistics what 5 billion humans are doing every sixty seconds. The catalogs of death and misery, the computer-generated lists of facts without meaning, are finally overwhelming. "For instance, the stream of sperm, 43 tons of it, discharged into vaginas each minute—its 430,000 hectolitres is compared with the 37,000 hectolitres of boiling water produced at each eruption of the largest geyser in the world. . . . How can one come to terms" slyly complains Lem-the-reviewer, "with an image of humanity copulating relentlessly through all the cataclysms that befall it, or that it has brought upon itself?" (p. 14). This Swiftian disgust is only somewhat moderated in "The Upside-down Evolution" (p. 37), which argues—plausibly enough, in this day of emerging nanotechnology—that armies and their generals will soon to be replaced by dustmote microchip invaders with the intelligence of insects, self-guided and invulnerable to nuclear or other attack. "The World as Cataclysm" (p. 69) sums up Lem's unromantic yet uncynical view of the universe we chance to inhabit, although not necessarily for much longer. Lem's verve makes sparkling refreshment of these chilly draughts, if one can swallow it without gagging. But there is more in Lem's oeuvre than games and hilarious verbal agility; it is hard, as yet, to imagine Egan writing a book to equal Lem's first novel, *The Hospital of the Transfiguration* (to which we shall return), at once formally engineered with great cool beauty and heartbreakingly moving.

MECHANISMS OF DESIRE

Egan's short fiction is certainly important in its own terms—terms that are helping to reorient sf once again in the direction of hard thought and away from squishy self-indulgent consumerist wish fulfilment. It catches an aspect of the cusp of the millennium in just the way that Wells's sf did for his own two centuries. Wells embodied Victorian desires of the nineteenth, while reaching forward to a twentieth of fantastical technologies. The machineries in Wells were external, even if often they were palpably expressions of wish or mental states: time travel (memory and anticipation), invisibility (voyeurism and camouflage in a dangerous, puzzling world), terrifying military threats and opportunities that staged and foresaw the upheavals of class near to Wells's own torn soul.

The mechanisms in Egan are on both the grandest scales (the substrates of space and time, beyond the infinitesimal Planck intervals that define the quantum) and the most intimate (those intimations of the machine in the ghost we must all share, if we dare to learn what science is now exposing, as functional magnetic resonance imaging (fMRI) and PET scans reveal the flux of our brains even as we see, hear, think, imagine, dream). Egan need not look to invaders from Mars; his own gaze and intellect are already vast and cool and, if not unsympathetic, *diagnostic*. Idea is almost all; his fiction has just barely enough domestic business to establish and convey the salience to human persons of these high biological and cultural abstractions. In the end, almost always, we are left with a fatal sense of having had an allegory foisted on us. What Egan's fiction needs, I suggest, is a strong dose of transrealism.

Consider a fairly slight story, "Transition Dreams" (*Interzone*, 1993), which dealt effortlessly with conceits only now coming into focus in other writers' fiction as well as in forecasts from the real world of scientific research: uploading your mind from fallible protein into a durable computer platform and ultimately an independent robot body (the Gleisners of *Diaspora*) free of the limitations of flesh but with all its advantages and more. If mind is itself a vast computation, what is its fate during that transition? A sleep akin to coma? A protracted nightmare of unhinged hallucination? Egan tells a neat horror story with mild philosophical implications, but that's all. It is a theme close to the center of Egan's work from "Learning to Be Me" (*Interzone*, 1990), in which an implanted computer routinely replaces the frail brain in late childhood—but which of the two, as they are uncoupled, embodies the "true" self?

The intellectually sinuous "Mitochondrial Eve" (*Interzone*, 1995) is a typical ideational escapade in which a bombastic high-tech bid to rid the earth of traditional racisms and sectional strife backfires, inevitably, and spawns a brand-new fire-flickering, bloody means to bolster old tribalisms and new. The tale is worked through in a schematic, convenient conjugal conflict that enacts in small that battle of the sexes its theme accelerates and detonates. Egan is bleak in his dark humor; you get the feeling that he doesn't see much hope for people, poor people, poor damned mired hard-wired people. "Chaff" (*Interzone*, 1993) makes that explicit. An agent flies into El Nido de Ladrones, a microecology of lethal designer pharmaceuticals between Colombia and Peru owned by biotech drug cartels and utopians, and learns what Egan's protagonists always learn, sooner or later, captured in a quote from Conrad's *Heart of Darkness*: "as to superstitions, beliefs, and what you may call principles, they are less than chaff in a breeze." It is a scarifying assertion, one that undermines everything that makes us human (if we take it seriously, and Egan tries again and again to force us to do so). The story's landscape, its detail filigree, is assured, convincing, the very model (like, say, those of Lucius Shepard)[11] of a modern major genre *Weltbild*. His values-are-chaff, meaning-is-contingent case is tested again in this melodramatic setting, which is really just a narrative gadget to keep us tracing the logical exercise. Imagine a drug that allows you to re-write the mental maze that is yourself. What happens when you are unhooked from the tyranny and structural solidity of "human nature," of genetically contrived codes and tropisms of conduct? Here is a radical freedom as even Sartre and Camus and Biswanger never dreamed it. Here is utter self-fashioning. Yet who is the self performing this self-levitating feat of construction? We step into an Escher-void once we grant that "all the 'eternal verities'—all the sad and beautiful insights of all the great writers from Sophocles to Shakespeare—are *less than chaff in a breeze*" (Egan, *Luminous*, p. 23).

What burns through these minimally dramatized demonstrations in epistemology and indeed ontology is Egan's own problematic or quest: how *can* we know the world, or ourselves as a sliver of it, when everything comes to us via the mediation and construction of parochial upbringing, of genetic and cultural history, of contingent biology, of the arbitrary settings (or are they quite so random as they seem?) of the cosmos itself? This is explored in a sketch, "Mister Volition" (*Interzone*, 1995) and more wittily and painfully in "Reasons to be Cheerful" (*Interzone*, 1997). The poignancy of that question is made especially piercing in "Silver Fire" (*Interzone*, 1995), where Claire Booth, a kind of epidemiological private eye, tracks an outbreak of the twenty-first-century equivalent of AIDS. Her conflict with 14-year-old daughter Laura, involved (this week, at least) with the New Hermetics cult, is exact:

Laura said, "Did you know that Isaac Newton spent more time on alchemy than he did on the theory of gravity?"

"Yes. Did you know he also died a virgin? Role models are great, aren't they?" Alex gave me a sideways warning look, but didn't buy in. . . .

"But sure, it's fascinating to see some of the blind alleys people have explored."

Laura smiled at me pityingly. "*Blind alleys!*" She finished picking the toast crumbs off her plate, then she rose and left the room with a spring in her step, as if she'd won some kind of battle. (Egan, "Silver Fire," p. 159)

Claire's world is our own, turned up a plausible notch. As the dreadful, incurable disease Silver Fire spreads, every fashionable poseur and media loony advances a mystery theory. In a fine pastiche of such "theorists" as the French Jean Baudrillard and the Australian McKenzie Wark, and a thousand graduate students who have learned the kind of pomobabble debunked so hilariously by Alan Sokal and Jean Bricmont, Egan's glib talking heads embrace the scourge as a postmodern medical condition, "the very first plague of the Information Age" (p. 168). That turns out, hideously, to be correct, in a way. But the disease is symptomatic of a worse blight, a recurrent collapse of even advanced technological cultures into blind and blinding belief systems of astounding stupidity. "All it took," Claire realizes, "was the shock of grief to peel away the veneer of understanding: *Life is not a morality play. Disease is just disease; it carries no hidden meaning* . . . At some level, we still hadn't swallowed the hardest-won truth of all: *The universe is indifferent*" (p. 171).

Yet if that is so, if we see faces in clouds and cracks just because our brains are hard-wired by mindless selective reproductive filters to give priority to any shape that *looks like* a face, to impose meaning on any pattern that *looks like* an intention, what happens to our self-estimate? Suppose homosexuality is, after all, most often a developmental pathway switched on by an unusual stressor in the mother's environment, triggering elevated levels of some hormone bathing the fetus? That makes gayness "natural," true, but also provides a way to prevent growing brains from turning along that path. What then of all the hard-won political victories, the heroic and joyful Gay and Lesbian Mardi Gras, the brave, tortured cultural history obliterated within a generation in a kind of preemptive genocide? That's the quite realistic issue at the heart of "Cocoon" (*Asimov's*, 1994), a cerebral *policier* that in other hands might have been a multimillion seller by Michael Crichton or Robin Cook, or indeed Martin Amis or Peter Ackroyd.

But then fiction written in the slipstream and illumination of advanced science is sometimes obliged, in being true to its own strengths and possibilities, into an oppositional stance to traditional literary devices that faces off its forebears high and low. For the adventurous, Egan's approach is worth persevering with, even if learning that we are not inviolate selves but a pandemonium or parliament of contesting inner voices, that we are constructed not given from eternity, that even universal mathematics might be as gapped and fissured as any poststructural text ("Luminous" *Asimov's*, 1995), once deeply shocking, has become familiar news.

And when the shock of the new starts to turn into the yawn of the been-there-done-that, surely a writer as important to sf as Greg Egan will start to notice, turn away from austere fable, move—as Greg Bear and Greg Benford and Greg Feeley have been doing, not always successfully—in the direction of more sumptuous literary and imaginative values, those contingent but time-tested techniques, which Egan parodies so cruelly in Prospero, that touch the heart on their way to the brain and back again.

Arguably, *Teranesia* is Egan's attempt at a rounded character study in a setting richer than usual with smells, vivid naturalistic imagery, social nuance, psychological inwardness, familial density: a kind of breakout "literary" novel. Read this way, it can be disparaged, since Egan is still not especially adept in these areas (although the sensory detail of many scenes is cinematic and generous). There is too much expositional dialogue to satisfy the literary reader, even though people as smart and goal oriented as his really do talk this way. Their passion is in their grasp of the abstractions underlying the endless particulars of the universe, which they struggle to weave together by examining closely many of those particulars at a level of intense scrutiny not usually applied to *anything* by less reflective folks. Still, we have learned how to read novels by reference to other novels, most of which teach us that long exchanges of compressed information, however plausible, are ungainly, ill-fitted to the medium. So much the worse for canonical forms, of course—but a writer needs to be very, very good to manage it, and doing it *well* is almost inevitably a triumph, as in certain Nabokov and Burgess novels. Egan is not there yet, and probably he is not interested in going there.

Still, *Teranesia* is largely focused through the viewpoint of a charming prodigy, the vulnerable, loving, conscientious and tormented Indian boy, then man, Prabir Suresh, so it seems to be a *Bildungsroman*. Prabir's parents are doomed biologists Rajendra and Radha. His sister Madhusree, eight years younger, is smarter still, and the moral center of his universe. His parents move to an uninhabited island not far from Timor and New Guinea, a region in even greater postcolonial turmoil several decades from now than it is today. The Sureshes are drawn by a mystery: mutated butterflies with impossible properties. What is causing the mutation? It's the life-long quest Prabir finds himself entangled in—that, and his protective obsession with his sister's welfare.

The island setting, and the places Prabir and his kin travel, are deftly if dutifully sketched. So too is Prabir's guilt-driven consciousness, although his relationships with colleagues, lover and even Madhusree are scant and functional, like those of most Egan figures. Just as it seems some aspect of his life is truly contingent, gratuitous, surprising, in the transrealist way of actual people, the detail snags on a plot hook and unravels into convenience. In the 1960s, dull structuralist academics used to graph every fictive action and actor into semiotic squares and lists of oppositions and vectors, draining the vivid life from fiction and rendering it into algebra. It is all too easy to conclude that Greg Egan's method works the other way around. He finds a superb science fictional idea, then cudgels his considerable brain until he has a batch of suitable puppets to work through as many of the optional action-figure stances as he can manage, ending by blowing them back into a set of selfish genes or memes, as advertised.

Egan is crucifyingly nasty to Prabir's noxious and modish Canadian poststructural aunt (Masters in Diana Studies and authority on the "gendered megatext of technology and science") and uncle (Ph.D. in X-Files Theory) (p. 95). Paul Sutton's Paul Davies–style "twenty-first-century science of *ecotropy*" is destined for a book called *The Seventh Miracle* or perhaps *Gaia's Bastards* (p. 120). The detestably self-satisfied Hunter J. Cole claims that his "analysis of the relevant cultural indices across a time span of several centuries reveals that the predominant passion changes cyclically, from deep filial affection to pure xenophobia and back. Pastoralism, industrialism, romanticism, modernism, environmentalism, transhumanism, and deep ecology are all products of the same dynamic" of anxiety (p. 224). Egan is scathing about "Big Dumb Neologisms and thesaurus-driven bluster" (p. 115). Oddly, though, the transformative history of young Prabir, a floating signifier of a character, is exactly a sequence of gazumped narratives written like a palimpsest atop each other. The McGuffin driving the mutations on Teranesia ("monster island") is a superb narrative/scientific figure, combining quantum theory's Many Worlds interpretation with molecular evolution, for the endless rewriting of a constructed, always-already transitional and superposed self. I suspect the loathsome Cole might give a better account of the book's own dynamic than Egan would choose to admit.

In short, Egan's characters remain cunningly constructed stick figures, deployed elegantly to the ends of a given story's thought-experiment. Their world is just detailed enough to capture the notion or conceit under stress. And that conceptual apparatus at the core of each Egan story is nearly always inventively, brilliantly conceived and worked out step by surprising but satisfying step to a philosophical conclusion that can be summed up thus: *we humans are rewritable gadgets with no transcendental meaning acting in a meaningless universe—get over it.*

Since we know the message never changes (as in a romance, but less fun), the pleasure comes from the ingenious way we are led, once more, to its stoical appreciation. The primary paradox working at the heart of any Egan story is a profoundly intelligent forensic consciousness at his narrative focus—private investigator, quantum dabbler, artificial life programmer—who is assailed by searing ontological doubts of a depth and horror to make Rene Descartes's meditations on security of knowledge seem cozily comforting. What counts in assessing an Egan fiction remains the precise details of this epiphany, the sequence of ascending and mutually swallowing insights implementing it.

Selecting Egan as a test case is a frank admission that the narrative values built into core science fiction will tend inevitably to repel "literary" readers or indeed most general fiction readers who pick up a book for the solace and provocation that has always gratified those who enter an invented life. What might a sophisticated but unapprenticed reader and writer make of sf's special ways of doing things with words? I have been drenched in sf and its associated textualities for nearly half a century, during at least three decades of which I have been slowly, consciously constructing an aesthetics and reception theory for the mode. That leaves me at a distinct disadvantage in trying to understand why other people neither smarter nor duller than I should find sf so aversive—or at least simply uninteresting.

WHY PEOPLE DISLIKE SCIENCE FICTION

I asked a friend from my undergraduate days, Rory Barnes, a writer with whom I have collaborated on five books but who has himself read very little sf (finding it uninteresting or aversive), what he had been reading recently, and how he thought the novels on his list might illuminate the problem at hand. He provided this useful snapshot, this parallax view:

Joan Didion's *Democracy* is certainly the only book I have read from cover to cover at least three times this last decade. Why? Mainly for the language and the world evoked by the language. Didion's artful compression of the idiomatic ramblings and jargon-filled dialogue of her spooks, crooks, politicians, wheelers and dealers gives the whole scene a murky verisimilitude. Which is a word my dictionary defines as "the appearance or semblance of truth or reality." Maybe this world exists or maybe it doesn't—it doesn't matter; it's a zeitgeist one would not wish to inhabit but is fascinated to have evoked by the printed page. Admittedly, the novel has little warmth. One identifies with none of the characters, despite the complexity of Didion's main character, Inez Victor neé Christian, at once victim and player within the demimonde of power politics; Didion is at pains to ensure one doesn't. Alienating the reader is the name of the game. Didion's husband, John Gregory Dunne, is even more over the top with his creation of cynical, corrupt, venal, hypocritical, double-dealing denizens of a literary nether-world; as with Didion, one reads for the language as much as anything.

Which can't be said for, say, Margaret Drabble (*The Radiant Way, A Natural Curiosity* and *The Gates of Ivory* especially), who feels great warmth for her cast of middle-class Hampstead types and even the working-class north country types as well, although the more interesting of these have the wit to migrate to London and become Hampstead types instead. A soap opera quality to the writing would irk a Great Literature hound: no compression at all; plot, dialogue, description all sprawl. One does not stop, as one does with Didion, to re-read a paragraph. The fascination is all in the interaction of the characters, who speak in realistic everyday sentences and, for the most part, experience ordinary everyday events. It's a world I know well myself. Even Drabble's postmodern exercises in discussing her characters and their foibles with the reader have little or no alienation effect: "I suppose you think it's a bit off, the way I keep seeing things from my own point of view, what with Stephen dead and all. But what other POV can I see things from but my own? As Saint Joan said at the Inquisition, if I remember rightly" (*Ivory*, p. 412).

A. S. Byatt writes with a more waspish Oxford donnish asperity but the fascination is still with the whole network of interacting characters. One wants to know what her chief character Frederica will do next, what will be done to her, how she will react. Byatt actually gets it wrong every now and then. If the plot demands that Frederica cut herself off completely from her north country family, then Byatt will do it, despite this being so out of character as to be completely unbelievable. Indeed, it induces a slightly possessive rage—how dare Byatt slander poor Frederica by suggesting she'd do this thing? Drabble, for all her own use of improbable coincidence, wouldn't have forced things like that.

Ian McEwan works with tighter, bleaker plots; his characters go through a greater number of emotional hoops and end up far more changed. But the source of the compulsion to read is still in the psychology of the interaction. "Yeah, that's right" one thinks, "that's how X would feel under those circumstances." And that those circumstances are often pretty weird only strengthens the compulsion to read.

Toby Wolf, too, one reads for the ease with which he shifts ambience by modifying language. At random, one could add Iris Murdoch, Pat Barker, Peter Carey, Kate Grenville, Doris Lessing, V. S. Naipaul: whatever the zeitgeist invoked, whatever the cast of characters, they are for the most part interesting; their interactions make psychological sense. One hungers to know what will happen to them next. And the writing is, at least, up to the task.

There is, of course, no reason why any of the above cannot be incorporated into a world subject to sf's flights of imagination. You can have utterly believable everyday characters confronted by strange dilemmas—the product of weird or new science. You can have a totally mundane world subject to the goings-on of strange beings with slightly non-human personalities (the word *slightly* is important here—make your weird sisters too weird and they just become improbable and dull). You can mix the two scenarios. But for me, at least, you need to feel for the characters, you need to know them, even if you don't like them. I suspect the problem with many sf writers (but can't be sure, having read so little of the stuff) is that constructing and considering the fantastic or technological elements gets in the way of interactions among human beings with feelings and desires, rather than providing a useful background for them. But it's humans, after all, who provide the only known readership. However, there *are* many sf readers (and writers), so clearly some humans find satisfaction in fantasies of superhuman feats and qualities lacking the realities of small group interaction. A quick teleport through six galaxies and five millennia becomes the wonderful thing in itself, regardless of who does the teleporting or whom they meet on the way. Wheee, I'm flying.

Yes, but—Much of this is true in general of any popular form: big business and legal thrillers, CIA thrillers, submarine thrillers. Rarely do their writers emphasize the nourishment of the soul, the fine and sensitively delineated nuance of subtle, ambiguous emotion. No doubt this aesthetic choice has its own good reasons (beyond, to be blunt, the writers' inability to *do* nuanced emotion). The characters of most popular fiction and their emotional interactions, whether in print or on the screen, are perfunctory, stereotyped routines that momentarily satisfy without filling. Soaps, Mills & Boons and Gothic romances have the opposite or complementary failing from sf's austerity, dissolving into slushy bursts of *faux* emotion without the cognitive, critical, disruptive element of mature fiction to keep those emotions true.

Wheee, I'm flying? Certainly. Some of the appeal of science fiction is the rush of cosmic wind in the reader's brain. Some, the most lastingly effective, presumably taps into archetypes (whether archaic or locally constructed by one's contingent upbringing). Some is surely just the same buzz provided by any thriller, but conducted by means even faster, more powerful, more wish-fulfilling—which is presumably why today's mass media (and yesterday's comic strip) bigbucksters increasingly invoke science fiction-ish tropes. Sf movies are always far more sentimental, if rarely emotionally truer, than print fiction exiled to its specialized readership within sf's self-defined ghetto. That, at least, was true until fairly recently, when young college-educated writers turned to sf because it provided one of the few remaining markets for stories. They brought with them the tricks of the mainstream trade—to the annoyance of ghetto diehards, who found their tipple diluted by *feelings*, by a softening of the traditional troping on technology and "hard" science (most of it as spurious as faster than-light-travel, but convenient and comforting), by loss of generic memory.

Robert Silverberg, one of the sharpest sf professional commentators, complained lately that "since about 1975, when books based on popular s-f movies and television shows began to be published and to enjoy huge sales, a gradual debasement of the stuff we like to read has taken place. . . . Unsurprisingly, books of the more simpleminded sorts sold better—sometimes a great deal better . . . [T]here will always be more cash customers for Schwarzenegger-esque tales of violent conflict than for sober Campbellian examinations of the social consequences of technological developments."[12] He meant sf written by the strictures of John W. Campbell Jr. who as editor of *Astounding* overhauled the genre in the late 1930s and early 1940s, introducing the now-classic writers Isaac Asimov, Robert Heinlein, A. E. van Vogt and many others who built up the megatext that is now being lost, eroded or simply bypassed.

What of today's young writers "who have no access to those classics, and who may very well come to regard the crudely written and crudely conceived formula-ridden mass-market stuff of today's paperback racks as the proper ideal to follow?" Silverberg wondered. "Junk begets junk. So the newer writers will give us imitations of works that themselves would probably not have been able to see publication a generation ago." Silverberg adds in preemptive self-mockery: "So I am playing the part, I guess, of that stuffiest of old bores, the *laudator temporis acti* . . . I can't help it . . . I love [sf] for its visionary potential; I hate to see it turned into something hackneyed and cheap" (Silverberg, "Gresham's Law and Science Fiction," pp. 22–23).

That fate was almost inevitable, however, once science fiction turned into something hackneyed and very, very expensive.

NOTES

1. Cited from Part II of *The Sound and the Fury* (1929), Quentin Compson's monologue, by Hugh Kenner, *A Homemade World: The American Modernist Writers* (New York: William Morrow, 1975), p. 194. Compare two more monologue sentences for the same "high finish on the language" (pp. 194–95): "The shell was a speck now, the oars catching the sun in spaced glints, as if the hull were winking itself along" and "the last light supine and tranquil upon tideflats like pieces of a broken mirror." Yet that penultimate citation might readily be adapted, changing a word or so, to a sf context of space flight, in a story of a starship propelled by pulsed nuclear detonations written by Gene Wolfe or even Poul Anderson; but would we then find it quite as magical (being, suddenly, so much more literal)?

2. Vladimir Nabokov, *Lolita* (London: Corgi, 1961), p. 11.

3. Brian Aldiss, "*The Atheist's Tragedy* Revisited," in *The Detached Retina: Aspects of SF and Fantasy* (Liverpool: Liverpool University Press, 1995), pp. 170–71.

4. Banks publishes his quirky and much-noted mainstream fiction as "Iain Banks," and his sf as "Iain M. Banks." The two classes of novel, although they have much in common, tend bafflingly to be reviewed by distinct critical moieties, and in different parts of the literary pages.

5. Brian Stableford, "And He Not Busy Being Born," *Interzone* 16 (1986), reprinted in James Gunn, ed., *The Road to Science Fiction, Vol. 5: The British Way* (Clarkston, GA: White Wolf, 1998), p. 608; John Updike, *Toward the End of Time* (London: Hamish Hamilton, 1998), pp. 312–14.

6. Michaela Roessner, "Family Values," in *Nebula Award 31*, ed. Pamela Sargent (New York: Harcourt Brace and Co., 1997), pp. 25, 27.

7. J. O. Bailey, *Pilgrims Through Space and Time: Trends and Patterns in Scientific and Utopian Fiction* (1947; Westport, CT: Greenwood Press, 1972).

8. Greg Egan, "The Planck Dive," in *Luminous* (London: Millennium, 1998), pp. 276–78.

9. One is reminded a little of Leonard Lewin's extraordinary bleak hoax, *Report from Iron Mountain* (Harmondsworth: Penguin, 1967), which purported to be a major leaked U.S. study proving beyond argument the necessity of war.

10. In a slender book of essays passing as sf, *One Human Minute* (1986; London: Mandarin, 1991), pp. 99–100. Even more remarkable is a book of reviews of imaginary books, *Imaginary Magnitude* (1981; London: Mandarin, 1991), parts of which were first published in Poland in 1973 and 1981.

11. Collected in, for example, Lucius Shepard, *The Jaguar Hunter* (London: Paladin, 1988).

12. Robert Silverberg, "Gresham's Law and Science Fiction," in *Nebula Awards 31*, ed. Pamela Sargent (New York: Harcourt Brace and Co., 1997), pp. 21–23.

4

The Death and Deconstruction
of Science Fiction

> The science fiction field harbours an ingrained philistinism. . . . Most
> people really don't want new approaches or ideas. They do not want
> the sort of fiction of which real literature is made. Fictions, that is,
> with central balance . . . which traffic honestly with the tragic as well
> as the sunny side of life.
> —Brian W. Aldiss, *Trillion Year Spree* (p. 277)

Certain trajectories trace the development of the fiction of science from
the 1940s and 1950s (when Isaac Asimov, Robert Heinlein and the others
were hewing out "modern science fiction") to the postmodern present.
An important, perhaps paramount, dimension that alters its values along
each of them is the material conditions of writing, publication and distribution of sf texts. Since science fiction has gone from a set of practices
employed in a commercial-cum-artistic ghetto to a major component of
the entertainment industry, as Silverberg noted at the close of the previous chapter, it attracts all the benefits and blights associated with commercial megavisibility. It is not alone in this, but the mode has been
badly mauled by the coincidence.

So is sf, now at its apogee of commercial success, actually dead or
dying? *The New York Review of Science Fiction*, a monthly little magazine
produced by aficionados, seems to think its prospects might be terminal.
In March 1997, editor David G. Hartwell posed the bald, contentious
question: "Who Killed Science Fiction?" It is a topic first raised back in

the early 1960s, and it has not gone away since. (That is a good reason to doubt its force—dead and rotting for nearly forty years, and they're *still* prodding the carcass?)

Myth blames a terrible magazine distribution crash in the United States some four decades ago, at the very time when the launch of the first space satellites should have boosted a fresh enthusiasm for sf's "wild, far-out ideas." Now, as then, commercial sf is in a trough of decline. 1997 was the third year of a savage slump in the United Kingdom and United States: fewer magazines, fewer issues of those that have survived, fewer mass market books. 1998 was not much different. Is this just a random fluctuation? Or must sf devotees ask, as Hartwell did: "Are we all reading a dead or dying literature?"[1]

Money! While it might appear unseemly to launch an account of a new Don DeLillo or Peter Carey novel with the size of the author's advance, clearly it would be ludicrous to discuss a new supermarket blockbuster—the latest Tom Clancy, say—in any other terms. (Perhaps this is rhetorical overkill, and some Popular culture theorists would disagree. Of course the irony in my observation lies in art's valorization by a bourgeois establishment that still measures worth, by and large, precisely by the criterion of assessable wealth.) Until the last few decades, however, it would have been simply pointless to measure any science fiction book by *either* literary or financial standards. While the genre attracted a small devoted following, no sf novels (discounting Wells and Verne, Huxley and Orwell) ever came within shouting distance of the resting places of God or Mammon.

All this changed within the last third of the twentieth century, and especially since the U.S. college success of (to take a mixed but representative batch) Robert Heinlein's *Stranger in a Strange Land*, Samuel R. Delany's *Dhalgren*, and any number of unstoppable multivolume confections—speaking of money—by otherwise unremarkable and frequently deplorable authors. Now, too, Ursula Le Guin, J. G. Ballard, Stanislaw Lem and William Gibson are studied dutifully at the university in English and Popular Culture courses.

During the 1980s, Heinlein, Arthur C. Clarke, Frank Herbert and Asimov took turns at the top of major bestseller lists. In the 1990s, a different but equally select group also did quite well, but the big advances got a little smaller. Above and behind them were the true earthshakers: those movie, TV and computer game spin-offs, from *Star Wars* to *The Hitchhiker's Guide to the Galaxy*, the *Alien, Back to the Future* and *Terminator* movies, *Dune* and *Myst*, and those many-paged epics of fantasy high and low, from Tolkien's *Lord of the Rings* to Stephen Donaldson's *Chronicles of Thomas the Unbeliever* and Tad Williams's blockbusters.

THE FREQUENTLY ANNOUNCED DEATH OF SCIENCE FICTION

Glancing at any recent list of bestsellers and top-grossing movies, then, one might easily suppose that science fiction is a genre in the rudest of health. In fact, as we've just seen, aficionados are bewailing its death, or at least its ruinous maiming at the hands of the infidel. Is this merely desperate mimicry of high culture's regular brooding on the death of the novel? After all, the term "sf" is primarily a *marketing* category, not a usage from the literary canon. Can a marketing category be alive or dead?

You can say that decorative piercing is dead when nobody does it any more. With equal justice, you might declare it dead if *everybody* waggles metal bars inside their mouths and mutilation loses its shock value. Still, why pose the matter in terms of death rather than (say) transfiguration? Children change into adults without dying. A quite different standard metaphor asks whether sf's narcotic has been adulterated—or the addict become tolerant of its influence. The very fact that texts old and recent by Isaac Asimov and Arthur C. Clarke and Robert Heinlein continue to sell like crack cocaine, even though two of those three old masters have been dead for years, suggests that naive readers still get exactly the same kick from these exemplary works. (Which suggests that even when sf *writers* are dead, the genre or mode they implemented can linger on with a merry blush to its cheek.)

Indeed, despite his earlier Jeremiad, editor David G. Hartwell subsequently found "reasons to be cheerful," as his editorial in *The New York Review of Science Fiction* put it at the close of 1999. With "the decade and the millennium building to a climax of some sort, and everyone confused about the future, it seems to me a time to rejoice and embrace change. SF is alive and well and so, I hope, are we all" (Hartwell, "Reasons," p. 21)

Yet, as I have noted, even the most sophisticated sf is still treated with disdain by the cultivated—unless it is the assimilated variety produced by a Doris Lessing, and even Lessing abandoned sf in fairly short order. Why should this be? We can't blame Luke or Annakin Skywalker for everything. Surely it is because the codes and strategic moves of sf's accumulating megatext have never been learned by the custodians of cultural legitimation.

This view is not universally accepted. In *Trillion Year Spree*, Brian Aldiss and David Wingrove put the objection in these terms:

That such writers as Gore Vidal in *Messiah* . . . or Doris Lessing in her *Canopus in Argos* series, knew nothing of the continuity of science fiction, of its traditions, or of its rules (which mean in fact a few prescriptions laid down by a small clique of, in the main, non-writers); and in consequence cannot be said to be a part of science fiction at all.

This is a fallacy. If we imagine that a playwright like Eugene O'Neil ... or a novelist like Gabriel Garcia Marquez, knew nothing of the history of the drama [etc.], the fact would in no way lessen the contributions those writers made to their chosen medium, or to the influence they had on those who followed them. (P. 20)

"There is no such entity," they declared with a flourish, "as science fiction" (p. 20).

But there is a fallacy in the fallacy, the fallacy of the wolf-child. No discourse happens outside of a context, a history. In fact, those great innovators *did not* work in utter isolation; their texts, especially at their most challenging, were always produced against the grain of certain collective, established reception codes.

There is no "entity" named sf, but it is clearly feasible to identify regular writing and reading practices that cause us to "chunk" these texts together, to identify prototypical "good examples" of sf and to expel some cases as hopelessly botched, maimed or sterile.

But even if we accept the usefulness of generic labeling, there are more varieties than one. Yes, mass markets may see a shift back to politically conservative adventure narrative, with cardboard characters and epiphanies, churned out by hacks. At the same time, more literary sf moves toward elusive, radical, rich, subjective, dirty-mouthed, deconstructed works written by stoned street poets (and perhaps the occasional after-dinner academic).

Yet again, Brian Aldiss, Iain M. Banks, John Crowley, Jack Dann, Greg Egan, Gwyneth Jones, Ursula Le Guin, Paul McAuley, James Morrow, Michael Swanwick and Gene Wolfe also keep their heads above water. So there are sufficient readers primed to sf's specialized codes—and capable of using them in more sophisticated forms of discourse—to support at least *some* postprimitive sf. But it is the problematically ambiguous status of that central supply I am worrying at just now.

Long before it became an industrial machine for converting cute furry aliens and gobbets of gory flesh and pus into hundreds of millions of publishing and media revenue dollars, science fiction had a rude, homespun appeal to it. Stifled by all those factors that poets rail against, imagination (or, as we have seen, perhaps "fancy") found in sf a byway that poets were usually too tender to risk. Hence, what was produced was lumpy as gruel, but on close inspection it proved to be nourishing to those hungry with an appetite for wonder.

Sf fans, like proselytizing missionaries, wished that their astringent diet might some day grace every table. By a fateful irony, this came to pass. For Brian Aldiss, the sf boom has turned it into Instant Whip. While some sf is published in languages other than English, or outside the United States, the central market place "demands a simpler product, easily packaged, something as reassuring as homogenized food." Science fiction, he adds wryly, "has finally got into every home, just as the older fans hoped."[2]

Trillion Year Spree demonstrated how deeply the icons of sf have permeated the cultural and media landscapes—though often, sadly, with down-market chic. Aldiss, like me, is torn between two loves: for the tatty images of all the futures we've left behind and for genuine literature able to embrace the tragic. One might suppose that a genre drenched with tales of postnuclear devastation and amok technology is tragic, but of course it is rarely that. The reader becomes a bold survivor amid the radioactive ruins, inheritor of the bombed supermarket and all the free tinned caviar. Costner's version of David Brin's cosy catastrophe *The Postman* failed to exceed this dismal expectation.

In 1996, Susan Sontag published a notable essay, "The Decay of Cinema." It told a tale with a plot along the lines of the one I have just told. Movies are losing vitality, stuck in fashionable formulae, driven by brainless adherence to momentary trends. The experiments of the sixties—like sf's experiments of the fifties—enlarged the ambitions of jaded audiences; they refreshed, even revolutionized the cinema. Now the damned bean-counters have ruined it all. Or so claimed Sontag, who has always been something of a Jeremiah.

Susan Matthews, a new sf author once compared with Dostoievski, bridles a little at this claim. An MBA, she *is* a bean-counter, and disapproves of writers complaining about readers' tastes—purchasers pay their money and make their choice, and we have no right to try to dictate their aesthetic criteria (although we ought to write as well as we can and hope to influence them by example). Amy Stout, an editor with fifteen years' experience in the sf and fantasy field whose second fantasy novel was recently published, commented: "I think tie-ins are just the pulps of our day. It's far better that people read something than nothing at all. Probably very few of these readers cross over into the main sf/f field but some do wander over now and then. On the other hand, I admit it's tough to go into a bookstore and know that my first novel would probably be holding a lot more shelf space if I'd chosen to do a book in one of the *successful* tie in series."[3]

Sontag nonetheless has a point, and it is one that transfers all too easily to sf. We can hardly expect businesses to act deliberately against the interests of their stockholders, and apparently it is concluded that the only objection to marketing fiction as "product," each book as reliable as the last in the way we expect of a tube of toothpaste, is to the policy's pragmatic boom-and-bust weaknesses. So at root, this being the "real world" (as we are told repeatedly by knowing authorities through one clumsy convulsion and ham-fisted crisis after another), the question is— can we ever again expect to find more than a handful of sf writers earning a decent living without being obliged to debase the genre?

Strictly generic sf, then, is spoiled by two factors at least: its dependency, even to the point of near plagiarism, on previous exemplary works and interests, and its tendency to repetition, almost to entropy. In part, of course, these traits are automatically entailed by the notion of generic categorization, but it is instructive to turn now to an examination of the constrictions and liberations available to writers wishing to be read outside the makeshift sf canon but who nevertheless work—as John Calvin Batchelor and Thomas Pynchon, say, do not—*within* the web of the sf megatext. In the remainder of this chapter, we shall examine two books each by two writers—one, Mary Doria Russell, a recent newcomer marketed not to sf fans in the first instance but to mainstream and book club readers, the other, Kurt Vonnegut, a classic sf author who with some effort escaped generic labeling.

A CALCULUS AT GOD

Richard Grant stingingly encapsulated, in a 1990 *Foundation* piece on the profession of sf, the commentator's trajectory.[4] Prior to the critic's arrival, the act of writing and reading: tens, maybe hundreds of thousands of words have been emplaced with some precision into sentences, paragraphs, the syntagmatic ascension, to interact with the reader's complex consciousness, working by rhythm, implication, mood and nuance, coloring and contorting the actively receptive mind until, cumulatively, their persuasion evokes, as if in memory, "the experience of being with real people over a period of time" (Grant, "Git Along, Little Robot," p. 188).

Partial and contentious as it is, grant Grant's story of story-telling and re-creation as an emblem of the rich multidimensional process that fetches us again and again to the printed page. And when reading is complete, at the final escalation of complexity, here is the exact violence inflicted by a critic: s/he "closes the book, sighs in relief . . . and bangs out something along the lines of 'The society here is not entirely plausible,' or 'This book is an environmental tract.' With this, the intricate matrix of interactions mediated by the work collapses to a small subset of observed properties" (p. 188).

In Mary Doria Russell's *The Sparrow*, and its sequel *Children of God*,[5] Jesuits in the moderately near future find themselves tested like Job to destruction, or nearly so (especially Father Emilio Sandoz, S. J.), under three suns, amid exotic intelligences perhaps ensouled or perhaps in some way diabolical, strangers in the strangest of strange lands. Nearest star system to our own, Alpha Centauri is two stars, A and B, nearly twin to our own sun, revolving around a common center of gravity, attended very distantly by duller red Proxima. One of the two has a planet nearly twin to Earth, Rakhat, where dwell twin intelligent species, visited at last by humans early in the twenty-first century. Point, counterpoint; plaintive, plangent antiphonies. Wherever two are gathered together, there shall be a third in their midst, the mediating and transcending term.

We cannot avoid the drumming of megatextual archetypes formed quite recently (measured by the long yardstick of art and its history): C. S. Lewis's unfallen intelligent beings on Mars and Venus, and the twisted fiend inhabiting the night side of Thulcandra, his Earth (1938, 1943); Lester del Rey's gusty, gutsy blasphemy, "For I am a Jealous People" (1954); Walter Miller's *A Canticle for Leibowitz* (1960) and its long-delayed sequel *Saint Leibowitz and the Wild Horse Woman* (1997); James Blish's magisterial *After Such Knowledge* trilogy (1991), especially its earliest stanza and closing part, the novel *A Case of Conscience* (1958); Arthur C. Clarke's *Childhood's End* (1953) and *2001: A Space Odyssey* (1968); half the corpus of Orson Scott Card, shaded everywhere by his Mormon faith yet cast sometimes into forms of Catholicism, perhaps for greater bite; Gene Wolfe's grand tetralogies of Urth and Parousia, Catholic to bedrock; and perhaps most poignantly, to those who first knew their thrilling exoticism forty years ago, Cordwainer Smith's High Episcopalian allegories of Incarnation and Redemption. Writing under that implausible mythic pseudonym in the 1950s and early 1960s, a conservative psychologist actually named Paul Linebarger created a radical kind of lyric science fiction. Many of his romantic images painted highly Anglo-Saxon Australians of the future, stern and staggeringly wealthy pragmatists in an abundant but cruel post-utopia.[6] Smith dubbed his imaginative epoch The Rediscovery of Man. For sf, it was the rediscovery of poetry—of a sort—and of a sentimentality later found triumphant in mass media successes such as the TV fantasy-soap *Beauty and the Beast* ("I knew that though we could never be together, we would never, ever be apart . . .") or the harder-edged *Buffy, the Vampire Slayer*.

A generation was to pass before sf had the benefit of the Rediscovery of Woman. Certainly transrealist Philip K. Dick, for all the brutal delineation of his female characters, was not a useful contributor, due to a persistent (if culturally pervasive) misogyny. As well as classic works, sometimes overlooked, like *Herland* ([1914], 1979) by Charlotte Perkins Gilman, the object of women's studies in sf includes the brilliant and genre-reconstituting *oeuvres* of Ursula Le Guin and Joanna Russ, especially Le Guin's *The Left Hand of Darkness* (1969), *The Dispossessed* (1974), the extraordinarily densely wrought eco-utopia *Always Coming Home* (1985), and a recent suite of shorter fictions wryly and movingly exploring the nuances of sexual variation across her Hainish galaxy; and Russ's *The Adventures of Alyx* (1983), its companion *Picnic on Paradise* (1968), and perhaps the most confrontational of all second-wave feminist sf, *The Female Man* (1975) and *The Two of Them* (1978). Joan Slonczewski's *A Door into Ocean* (1986), and Connie Willis's *Lincoln's Dreams* (1987) were winners of the prestigious John W. Campbell Award; by 1993, Willis was so well established in the reputation of sf fans that she took the Nebula Awards for both Best Novel (for *Doomsday Book*) and Best Short Story (for "Even the Queen"), a tale about menstruation.[7] In the same year, Marge Piercy's *Body of Glass* won the Arthur C. Clarke Award, beating one of the male triumphs of traditional sf in recent years, Kim Stanley Robinson's *Red Mars*. Each of these books by women, unlike much routine space opera fodder written largely by males for males, is at once entertaining and provocative, and all deal with what the male gay writer Samuel R. Delany has somewhere termed the most important political issue of our time: sexism and its biological and cultural underpinnings.

NEW CASES OF CONSCIENCE

For knowing readers (few of them, perhaps, accredited students of literature, many more programmers, motor mechanics, public servants) all that long argument inevitably hangs above the text of the rapturously noticed novels of Mary Doria Russell. A Ph.D. in biological anthropology, she was already a married mother in her midforties—unusual for a newcomer to the sf mode—formerly Christian, then atheist, now convert to Judaism. Her first book immediately won several distinguished awards, including the 1997 Tiptree prize for best sf novel exploring gender issues (in this case, largely the problematic of elected celibacy and the muted varieties of conventional sexual identity). Read against the richness of sf's history, what one finds is *2100: A Space Theodicy*. Read otherwise, it is a triumph of diversionary marketing.

"*The Sparrow* is an incredible novel," a crunching quote from the *Milwaukee Journal Sentinel* assures us, "for one reason. . . . it is not written like most science fiction"—a wincing opinion based, presumably, on *Star Trek* episodes, or best-selling *Star Wars* sharecrops, or perhaps merely that sedate ignorant prejudice held by many of Russell's mainstream supporters. Her caramelled and decorated plot alternations, we learn, are "driven by her characters, by their complex relationships and inner conflicts, not by aliens and technology." In this respect, then, it differs, we are given to understand, from the work of Michael Bishop and Gene Wolfe and Ursula Le Guin and Gwyneth Jones and M. John Harrison and John Crowley and James Morrow and a hundred others who have gone before.

"And how can we decide," Richard Grant had asked, "if the [sf] work is any good? . . . By how strongly it alters the reader's consciousness. . . . Many sf works are roundly praised because they fit the conventional paradigm to a T—good 'plot mechanics', et al.—yet their prose is anaemic and the experience of reading them is worthwhile only on a shallow level" (Grant 1992, p. 197). Mary Doria Russell's prose and emotional effects do well enough, in some places beautifully, in others after the manner of a slick fifty minutes of television ensemble work. Yet the reader is frequently jolted by point-of-view whiplash, as she snaps her focus away from behind one character's eyes and into the inner reactions of another, pulls back for a moment of omniscience, then dives again into whatever viewpoint or editorial aside seemed convenient. Blish would have been appalled—as William Atheling Jr. he smote Frank Herbert for "jumping from one point of view to another like a maddened kangaroo."[8] Perhaps this technical complaint is simple generic prejudice on my part; Henry James would not object. But it is easy to agree with Blish that such "handling is maladroit" (Atheling, *More Issues at Hand*, p. 6).

The most insistent voices apparently contesting behind the words of the text are those of Dr. Baines, from Blish's *Black Easter* (1967), and Father Ruiz-Sanchez, from his *A Case of Conscience*, yet Russell denies being influenced by those texts—although the similarity in names of Blish's Ruiz-Sanchez, S. J., and Russell's Sandoz, S. J., smacks of honest *hommage*. These volumes from the post facto thematic trilogy *After Such Knowledge* (the remaining volume is the historical treatment of Friar Roger Bacon, *Doctor Mirabilis* [1964]) take their title from a line of T. S. Eliot: "After such knowledge, what forgiveness?" Baines, who precipitates War in Heaven and if not the death at least the departure of God, notes: "A large part of the mystic tradition says that the possession and use of secular knowledge—or even the desire for it—is in itself evil."[9] In his own 1972 *Foundation* piece on "The Development of a Science Fiction Writer," Blish put it more sharply still: each of the volumes "was a dramatisation in its own terms of one of the oldest problems of philosophy: *is the desire for secular knowledge, let alone the acquisition and use of it, a misuse of the mind, and perhaps even actively evil?*"[10]

There is a case of conscience at the core of *The Sparrow* and *Children of God*: a case, that is, not just of moral scruple, of sin and forgiveness, or good and evil, but of mortal consciousness itself—awareness of self, and perhaps of deity, of transfiguring spirit or its absence, of the pain and glory of exquisite sensitivity in a world where God has, notoriously, absconded.

Mary Doria Russell's own key is this: "What happens to Emilio Sandoz is a holocaust writ small. He survives, but loses everyone. Now he has to live in its aftermath." The moral? "Maybe it's 'Even if you do the best you can, you still get screwed.' "[11] Well, quite—Sandoz is repeatedly sodomized by very large and punishingly equipped aliens, like some awful *fin de siecle* parody of the brass-bra'd space kittens traditionally ravaged by monsters on the gaudy covers of space opera pulps. But aren't martyrs and mystics meant to seek (or at least submit to) the chastisements of God's foes? Isn't that part of the deal? Dr. Russell is wiser than that, although her novel dances prettily in the boundaries of that disgraceful delusion. "We seem to believe that if we act in accordance with our understanding of God's will, we ought to be rewarded. But in doing so we're making a deal that God didn't sign onto" (from "A Conversation," in *The Sparrow*). Surely that's not the bumper-sticker customary religion leaves us with, despite the odd in-your-face shocker like the travails of Job? No, but "if you read Torah, you realize that God has a lot to answer for. God is a complex personality" ("A Conversation,") This, like the twinned Gethsemanes of Father Sandoz (in heaven, which is hell, and on earth, which is purgatory), is, as another convenient review snippet (from *Entertainment Weekly*) informs us, a stricture of "tough love."

But what if God's neither in His heaven nor absconded? What if He's a delusion and a snare, a folly for trapping the vulnerable into cruel absurdities like the voluntary abandonment of sex, children, the simplest comforts of attachment, physical embrace?

Reading such a novel, we are naked to all the subtle solicitations Richard Grant urges upon us, but we're also marched through a design. Any theological tale has design upon us. Of course, like the venerable (and fallacious, because pre-Darwinian) Argument from Design, we are fetched up out of the pages to find ourselves staring into the face of a Demiurge: in this case, the engagingly smiling face of Mary Doria Russell. Emilio Sandoz and his luckless colleagues become the snake in an old garden, or rather the culpable gardeners in an old snakepit, and sense the hand of God directing their path. They're right, in a way, but theophany is inserted into them, from behind, by old goddess Russell. Does that make her some kind of Satan? No—as she notes, such comforting duality misses the true fearful complexity of the Torah's deity, the one William Blake glimpsed.

Symbolic loading is everywhere and often the characters are cynically conscious of it. Broken Sandoz, body ruined by scurvy, mutilation and insupportable grief, stumbles as he climbs a cliff to meet his Father General. ("Really, Emilio," Vincenzo Giuliani said in a dry, bored voice, "why not stumble again, in case someone has missed the symbolism? I'm sure Brother Edward has been meditating on Golgotha all the way up" [*The Sparrow*, p. 78]. And minutes later Giuliani lashes out at the spoiled priest, changing the metaphor (or perhaps invoking a different garden of suffering): "Did you think you were the only one?. . . . Do you honestly believe that you alone, of all those who have gone, were the single man to lose God? Do you think we would have a name for the sin of despair, if only you had experienced it?" (p. 79).

Sandoz bends beneath a crueler doubt than the loss of God. He suspects that deity is not absent but active, smashing us at random or for spite. He has had plentiful proof of God's intervention, coincidences that stretch chance as an explanation. He's correct; it is the hand of the author at work, skewing the probabilities, setting up the design and kicking it to splinters, in the hope (one imagines) of performing an invocation in the next world up, the world we readers share with her. A world in which, at the end, we may learn courage and meaning in the ancient poetry of Aeschylus: "In our sleep, pain which cannot forget falls drop by drop upon the heart, until, in our own despair, against our will, comes wisdom through the awful grace of God" (*The Sparrow*, p. 404). Tough love, again. The fearful shadow of the Blakean tyger, the Rilkean angel which is terrible. But in this case, as always in sf and perhaps in art, it's a contrivance. No child has really coughed, torn, in the night, blood frothing at her lips, and died. If we weep for the slaughter of innocents (the recurrent trope at the heart of so many of these Jesuit tales), still it is in the knowledge that they were never more than shadows, really, less substantial than those colored shadows we watch each night on television, gaunt figures stumbling in Somalia and Kosovo and East Timor. And we have forgotten, if we ever knew, how to weep for those. There are limits, after all, to endurance, at least, if not simply to attention span.

Russell's attempt at the grand metaphor cannot be accounted a success, although many moments in the journey are rewarding, and heartstrings twang obediently now and then. Before anything else, after all, the books are sf novels and need to meet sf's difficult requirements, even if we do see the shadow of, say, Brian Moore's *Black Robe* flapping over their plots. Is it trivial, entirely beside the point, to object that nobody could possibly be mining the asteroids by 2019, let alone refitting them with mass-drivers capable of driving a cored mountain at one gee to near light-speed within a year. Throw rocks out the back, so that "from the moment the engines were fired, they had full gravity" (*The Sparrow*, p. 148)?[12] Certainly it is not trivial to object that her astronomy of the Alpha Centauri system is plain cockeyed.[13]

Plainly, Russell did not wish to lose her purchase on the present by placing her opening scenes in, say, 2059, forty years later, when this scenario might be somewhat more plausible. As it is, Emilio returns to Earth in that year, four decades after his departure, and non-sf readers would be profoundly discomfited by the radically discontinuous world and *Weltbild* to be expected by 2100. (In fact, the sequel ends near the close of the twenty-first century, and little seems to have changed in technology or culture.) Plausible technologies of fifty years or a century hence would make hash of the plot, as we shall see in chapter 6 when we discuss the likely hypertechnologies of the twenty-first century. Father Sandoz struggles agonizingly with clumsy prostheses that will be obsolete by 2020, let alone the 2100 a believable plot line would mandate. As always, playing sf with the net up is *incredibly* harder than it might seem at first glance.

LAMBS AND LIONS

A fan critic, Nancy Leibowitz, has called *The Sparrow* a Poul Anderson story for the 90s. This is just, although I'd splice on Morris West (*The Devil's Advocate, The Shoes of the Fisherman,* etc.) for the portentous theological brooding—although that is somewhat unfair, as Russell is much lighter in touch than that old Vatican-besotted midbrow potmeister. Her people do not sparkle quite as much as she supposes, but they are pretty good fun. Poul Anderson's spirit hovers ever more closely over the novel after it reaches Rakhat, fully halfway into the text, and the two fatally entangled sophont species are disclosed. Runa and Jana'ata, nicely imagined and deployed, are co-evolved prey and predator, the masterful 4 percent literally cultivating and eating the babies of the lovable but docile 96 percent. Innocents are always being gnawed in this generic crux. Blish's Father Ruiz-Sanchez, S J, learns that the whole planet Lithia is a put-up job by evil incarnate when he finds that the intelligent but sinless Snakes comprise an entire ecology, their aquatic children literally food for each other in a savage, godless Darwinian recapitulation. Orson Scott Card's religion-drenched plots often turn upon planetary murder and expiation.[14] If Father Sandoz had bothered to read any sf before he left to follow the beautiful songs of the Centauri system, he'd have been waiting in dread for the sinister dinner setting.

The chief obstacles to acceptance of the plot—crucial if one is to take seriously the moral urgency and gravitas proposed by the plot's design—are less whimsical than any of these considerations. The Rakhat lion has not just lain down with the lamb but morphed into sheep's clothing. The lion people are an exquisite warrior race, Muromachi *bushi* perhaps (those samurai aristocrat warriors as deft with tea ceremony and flower arrangement as they were with the sword), the sheep—well, a funny lot, the sheep. The sequel reveals that lions not only subsist on the succulent lamb but employ their sheep as civil servants, historians, eyes and ears, the whole mercantile infrastructure. No warrior Roman farmers and their learned Greek slaves, these are two distinct if entwined species, whose DNA each speaks its singular but complementary message. Yet the ruin brought upon Rakhat's ecological balance is one that must have happened by chance many times in the planet's history. The Runa population is held in precarious check by their failure to develop agriculture (as was ours, until a few thousand years ago), but surely fat years would provoke runaway population booms, cropped by a concomitant boom in Jana'ata numbers, as chaos dynamics instructs us. The difference is that both these species are intelligent. We are told that the revolutionary invocation, "We are many. They are few," is enough to trigger a cascade of resentful rebellion across the planet, disrupting the age-old accommodation of eater and eaten. Just say no. I don't think so.

A second qualm: Sandoz is found imprisoned, his hands cut to shreds, dissociated and traumatized, his body unpleasantly damaged by repeated buggerings—and worldly, charmingly profane Jesuits recoil like shocked maiden aunts, assuming without question that he has voluntarily chosen a depraved life as a homosexual prostitute. Only through the most contrived of juggling acts is Russell able to render Sandoz effectively speechless in his own defense, but still the reaction of his brothers in Christ is simply inconceivable. The nearest we come to an explanation is Father General Giuliani's avowal that this vile interrogation "was necessary. If he were an artist, I'd have ordered him to paint it" (*The Sparrow*, p. 399). As a linguist, specialist in tongues, he must speak his travail (luckily for us). And why? Because despite his apparent apostasy, Emilio Sandoz is "the genuine article," a true mystic given sight of God. "He is still held fast in the formless stone, but he's closer to God right now than I have ever been in my life" (p. 400). If this is correct, God has first tested His victim in a replay of the torments of Job, John the Baptist, Christ, and the Jesuits maimed by Native Americans, and then by an unremitting psychic scourging (for his own good, naturally) at the hands of his Order. It is a proposition so bleak that I can only assume the novel's many sentimental admirers have missed the point.

A third qualm: Father Sandoz was once a hard, street-smart, good looking little Puerto Rican kid, whose many droll impersonations hint at an insecure sense of his own identity. This is a man poised to crumble, perhaps—but is the indignity of anal rape sufficient to smash him apart? That is a reductive question, admittedly; his anguish is hugely overdetermined, compounded of guilt in the deaths of all his friends, the ruination of a peaceful planetary community, the murder in utero of a child that he might wish with all his heart had been his own, the cannibal daily sustenance he takes. Yet drama fixes our gaze on his "unmanning," his being-done-to. Yes, there's a certain artistic adequacy to the metaphor, but also a measure of offense to those many of the novel's readers who regard receptive homosexual sex (but not, usually, rape) as powerfully desirable, not aversive, certainly not mind-killingly ugly. Do I merely fall into the dreaded sin of political correctness? Am I compensating too hard for my vanilla heterosexuality? Maybe. Still, using homosexual practices as a figure of unparalleled evil, even under the guise of rape, strikes me as suspect.

MUSIC OF THE SPHERES

Father Sandoz and his friends begin their first mission in pursuit of the ravishing music (ha!) SETI astronomers detect from the Centauri suns. When their clumsy work is done, the broadcast music has been silenced. One human adult and one damaged child survive the carnage after Sandoz is returned in mute disgrace to Earth. Runa, challenged by horrific attack, learn that the lamb can best the lion given sufficient numbers and resolve. Lion society is effectively destroyed. It is a mess of biblical proportion. By the time Sandoz the apostate is hauled kicking and screaming from Earth back to hell, torn from his new love and her own child, leaving behind all unknowing a new life, the Romans are almost extinct and the Greeks are everywhere.

What kind of theodicy is an ex-Jesuit to find in this nightmare? Luckily, the force is with alienkind, human race and Sandoz alike: two human holy fools, one a slow learner Camorra thug who sings opera beautifully, named (rather blatantly) d'Angeli, the other an autistic savant genius who unpacks a Philip Glass–like Music of the Spheres from the comingled genomes of all three species. God has worked, as usual, in mysterious ways, and all's well that ends well, even if the deep harmony of the choir of angels is brought forth from the tormented evolutionary succession of two whole planetfuls of anguished souls. Is art redemption in a fallen world? Not here on Earth, we know, when the cultivated Germans shivered with joy at Bach and Mozart before pulling on their boots for a long day at the gas chambers. Or is that a philistine objection, smugly or even Satanically pleased to find any pollution of the beautiful? Either way, this happy ending is not *absolutely* persuasive.

Still, *Children of God* is a more satisfactory (sf) novel than its better-received forerunner, whose gratifying, if insinuating, cast are mostly dead, leaving Russell without their slightly cheesy if always dazzlingly intelligent winsomeness (*Party of Five Goes to Mars*, as it were), so she has to work harder. What's more, if sf's vocation is "a symbolic meditation on history itself"—as critic Fredric Jameson insists[15]—Russell comes closer here to that large-scale canvas. Drawn in to her complex antiphonies, the richly imagined and described lives of these twinned aliens and their human tempters, one is able to ignore the inconsistencies and absurdities. "As fish are caught in a net and as birds are trapped," saith the Prophet, "so are the children of men entrapped" (*Children of God*, p. 241). True enough, but perhaps, as a noble carnivore reminds her doubting, heart-sick charge: "I listened to you say we are all—Jana'ata and Runa and H'uman—children of a god so high that our ranks and our differences are nothing in his far sight" (p. 326). If so high a god had actually woven into our genomes a celestial music, etched in the vast odyssey of travail and love, antipathies and generosities of conscious history and its billion-year mindless antecedents, we might stand under heaven in both conditions simultaneously: trapped in sacred nets, privileged to be the instruments upon which the twinned and trebled musics are sounded. Even redeemed Sandoz, I suspect, is left at the end holding doubts in his tattered hands. We hold only a fairytale in ours, but it is an impressive one, in its way. It is not, though, I think (despite Russell's obvious immersion in her created world, and the distinct resemblances between her own biography and the married characters Anne and George) a transrealist one.[16]

SO IT GOES

Are these reflections themselves nothing better than an instance meriting Richard Grant's stern rebuke? "The society here is not entirely plausible" "Rockets and ecologies don't work like that," "Jesuits are made of sterner stuff." Perhaps. A standard apologia for sf takes this form: If the past is another country, so is the future—and it will be our place of exile. Not only do they do things differently there (*whichever* future it is), they are imperialistic with it. The future has its fifth column in our midst. At best, we can take language lessons and hope we are memorizing the lexicon of the correct future.

Of course, if it really did make sense to say that the future had placed a fifth column in the hapless present, I am far from certain that science fiction would be the proper cartographer of its spaces. But perhaps the one thing science fiction writers and readers know is the immense lability of what everyone else tends to regard as solid reality. Indeed, in a 1980 interview Philip K. Dick acknowledged exactly that: "SF presents in fictional form an eccentric view of the normal or a normal view of the world that is not [our] world" (interview conducted with Frank C. Bertrand, in Sutin *Shifting Realities*, p. 44). That is the very eccentricity, the necessary off-centeredness, at the heart of transrealism.

The desire to find purpose and significance in life, however it is expressed or thwarted in a given language, might be the most persistent characteristic of the human condition—which is to say, of mind conscious of the time and confinement. We shall now step back from those ambiguous recent bestsellers and anatomize two linked novels from that interesting transitional period when a few sf authors began to write as if they were first and foremost game-playing *literary* novelists, while those from the right side of the tracks began to appropriate themata, enabling devices and even neologisms from sf (as we shall see in the next chapter on slipstream).

If there is indeed a specifiable human condition, its limit cases are the numinous and the nihilist, figured in the extreme as apocalypse and absurdité. But these limit cases, apparently binary opposites, are in turn a suitably classic site for deconstruction. They share an intimate relationship, for their polarity curves back upon itself like the two-in-one surface of a möbius strip, or the mandala integrity of a Yin-Yang form where black and white curve about one another in a closed circle, each a fish sibling swimming within the amnion of the other's identity. Plato wondered of his utopian Republic whether a society could contrive some magnificent myth that would carry conviction to its whole community— a lie that might serve the greater truth of community. Kurt Vonnegut's early sf novels *The Sirens of Titan* (1959) and *Cat's Cradle* (1963), like most of his subsequent acerbic fiction, are a concerted investigation of that putative identity of truth and falsity, outrageous gambles at the margins of transreality.

"All persons, places, and events in this book are real," declares an author's note in the front of *Sirens*. This disarming lie seems merely comic, a sort of stand-up jest at the expense of the usual pious formula that hides every writer's disguised borrowings from real life. Then we find its complement in the front of *Cat's Cradle*: "Nothing in this book is true." No reader wants to believe that, even of a sf confection. Taken together as antitheses, both declarations strain in mutual contradiction— and mutual invalidity. Vonnegut has his readers by the throat, from the outset, and we laugh while we choke.

At its core, of course, *The Sirens of Titan* is perhaps the longest shaggy-dog (or shaggy-god story) ever told. The whole of human history proves to be no more than an engineered communication device for an extra-terrestrial robot stranded on Saturn's moon Titan. *Cat's Cradle*, in which the Earth is destroyed in a clumsy accident, is a vaudeville pratfall with the whole world as metaphor. Both are huge intellectual gags, in bad taste, sick jokes of such gentle bitterness, painful as a spastic's steps, that they provoke tears. When our laughter has eased, we sometimes find with surprise that we are weeping.

ANTI-BODHISATTVAS

Vonnegut's novels are impossible to categorize, which is exactly what makes his work a suitable site for investigation despite the recent slump in his literary stock. While his early short stories and books were sold as science fiction, the body of his work is regarded by his mass audience as something akin to magical realism. Still, *Sirens* and *Cat's Cradle*, at any rate, plainly evoke the mystique if not the methodology of science. Both plots hinge on sf tropes: time travel, flying saucers, robots, the fatal iso-tope of water called *ice-nine*. At a deeper level they satirize sf devices specifically (the "chrono-synclastic infundibulum" which links past and future)[17] and scientism in general (especially in the person of Dr. Hoen-ikker, atomic bomb designer and absent-minded killer of the world).

Yet their appeal has proved vastly greater than the in-group of sf fans. In the 1950s and 1960s, when Vonnegut was shaping his own strategic blend of anarchic satire and sf, the literary vogue was for "antiheroes" and "antirealism."[18] Both tendencies retained an affinity for the blackly comic, from Kingsley Amis's *Lucky Jim* to Joseph Heller's brittle, sorrow-ing cynicism in *Catch-22*. Vonnegut's method suggests a more audacious antinomianism, or refusal of conventional moralism: let us call his figures "anti-bodhisattvas." Its protagonist is a man (almost always, at least when these books were written) who gains a putative enlightenment but declines any obligation either to pass beyond illusion into nothingness or to remain behind for our succor and guidance—the traditional role of the bodhisattva.

His liberation stands against an ontological aporia, for the world is undecidable either vastly and cruelly ordered, a dominion of unappeas-able causality, or alternatively a realm where order itself is no more than a local mirage within general lawlessness. The former might be figured as the world mapped by relativity, which proposes a four-dimensional "block universe" of space-time world-lines where everything that will ever occur has already happened, so to speak, under the aspect of uni-versal closure. The latter might be figured by the radical contingency of quantum theory, where at bottom nothing whatever is predictably sub-ject to causality.

To catch the mood of Vonnegut's college audience in the late 1960s when his books first attracted cult following, we might consider a 1961 passage from Alan W. Watts, a sort of hot-tub Zen Christian ecumenical minister, who interestingly cites Herbert Marcuse some years prior to that philosopher's own fifteen minutes of fame:

The adult or mature version of primal narcissism is, of course, "cosmic con-sciousness," or the shift from egocentric awareness to the feeling that one's iden-tity is the whole field of the organism in its environment. But if this is not to remain a purely contemplative state; if, in other words, the liberated man is to return to the world like the bodhisattva, he will seek the means of expressing his sense of being "at one with the whole world in pleasure and love." Because the means are aesthetic his approach to the world is as Marcuse suggests, that of Orpheus, "the priest, the mouthpiece of the gods" who tames both men and beasts by the allure and magic of his harp . . . For in the value system of civili-zation, the artist is irrelevant. He is seen as a mere decorator who entertains us as we labor.[19]

Watts suggests here some of the existential implications of Taoist liberation, what a Heideggerian would call *Dasein*-analysis. Tao, being-in-the-world, is made impotent by attempts to split it apart, by categorization and reductive manipulation. Spontaneity cannot be forced, for then it is nothing better than deliberation. It is out of spontaneous lawlessness that the ineluctable Tao emerges, a condition of serenity in an absurd state that transcends itself into an integrated unfolding of its own implicate order. Watts adds:

The liberative artist plays the part of Orpheus by living in the mode of music instead of the mode of language. His entire activity is dancing, rhythm for its own sake, and in this way he becomes a vortex which draws others into its pattern ... The high art, the *upaya*, of a true bodhisattva is possible only for him who has gone beyond all need for self-justification; for so long as there is something to prove, some axe to grind, there is no dance. (Watts, *Psychotherapy East and West*, p. 152)

I do not know if Vonnegut had read Watts, or Marcuse, or any of the modish Frankfurt School Marxist and sub-Eastern doctrines available when he was writing *Sirens* and *Cat's Cradle*.[20] Nonetheless, these paired novels wind skeins drawn from just such a schema of the world—later articulated explicitly by the alien Tralfamadorians in *Slaughterhouse-9* (1969)—and its reverse, the anti-bodhisattva theme. Winston Niles Rumfoord in *Sirens* is the very mirror negative of Watt's bodhisattva-artist: skewed, reversed, yet clearly recognizable in his *upaya*. He is the "mouthpiece of the gods": "You should believe," says Rumfoord. "... because I, as head of this religion, can work miracles. ... I can work the miracle of predicting, with absolute accuracy, the things that the future will bring" (*Sirens*, p. 128) He has been placed, by the infundibulum, "beyond all need for self-justification," and indeed "his entire activity is dancing": he dances a spiral from the Sun to Betelgeuse, dances "over his golden jungle gym in Newport" (p. 175) for the reverent delight of "the same idiots one finds in toy stores" (p. 175), dances the dreadful *leitmotif* piped across the light-years by the Tralfamadorians to their "disgustingly paltry ends."

And if any bodhisattva experienced cosmic consciousness—"the feeling that one's identity is the whole field of the organism in the environment"—it is Rumfoord, whose node is "a place where all the different kinds of truth fit together as nicely as the parts in your Daddy's solar watch," where "everything that ever has been always will be, and everything that ever will be always has been" (p. 12). He has been liberated from linear time into ubiquity, yet his characteristic adjective is "punctual" (e.g., pp. 19, 41). In his cosmic consciousness he instigates deceit, destruction and death. As a final irony, Rumfoord never learns just how paltry the ends of the Magellanic machines were.

DOUBLES

The Sirens of Titan shimmers with *doppelgangers,* signifiers of both unconscious and ontological reduplication. Malachi Constant, the man who yearns to fulfill his name, to carry "a first-class message from God to someone equally distinguished" (*Sirens,* p. 14), figures the entire human species which has labored for its history to carry the replacement part for Salo's broken spaceship. Humanity is itself merely a figure of Salo, the messenger designed (rather like DNA) to be completely dependable, efficient, predictable and durable (p. 192), to carry a message without degradation for eighteen and a half million years. The novel plainly maps a Tao, albeit a flawed and mean Tao, and its path is as ineluctable as might be wished.

That Tao, of course, does not serve human ends or truths. The novel aches with lies and deceptions. With the robot Salo's aid, Rumfoord designs the Church of God the Utterly Indifferent. Its motto (which Vonnegut's oeuvre persuades us is the writer's own doctrine) is *I Was a Victim of a Series of Accidents, As Are We All* (p. 161), and for the compass of the book it is precisely, and on a scale previously unimagined since the high tide of Calvinist predestination, what we are not. Its ethical practice, ensuring equality by handicaps, is the essence of fraud. Its prolegomenon, the Martian War, is no better than an inhuman publicity stunt. Its telos, the delivery of the replacement part, serves a Higher Power's definite, if grotesque, purpose.

When happiness ensues, its roots are equivocal. "Look forward to being in love for the first time, Bea," Rumfoord promises his estranged socialite wife. "Look forward to having nothing but the dignity and intelligence and tenderness that God gave you—look forward to taking those materials and nothing else, and making something exquisite with them" (p. 45). Yet the continuity of personal memory, the best humans can attain of the four-dimensional extended present of the aliens, the continuity that would underpin such an achievement is just what is filched from Bea. Certainly in her moment of triumph—"when my son and I walk together to that ladder and climb it, we will not be doing it for you, or for your silly crowd" (p. 184)—transcends Bea's earlier spurious social dignity. But the theft of linear identity prevents her from rejoicing in the moment of choice.

The closing, moving scene occurs within the frame of an illusion. Unk is no longer what Malachi Constant was: aggressive, loud, childish, wasteful, parvenu. By the standards of canonized literature, Constant has passed through a redemptive passage into maturity, and by the stan-

dards of Eastern enlightenment he is emptied of false identity and ready
to enter into the status of a bodhisattva. Both standards are inappropriate
in the ontology of *Sirens*, for Unk is no longer a man. He dies in a simulated reality, as programmed by hypnosis as any computer. The book
folds back into itself like a box of mirrors. The final stanza is a kalei-
doscope of fragments, more Pangloss than Candide as we are fetched
back to the opening:

Everybody now knows how to find the meaning of life within himself.
  But mankind wasn't always so lucky. Less than a century ago, men and women
did not have easy access to the puzzle boxes within them.
  They could not name even one of the fifty-three portals to the soul . . . [But]
Outwardness lost, at last, its imagined attractions.
  Only inwardness remained to be explored.
  Only the human soul remained *terra incognita*.
  This was the beginning of goodness and wisdom. . . . (P. 7)

Indeed, outwardness—the desire to know "who was actually in charge
of all creation, and what creation was all about"—brought humanity
only three results: "empty heroics, low comedy, and pointless death"
(p. 7).

While this is the philosophical teachings of the text, we might easily
question it. The desire for objective knowledge, however thwarted, has
brought liberation in the end from the control of the Tralfamadorians.
The false bodhisattvas danced their directed dance to the freedom of the
human race. Even the interstellar message in whose service this cosmic
pratfall has been arranged is perhaps not so risible or empty. It is simply
this: *Greetings*. Is it really as insane or inane as one is tempted to take it,
driven as we are by the teleological impulse of narrative? It could easily
have been (as it has usually been in human history): *War!*

INVERSIONS

If Vonnegut is teasing us, he is apt to whip his tongue from one cheek
to the other. *Cat's Cradle*, inverse of *The Sirens of Titan*, is no more con-
clusive in its autodeconstruction. Nobody is as malleable as the person
who believes herself undetermined. In *Sirens*, God the Utterly Indifferent
was invented precisely for this use: "Oh, Mankind, rejoice in the apathy
of our Creator, for it makes us free and truthful and dignified at last. . . .
Oh Lord Most High, what a glorious weapon is Thy Apathy, for we
have unsheathed it, and claptrap which has so often enslaved us or
driven us into the madhouse lies slain!" (*Sirens*, p. 152). In *Cat's Cradle*,
the equally spurious religion of Bokononism teaches the reverse. "Humanity is organized into teams, teams that do God's will without ever

discovering what they are doing. . . . Nice, nice, very nice—So many different people in the same device" (pp. 7–8). This religion is explicitly and intentionally an opiate of the people: "Bokonon, cynically and playfully, invented a new religion. . . . Truth was the enemy of the people, because truth was so terrible, so Bokonon made it his business to provide the people with better and better lies" (p. 109).

When all life on Earth is destroyed by the apocalypse of *ice-nine*, no divine judgment has been rendered: this is brute contingent absurdity, facilitated by the irresponsibility of its inventor and the philosophy of industrial militarism. While "no cradle, no cat" is precisely and chillingly the metaphysical truth of the world, lies like *karass* (the secret affinity team God has put you in) and *Pro Patria* enable human beings to abandon any sense of personal responsibility. Perhaps Vonnegut's own reluctant message, as an atheist, is this: if there's Somebody Up There, whether or not They like you, there remains some chance of discovering the fifty-three portals of the soul. When the only outside entities are *foma*, sacred lies, the world itself locks into eternal winter and death.

Bokonon, originally a black British Episcopalian from Tobago named Lionel Boyd Johnson (*Cat's Cradle*, p. 68), is a full-blown anti-bodhisattva. He even resembles the Eastern original. Yet, fantastically, he hurls his mountebankery in the world's face: "Don't be a fool! Close this book at once! It is nothing but *foma!*"(p. 165) and " 'I thought this was trash.' " " 'Of course it's trash!' says Bokonon" (p. 166). The final paragraph of the novel, itself the final sentence of *The Book of Bokonon*, seems explicit enough:

If I were a younger man, I would write a history of human stupidity; and I would climb to the top of Mount McCabe and lie down on my back with my history for a pillow; and I would take from the ground some of the blue-white poison that makes statues of men; and I would make a statue of myself, lying on my back, grinning horribly, and thumbing my nose at You Know Who. (P. 179)

It is the typical final resort of the escapist to shift blame, to salve one's own conscience in projection. Is this Bokonon's admission? Has the "spurious holy man" slipped into his own mythos, or is the paragraph one final enormously ironical gloss on self-deception? Whichever is the case, the last responsibility has been renounced.

Dr. Hoenikker, deviser of *ice-nine*, is no less an anti-bodhisattva. Genius and moral imbecile, he is the spirit of spontaneity, the Tao in flawed action, an unconscious without an ego to control it. His dubious humanity needs no Bokononist lies to distract itself from the miseries of temporal life: "Why should I bother with made-up games when there are so many real ones going on?" (*Cat's Cradle*, p. 13.) This is an eminently liberated remark, since human existence is for the bodhisattva the Great Game, *Maya*. Regrettably, the real games for Hoenikker (as for Dr. Edward Teller, inventor of the H-bomb and promoter of the now defunct Star Wars orbital weapons systems) include developing nuclear weapons and *ice-nine*. As Watts remarks, "Not caring is the parody of serenity" (*Psychotherapy*, p. 96).

In *Cat's Cradle*, anomie, normlessness, is defended by the anti-bodhisattvas into a religion of resignation. Genuine moral anxiety is cathartized by ludicrous fears—practice the *boko-maru*, an innocent rubbing of the feet, at the lethal risk of the Hook (*Cat's Cradle*, p. 87). Ragnarok moves forward inexorably, not out of warfare between gods but from "a thrilling show" (p. 159). Jonah's pet cat lies murdered as a joke (p. 53). "What" (indeed) "Can a Thoughtful Man Hope for Mankind on Earth, Given the Experience of the Past Million Years?" (p. 153). Nothing but empty heriocs, low comedy, pointless death? It is a case urged with even more brutal certainty in Vonnegut's late novel *Galapagos* (1985) where humanity's descendants a million years hence frolic in an innocent Darwinian garden, deprived by evolution of our fatally hypertrophied intelligence and imagination.

The issue of moral responsibility, of humans individually and in concert, has never been more in need of clarification than at the close of the twentieth century and the opening the new millennium. The putative identity of the Noble Lie and the Good Life, however attractive to a world struggling once again with the clash between science and fundamentalism, species identity and local nationalisms, threatens the existence of species and planetary ecology alike. The two most dubious responses are surely these:"I guess somebody up there like me" (*Sirens*, p. 16) and "I would make a statue of myself . . . thumbing my nose at You Know Who" (*Cats Cradle*, p. 179). The mandala is stark: the inevitability of illusion, the illusion of inevitability. At such a crux, any retreat from realism might seem an abdication, yet its embrace remains always out of reach. Transrealism may prove one way forward. Another has been called slipstream, though rarely by those identified as practicing it.

WADING THE SLIPSTREAM

When retired scientist and middlebrow novelist C. P. Snow diagnosed a major gap between the numerate and the literate around the middle of the twentieth century, it certainly did not occur to him to see science fiction as a Vonnegutian rope ladder thrown across the chasm. This is hardly surprising, since most sf to that date lacked both literary dash and scientific validity. Philip K. Dick was unmerciful, at his own expense: "Science fiction writers, I am sorry to say, really do not know anything. We can't talk about science, because our knowledge of it is dreadful. . . . [S]uddenly, the academic world noticed us, we were invited to give speeches and appear on the panels—and immediately we made idiots of ourselves. The problem is simply this: What does a science fiction writer know about?"[21]

Since Snow's time, however, two generations of inventive writers have replaced rope with computer-designed girders and reinforced dreams. Their names are not those associated with popular sf success: not Robert A. Heinlein, Isaac Asimov, Frank Herbert, Dick himself (dead white males), or icons such as Vonnegut, Arthur C. Clarke, Ursula Le Guin, Gregory Benford, or Anne McCaffrey, nor yet the likes of Russell and Vonnegut. The books I mean are not sf at all—rather, they range from a kind of techno-Gothic to what the writer R. V. Branham has sarcastically dubbed Gringo Magic Realism—but they could not have existed without it. Or perhaps their special spin comes not via the advance mediation of sf and its painfully evolved narrative strategies (appropriated by the two writers we have examined in this chapter), but from standing directly in the slipstream of science itself. In any event, for many jaded science fiction readers, they are replacing a burnt-out genre. Perhaps slipstream is transrealism's sibling, or perhaps it is indeed transrealist sf seen from a slightly different angle. Let us consider some examples of this hybrid form.

NOTES

1. David G. Hartwell, "Who Killed Science Fiction," *New York Review of Science Fiction*, no. 103, vol. 9, no. 7 (March 1997): p. 24.

2. Brian Aldiss, *Trillion Year Spree* (London: Gollancz, 1986), p. 279.

3. Both these comments were made during an on-line discussion organized in 1998 by AvonEos, their U.S. publisher and are reproduced here slightly edited by the authors, by permission of Susan Matthews and Amy Stout.

4. Richard Grant, "Git Along, Little Robot," in *The Profession of Science Fiction: Writers on Their Craft and Ideas*, ed. Maxim Jakubowski and Edward James (London: Macmillan, 1992).

5. Mary Doria Russell, *The Sparrow* (New York: Fawcett Columbine, 1996; New York: Ballantine Books, 1997) and her sequel, *Children of God* (New York: Villard, 1998).

6. Especially in Smith's novel *Norstrilia* (New York: Ballantine, 1975).

7. Is "Even the Queen" a transrealist story? It is a superbly witty, plainly heartfelt short dramatization of the family ructions that ensue when a modish young woman in a Liberated near future decides to join a cult and have her menses reinstated. The cross-generational chorus of women denouncing the unpleasantness of this biological imposition—in the face of cant from a floratorian or flower-eater who extols menstruation's natural merits—presumably enacts Ms. Willis's own life experience of "the curse." Since the tale depends on a new drug, ammenerol, and a medical procedure, the shunt, the story is surely "writ-

ing in the slipstream of science." I am not quite persuaded, however. The form of the tale is a little too neat, shaped, declarative—too Wildean.

8. William Atheling Jr. (James Blish), *More Issues at Hand* (Chicago: Advent: Publishers, 1970).

9. James Blish, *After Such Knowledge* (London: Legend, 1991), p. 483.

10. James Blish, "The Development of a Science Fiction Writer," in *The Profession of Science Fiction Writers on Their Craft and Ideas*, ed. Maxim Jakubowski and Edward James (London: Macmillan, 1992), p. 32.

11. "A Conversation with Maria Doria Russell," *The Sparrow* (fifth page of unnumbered "Reader's Guide").

12. Well, maybe it's more complicated: "the engines broke down silicates to use as fuel . . . you could scale the system up for long-range travel" *The Sparrow*, (p. 96).

13. As astronomer Paul Thomas kindly confirmed for me when I asked him over the net, a tool surely available to Dr. Russell as well.

14. Indeed, in my own novella "The Magi," a Jesuit (a former Jew baptized following a second Holocaust) finds a madman slaughtering billions of viable human foetuses.

15. Fredric Jameson, in the symposium "Change, SF, and Marxism: Open or Closed Universes," in *Science Fiction Studies*, ed. R. D. Mullen and Darko Suvin (New York: Gregg Press, 1976), pp. 275–76.

16. In the "Reader's Guide," she states that some of the characters are "based on real people . . . Anne and George share a biography with my husband and me, with certain limitations. . . . Nevertheless, she speaks fairly clearly in my voice. I used my brother's voice for John Candotti . . . Emilio is his own person. I know nobody like him . . . Sofia is also her own person" (third page of unnumbered section in the Ballantine Reader's Circle edition).

17. Kurt Vonnegut, *The Sirens of Titan* (1959; London: Gollancz, 1986), p. 12.

18. See, for example, David Littlejohn, "The Anti-realists," *Daedalus* (spring 1963): 250–64.

19. Alan W. Watts, *Psychotherapy East and West* (New York: Mentor, 1963), p. 149.

20. Certainly Philip K. Dick seems to have modeled the Sufi teacher Edgar Barefoot, in his late non-sf novel *The Transmigration of Timothy Archer*, after Watts.

21. Philip K. Dick, *I Hope I Shall Arrive Soon* (1978; London: Grafton, 1988), pp. 7–8. This citation is from a speech given at a science fiction convention in Paris entitled "How to Build a Universe That Doesn't Fall Apart Two Days Later." Dick died in 1982, not yet 54.

5

Fictions in the Slipstream

Sf's failure to present its own best face, to win proper respect, was never so tragic as now, when its strengths are so routinely pre-empted. In a literary culture where Pynchon, DeLillo, Barthelme, Coover, Jeanette Winterson, Angela Carter, and Steve Erickson are ascendant powers, isn't the division meaningless?
—Jonathan Lethem, "Why Can't We All Just Live Together?" (p. 8)

By the end of the millennium, the flexible slipstream category had gained some important ground as an organizing principle that might escape the division Lethem deplored. Karen Joy Fowler, whose astonishing histor-ical novel *Sarah Canary* (1991) is a key instance, ran an annual slipstream writing workshop in Cleveland, Ohio, and panels attracted heated dis-cussion at science fiction conventions. It was not by accident that the packaging of Fowler's collection *Black Glass* (1998), comprising fifteen short stories mostly first published in sf magazines and original anthol-ogies, silently erased this history. Meanwhile, writer Justina Robson and Rozanne Rabinowitz, a founding editor of feminist newszine *Bad Atti-tude*, announced a new British anthology of women's slipstream writing, hoping to find "stories or pieces which are vivid with contemporary experience and which may use any genre or literary style to make their point." They defined their needs thus:

Slipstream stories are those which defy categorisation. They often contain varied elements of fantasy, horror or science fiction, but use them in a relatively mainstream manner to convey the themes of the story. Strange as they get, they're always concerned with real issues and real people. Their form is secondary to communicating insight and atmosphere. Slipstream is not simply a mixture of fantasy and realism, but something which lies between or even beyond the two. Whether telling a story or exploring a common situation slipstream is vivid, at the edge of reality and the heart of experience.[1]

In an October 1998 editorial in *The New York Review of Science Fiction* (having, a year and a half earlier, teasingly declared sf dead), David G. Hartwell sought a slipstream canon, and proposed that slipstream be redefined as co-extensive with "speculative fiction." That term had gained currency in the 1960s, deployed to catch the difference between the kinds of confronting experimental literary efforts coming out in *New Worlds* magazine in Britain, and then from flashy or adventurous sf writers elsewhere in the world, even in the United States. "Then we can appropriate any ambitious work in or out of sf we like," Hartwell wrote, doubtless with his tongue to some degree in his cheek, "and call it slipstream to distinguish it from the ordinary genre stuff that no longer gives us the kick it used to give."[2]

That was not the kind of austere or inflated critical language one would find in the academy, but Hartwell was writing for his fellow editors, writers and sophisticated fans of sf. "There is no new genre here, but a resurgence of an internal attempt to reform." He had no need to beat about the bush, even if the truth of the matter stung. "No one talks about slipstream but us sf genre geeks." (Hartwell, "Slipstream Slip Sliding," p. 24)

Bruce Sterling's original goal had been perhaps more ambitious than a simple redefinition. Slipstream he saw as an emerging genre—"a spectrum of work united by an inner identity, a coherent esthetic, a set of conceptual guidelines, an ideology"—rather than a marketing category, which he felt sf had become, with disastrous consequences. As a marketing category, sf was allocated a certain guaranteed rack space for reliable product. Slipstream was the work of "Postmodern Sensibility," "a contemporary kind of writing which has set its face against consensus reality. It is fantastic, surreal sometimes, speculative on occasion, but not rigorously so. It does not aim to provoke a 'sense of wonder' or to systematically extrapolate in the manner of classic science fiction."[3]

EARLY SLIPSTREAM

A representative forerunner might be Bernard Wolfe's scarifyingly funny *Limbo-90*, a 1952 vision of mass amputations as a moral equivalent to nuclear war (although Wolfe is not listed among the sample candidates that close Sterling's manifesto). Usually in this emerging genre there is a thread of black, bitter humor and absurdity: one thinks, pre-eminently, of Thomas Pynchon's *V* (1963), *The Crying of Lot 49* (1966), and the vast postmodernist *Gravity's Rainbow* (1973), of Richard Condon's tales of conspiracy and sex, passion and madness, Tom Robbin's *Another Roadside Attraction* (1975), Joyce Carol Oates's *Bellefleur* (1980), Edward Whittemore's tetralogy that started with *The Sinai Tapestry* ([1977], 1979), with its cruel jokes and fabulous characters: Plantagenet Strongbow, Victorian swordsman and botanist; the Szondi matriarchs, who owned and ran the Ottoman empire, and their delicate, artistic hus-bands; O'Sullivan Beare, and his friend Haj Harun, thousands of years old and looking every day of it, who concocted the Bible. Closer to ex-plicit sf were John Calvin Batchelor's first two novels, cousins of Pyn-chon, creative in the generous manner of many-voiced America. *The Further Adventures of Halley's Comet* ([1980], 1984), like the architecture of its central edifice, Means Manor, can be described aptly as "neo-Gothic blockwork strange" (p. 161). Grim Fiddle, narrator of *The Birth of the People's Republic of Antarctica* (1983) cites his birth-message from the Book of Proverbs: "My Son, fear Lord God and grow rich in spirit, but have nothing to do with men of rank! They will bring catastrophe without warning! Who knows what ruin such men may cause?" (p. 5). Batchelor knows, and in those two very different books tells us, until we marvel and howl, just how bloody and puffed-up are those men and women of rank who in the days of Mutual Assured Destruction seemed to be spur-ring us each day toward Armageddon. That same ambience suffused Don DeLillo's masterful early novels, especially *White Noise* (1985), and takes his recent success *Underworld* (1997) away from its notional sport-ing and organized crime setting into a dislocated *mise en scene* far more familiar to sf readers than to his enthusiastic and dazzled mainstream reviewers.

Sterling noted certain common technical features of slipstream tex-tuality, often the same features others (like Brian McHale [1987], Fredric Jameson [1991] and me [1995]) have regarded as evidence of postmod-ernism's intersection with both science fictional and surrealist strategies: audacious and playful appropriation of historical events and characters, flattened affect in the face of terrible or acutely disruptive events, *trompe-l'oiel*, blurring of frame and picture: J. G. Ballard meets Philip K. Dick in Kafka's Castle, under the zoned-out eye of William Burroughs or per-haps Will Self.

It seems to me that the heart of slipstream is an attitude of peculiar aggression against "reality." These are fantasies of a kind, but not fantasies which are "fu-turistic" or "beyond the fields we know." These books tend to sarcastically tear at the structure of "everyday life."

Some such books, the most "mainstream" ones, are non-realistic literary fictions which avoid or ignore SF genre conventions. But hard-core slipstream has unique darker elements. Quite commonly these works don't make a lot of common sense, and what's more they often somehow imply that *nothing we know* makes "a lot of sense" and perhaps even that *nothing ever could*. (Sterling, "Cat-scan 5")

In short, certain imaginative novels operate in a space opened in part by the general impact on our times of the vertiginous epistemologies and ontologies of science, in part by the narrative responses to that impact by science fiction itself, hitching a ride in the slipstream of both discursive subcultures as they advance. At the same time these books do not, somehow, feel to the aficionado or connoisseur like "real" sf. Marge Piercy's *Woman on the Edge of Time* (1976) is a feminist utopia, and a fine one, set partly in a surrealist psychiatric nightmare here and now, partly in the future, yet arguably it is not sf by any traditional accounting, nor, really, is her futuristic cyborg novel *Body of Glass* (1992). Margaret Atwood's *The Handmaid's Tale* (1985) is a feminist *dys*topia, no less impressive, and clearly not sf either, despite the wish one might acknowledge (apparently not a wish shared by Atwood) to appropriate it—indeed, it won the inaugural Arthur C. Clarke Award in 1986. So yes, call them slipstream. Other examples are even written by former sf authors (Kurt Vonnegut, Christopher Priest), others again by novelists adopting some of the usages of sf for ends that sometimes blunt their borrowed generic blade (Anthony Burgess, Doris Lessing, Martin Amis).

DADA

How, for example, might we position such marginalia as Lisa Goldstein's recreation of a surreal Paris in 1924, 1968, and the twenty-first century, *The Dream Years* (1986)? Its quiet, mildly sentimental tone seems at odds with sf's gaudy tradition. Goldstein's Robert St. Onge is one of the founding Surrealists, first friend of Andre Breton and his movement's first apostate. St. Onge, novelist-*manque*, comes adrift in time, as he is adrift in life. All the faintly silly enthusiasms of post-Dada Surrealism drift through the novel's structure like memories of a dream: *objets trouves* (these particular "found objects," one an LP record unplayable on a 1920s' phonograph, proving in fact to be cunning Barthesian lures from the France of May 1968 and its aborted revolution), mysterious signs and conjunctions, phantoms from nightmare, the dead father (at once bourgeois paterfamilias and defunct God), the strange woman; especially the strange woman. In this instance she is Solange, a name echoing his, as in, indeed, a dream, singer and revolutionary from St. Onge's future, in love with a man from her devotional history books.

The novel's actors largely comprise a Surrealist roll call: Breton himself, bruised by the Great War, hectoring and industrious in the cause of unreason, a Stalin of psychic license. Louis Aragon, not yet suckered into authentic Stalinism, nor his poetry yet traded down for social realism. Poor mad brilliant Antonin Artaud, whose Theatre of Cruelty was to pierce a thread of bright pain through our century's most complacent art form. Yves Tanguy, Paul Eluard, Jacques Rigaut who killed himself to honor a contract set exactly a decade earlier: the whole calculatedly sick gang (to adopt Pynchon's trope).

For Solange, St. Onge is a magus, a magician of the unconscious, one of the two genuine psychic revolutionaries—Breton is the other, of course— capable of leading the forces of spontaneity and joy against 2010's droning mechanical masters, themselves more Philip K. Dick than, say, Rene Magritte. For us, perhaps he is a listless shadow of the visionary poet, in that extraordinary Gallic tradition of artists-of-affairs, Saint-John Perse, sometime secretary general of the pre-Vichy Foreign Ministry. Or perhaps he is a blend of Breton and Eluard, driven by a hunger for the lost mother, the stolen paradise.

Here, we find ourselves at the slipstream intersection of genre and mainstream art. Goldstein had been all too successful in transmuting into an sf fable the *idees fixes* of the Surreal movement. The imagery, captured by automatic writing and the odd drug, was vivid and direct. As literal narrative, as plot and action, its force is weakened by the thousand debased media piracies we have since suffered. Is it possible to quiet the hammering of a hundred old *Twilight Zone* shows and perform, by an act of surreal faith, a pure, an *automatic* reading? Not easily. And so *The Dream Years*, in its simplicity and charm, is left altogether too close to, shall we say, *Jean Cocteau Meets the Terminator*.

Is this no more than an unseemly demarcation dispute? The questions at issue cut deeper than that, I think. Rap your knuckles against a culture's fantasies, listen carefully to the echoes. What you detect, if only rudely, is the shape of what's inside the shell.

Lacking reception cues in the outside of the book, it is not obvious how we might read the opening sentence from Geoff Ryman's *The Unconquered Country* (1986): "Third Child had nothing to sell but parts of her body" (p. 3). There are junkies in every Western capital city in the same boat, but never to the horrific extent as these victims in a poignant fantasy/allegory of the rape of Cambodia by America, Vietnam and finally its own fanatics.

Third rented her womb for industrial use. She was cheaper than the glass tanks. She grew parts of living machinery inside her—differentials for trucks, small household appliances. She gave birth to advertisements, small caricature figures that sang songs. . . .

When Third was lucky, she got a contract for weapons. The pay was good because it was dangerous. The weapons would come gushing out of her with much loss of blood, usually in the middle of the night: an avalanche of glossy, freckled, dark brown guppies with bright rodent smiles full of teeth . . . Thrashing in their buckets as she carried them down the steps, the guppies would eat each other. (Pp. 3, 5)

Its strangeness, the pain it catches, could scarcely be borne at greater than novella length. Not by accident is *The Unconquered Country* dedicated to John Lennon and Philip K. Dick, writers with a touch of surreal cruelty and a streak of wistful sentimentality. Certainly Ryman's book is not sf, for all its living houses and half-living Coke advertisements. "She hit it on the shoulder. The arm broke off. It was full of red, rather dry meat, and did not bleed. The thing kept singing ' . . . gives you life' " (p. 75). It is not fantasy either, but some blend of folklore and the nightmare of history. It is a fusion that Ryman was to bring to a kind of contemporary fabulism in his fantasy *Was . . .* (1992), a complex blend of The Wizard of Oz, the "real" nineteenth-century history of sexually abused Dorothy in the Midwest, and a late twentieth-century gay man seeking the understanding and forgiveness of memory in the final months of his slow death by AIDS.

SLIPSTREAM/TRANSREALISM

Sterling's own list of slipstream fiction, in his "Catscan" manifesto, is catholic, and some of his instances overlap with my own suggestions for transrealist fiction (though by no means all). He mentions, among many others, Kathy Acker and Peter Ackroyd, Angela Carter and Robert Coover, Raymond Federman and Russell Hoban, Kathryn Kramer and Ted Mooney, Toni Morrison, Marge Piercy, Thomas Pynchon and Salman Rushdie, Joyce Thompson and John Updike and Nancy Willard. More recently, he adds William Browning Spencer.[5] It is not difficult to think of others not on his list: the Nabokov of *Ada, or Ardor: A Family Chronicle* (1969), all of Umberto Eco's fiction, some of Jeanette Winterson, some of Peter Carey. One starts to wonder if there are any limits at all to the voracious appetite of this sprawling new genre. Is anything out of the ordinary fair game? Let us go back a step, probe once again at some commonplaces. What is the "mainstream" against which these notional new genres and categories are being mounted?

A novel, orthodoxy once instructed us, is a long invented story, told in a clear prose, that describes what we are to see in prompted imagination, transcribes what we are to hear, evokes the thoughts and memories of characters who do not exist in reality, and sometimes comments upon and evaluates these invented lives.

Actually, no. Of course that is not it.

For Vladimir Nabokov, a novel might be a longish poem attended by ever more bizarre footnotes (*Pale Fire*, 1962). Italo Calvino made one out of fragments of barely begun novels allegedly by other people (*If On a Winter's Night a Traveller*, 1981). James Joyce wrote one all of dreams, in a glossolalia that tempts even as it repels (*Finnegans Wake*, 1939). Martin Amis tracked his Nazi doctor backward through time to his innocent redemption (*Time's Arrow, or The Nature of the Offence.* 1991). Postmodernists generally scatter the literary landscape with oddities and triumphs of form, imagination working on language as a confectioner whips sugar and egg white.

Many stolid souls, yearning for a good nineteenth-century read, or even for a good Doris Lessing before she turned to turgid allegory, will agree with these demurrals. Yes, those are all novels, too—alas.

While not all departures from the canonical format are automatically slipstream, or transrealist in the sense I use in this book, some plainly stand at the boundary. Consider Stanislaw Lem's *Hospital of the Transfiguration* ([1955], 1989), which at first glance seems a strikingly realistic account of occupation life shortly after the German invasion of Poland but is nothing so simple.

FROM EARTH TO CYBERIA

Stanislaw Lem is the preeminent European sf writer, standing somewhere between the technical dazzle of Alfred Bester and the speculative sociology of Isaac Asimov. Better, perhaps, he is the Polish equivalent of Italo Calvino or Jorge Luis Borges, a fabulist whose invented worlds seem at once more opulent and clarified than the world of experience. His approach to fiction has grown more uncompromisingly intellectual with every book, so that his piercing melancholy seems unassuageable by anything warm, kind, generous in human life. A terrible Olympian laughter goes with the cool assessment, however, so that it is hard to know if Lem is a Martian adrift among people or a human lost among absurd aliens. His reputation and worldwide fame is founded on a kind of sf derived directly from Verne and Wells, bypassing commercial Western models. In his first published novel, *Hospital of the Transfiguration*, Lem's beautifully observed vignettes fold together, with exquisite placement, like the elements of a ritual, perhaps an exorcism, holding the past even as it purges its unbearable grief. This is territory trodden more recently, of course, by such writers as D. M. Thomas and Martin Amis, using much the same transgressive apparatus.

Stefan Trzyiecki, like Lem himself at the time a student doctor (though slightly older, so that he begins his practice in wartime), attends an uncle's funeral in a village where his family have been minor notables for centuries. As distant and alienated from his kin as Joyce's Stephen Dedalus, Stefan watches the obsequies with a certain distaste: all this confused bustle of life, family politics, evasion and warmth. By the novel's end, Stefan is lying in the arms of a cool, lovely woman whose name he does not know, in the hay of a stable, "as blank and empty as the moment of his birth" (Lem, *Hospital of the Transfiguration*, p. 207). That journey to nativity is Poland's funeral rites as well, his nation's uncertain rebirth into a condition of internal exile that it took fifty years to challenge.

Although *Hospital of the Transfiguration* was completed in 1948, it was not published until 1955—victim of the hegemony of "socialist realism"—nor translated into English until the late 1980s with the fall of the Soviet system. Yet it is not easy for us to see what the Polish communist authorities found technically offensive in the book, which evades realism only in its structure, and then only to the attuned eye. Even in his twenties, though, Lem was clearly struggling with those questions of form and narrative strategy that were to turn him away from the quotidian and into landscapes of the cognitive imagination. More recently he has written: "Those days have pulverised and exploded all narrative conventions that had previously been used in literature. The unfathomable futility of human life under the sway of mass murder cannot be conveyed by literary techniques in which individuals or small groups form the core of the narrative."[6]

If Thomas Mann found a tuberculosis clinic an apt metaphor for the decline of the West, many writers since have looked to a more extreme figure: the lunatic asylum, the cuckoo's nest. Almost by accident Stefan takes a job in a mental hospital named, with grotesque irony, for Christ in his transfigured state after the resurrection. There is little enough hope of rebirth for these poor souls. In the era before sophisticated psychoactive medication, Lem's site is the customary Bedlam of heedless, untrained orderlies and medical staff themselves on the verge of craziness. Each is sketched with precision and wit as Lem puts his carnival through its paces before the authentic madness begins, when the SS arrive to murder the doctors' charges, those supposedly less-than-human victims of disease, stress and the accidents of genetics.

At the heart of the novel is a truly horrifying Foucauldian rebus of the whole, a clinically described operation to remove a tumor from the brain of a patient who has been deteriorating under the enthralled gaze of his surgeon. Kauters (a suitable emblematic name) is the sole German physician among these Poles, destined to cower and blubber before his triumphant countrymen. At the operating table he delves and tears into the naked brain like a mining engineer dredging a sacred site, scorching tissue when an artery is cut, scooping out the cancer until, to his exasperation, the patient lies dead. Beyond the walls of the asylum, in a local power station, Polish patriots smuggle arms to partisans and brood upon the bodies of suicides charred black by electricity. Lem's world in this apparently realist first novel is at once pitiless and aching with pity, a small gem of a book gleaming across the decades like a drop of blood caught in a spotlight.

For the contemporary writer, like the young Lem perfectly equipped to notate the known in whatever naturalistic or symbolic register, sf retrieves simultaneously the additional fluencies of sacred or ritual art found in *Hospital of the Transfiguration*. It offers iconographies for the exploration of cognitive and metaphysical forms of life, by no means conveyed with the cool detachment often associated with the word "science," yet uncoupled in some measure from the supreme urgencies of naturalistic portraiture. Critic George Slusser notes:

The depiction of future things is normally considered the role of the science fiction "thought experiment." Through this analogy with the experimental method of science, SF is said to engage the future with a process that is epistemological in nature. And hopefully, as with science again, through creating future worlds science fiction can move from knowledge of being to affirmation of the existence of things. Like science, SF can make ontological claims, at least in the hypothetical sense whereby a descriptive term, once the presence of the descriptee has been verified, is considered by consensus to exist.... The compound *science fiction* is charged with tension. For here science's epistemological future, its sense of potential or hypothetical existence, must cohabit with the fictional sense of a present time in which ontology is reinforced by morality and law impedes change.[7]

Gregory Benford, a very fine and innovative sf writer who is also a professor of physics, argues that the traditional requirement of concerted psychological realism is not appropriate to science fiction: "We occasionally hear calls for higher standards in science fiction, which hark back to the bourgeois novel of character.... I wish excellence were so easy. One of our prime tasks is conveying strangeness. Portraying people in an altered future is harder than, say, getting into the mind of the mayor of Casterbridge." Indeed, as he asks tellingly, "How does the reader's need to sense the reality of the fictional world subvert the very oddness SF tries to convey? How much of what we "know" about people—the origin of 'good characterization'—is in fact passing conventional wisdom? (How can we know what the ordinary folk of Pharaoh's time thought? Or felt?" (cited in Slusser and Shippey, *Fiction 2000*, p. 228).

THE ATROCITY EXPEDITION

It begins to appear that the constraints of genre sf, while forgiving, will yield only in certain directions: preferred phenotypic distortions in generic mutational space. And the reverse transcription is always possible, as the instructive case of J. G. Ballard reveals.

An utterly innovative contributor to the late 1950s–early 1960s British sf "New Wave," Ballard has drifted ever further from the standardized science fiction tropes he never entirely accepted. Long before the punks and cyberpunks, the savage jump-cut video clips on MTV, the ever-present multichannel media landscape that raddles our brains and speeds our adrenalin spurts, J. G. Ballard wrote down, as a poetry of dream, the place we now find all around us: a poetry of entropy, of running-down, of amused disillusion. If his earliest novels drowned and burned and blew away the world, we did not read (or avoid) them because of their sensational thrills but for Ballard's awful focus, his middle-class sanity unruffled by overpopulation and global ruin.

If one posits John Updike as the late twentieth-century American ex-emplar of educated bourgeois nuance, exquisite spiritual doubt, randy ambiguity, his voice sweet and pungent by turns, his gift vaulting pre-cisely the fences we are tracing between science and fiction, encyclopae-dic and poetic, then across the Atlantic James Ballard is his strange antiecho: remote from domesticity (I mean, of course, the auctorial persona; the man himself is said to be domesticity's very resident),[8] wandering in hot sand under cloud sculptures, cruising some smashed motorway through Beirut-on-Tyne, enacting formulae from an algebra of the sky.

When Updike set *The Coup* (1979) in an imagined former French colony below the Sahara, it was, indeed, a coup of the imagination equal to Saul Bellow's invention two decades earlier of *Henderson the Rain King* ([1958], 1962) and his Rousseauian Africa. Beyond New Haven and into the trees! But when, a decade later in *The Day of Creation* (1987), Ballard sent his mad Dr. Mallory reeling on a drunken boat called *Salammbo* up a river new-sprung in the same stark suffering landscape, what for Updike and Bellow was a daring affront, an act of literary gall, was simply Ballard's meat and drink.

Too much has been made of Ballard's *Empire of the Sun* (1984), short-listed for the Booker Prize and gaudily filmed by Spielberg, another sometime-sf *auteur*. The cause of that book's celebrity seems evident: it worked within a generally accessible intertext, requiring no residues from science fiction for its decoding. Finally, it seemed, this Shanghai-born failed doctor, who had gone from childhood to adulthood in a Japanese prison camp, declared directly the horrors his metaphors had always conveyed with great power. Was this an artistic breakthrough? Only for those dull readers who cannot abide structural metaphor. (I bracket here the worth of the book on its own terms, which was consid-erable.)

In an interview, Ballard mentioned his alienation from the sedate Brit-ain he found on his repatriation: "The rural landscapes of meadow didn't mean anything to me. They don't seem landscapes that are psychologi-cally significant."[9] That much has been evident in his fiction since the late fifties. An Updike goes to Africa, one suspects, for fashion. Ballard *lives* in these overheated climates, these bleached apartment blocks and dried rivers: "Dreams of rivers, like scenes from a forgotten film, drift through the night, in passage between memory and desire" (Ballard, *The Day of Creation*, p. 1).

That opening line of the novel comprises, in essence, the novel's whole journey from first sentence to last. For Mallory—it is not necessary to replace many letters in that name to yield "Ballard"—the irruption of a temporary river in the heart of desert Africa is an outpouring from his own thirsty heart. And so he sees it, literally: Mallory comes to believe that he has created this great river, which an opportunistic TV documentary-maker names after him—and not merely created but sustained it out of his life and will. It is, in a sense, the transrealist postulate. Mallory is, indeed, a gnostic God, a demiurge whose voyage into the center not of darkness but of immense brightness is also a passage backward into the history of creation, an unpeeling of time.

Yet the luminous clarity of Ballard's conception is to make this a book all of interpretations. There is no indefeasible world here, to be witnessed and lived within: all is created, in the act of (mis)understanding. Mallory begins his voyage in Port-la-Nouvelle, the port of the news, framed in the viewfinder of a Japanese TV portapak, about to be executed by the guerrilla leader General Harare, an emblematically adoptive name. If it is Mallory's implausible ambition to sink artesian wells into the sands, it is his even more baroque destiny to trigger the release from a lost aquifer of a water source that changes everything it wets, an alchemist's solvent, a kind of *ice-nine* in reverse. Increasingly demented, Mallory attempts first to divert this intrusion, this flood of dubious life from within his own heart, and then to revive it when its natural source becomes exhausted. Animism and technology fuse with hermeneutics in a remarkable text, for Mallory's world is literally a palimpsest, a canvas erased and scribbled over, a document waiting to be written and interpreted.

Mallory is an Old Testament god with seamy television acolytes: Professor Sanger, "a sometime biologist turned television populariser. . . . He was well-groomed, but I noticed that his teeth were riddled with caries, a surprising defect in a television performer" (pp. 29, 31–32); Sanger's earnest Indian research assistant and explainer, Mr. Pal (another overdetermined emblematic name); the Japanese camerawoman Miss Matsuoka. These lesser figures perish, leaving only blind Sanger and crazed Mallory to follow Noon, the mute naked adolescent black girl who is Mallory's sexual fetish, toward the endlessly reinterpreted headwaters of creation. They are replaced by a phantasmagoria of mad dogs and English: Mrs. Nora Warrender and her floating world of whores, murderous Captain Kagwa and his French helicopter pilot who pursue the

Salammbo along the increasingly stagnant "mortuary stream," polluted by human desperation and stupidity.

It is not exactly a pleasure to read Ballard's *oeuvre*. His images are relentless, cruel and repetitive. From the start of his career, certain icons have recurred, reshuffled, a calculus of ennui. Yet, like the obsessive return to Surrealist paintings—Yves Tanguy's blue stones and desolate landscapes are never far away—this scratching boredom is bracing. When everything is given, inevitable, always as before, then the possibilities of interpretation are endless.

Ballard's work is a chess game of late twentieth-century fragments. *The Day of Creation* is postmodern sf at the farthest remove from its pulp beginnings, an intertext rather than a novel, a splicing of Ballard's curiously chill assessment and the geometries of all the TV programs that comprise our time. It is also a collage of his own detritus, especially those most piercing early works: *The Voices of Time* (1962), *The Terminal Beach* (1964), *The Crystal World* (1966) with its transmogrified Africa, *The Day of Forever* (1967), and the extraordinary condensed fictions of *The Atrocity Exhibition* (1970). Like all late Ballard writing—one thinks of *The Unlimited Dream Company* (1979) and his semiautobiographical sequel to *Empire of the Sun*, *The Kindness of Women* (1991)—*The Day of Creation* is not so much a traditional novel as a film script, a gallery of actinic images, a tone poem: astonishing pictures, in fact, at an atrocity exhibition.

LOST IN THE BARTH-HOUSE

But such alternatives to the main trajectory of science fiction since the 1940s slip always outward and away from its central generic vector. It might be that the best work derived from sf will have a Ballardian character, moving from outer to inner space, or from fantastic mimeticism to magic realism and transrealism. If so, it will no longer be simply sf. It will pass through the mutable boundaries, lexicons and grammars of the megatext so painstakingly laid down by the collective practice of sf writers in seventy or more years of quixotic artistry. Indeed, even when its debts to sf are visible only to the insiderly observer, much new writing inscribes sf's own lexical spaces. Consider the notable case of John Barth, author of the genuinely transreal *Giles Goat-Boy* ([1966], 1967) whose late recursive novels are exemplary efflorescences from a grafted stem:

> *Blam! Blooey!*
> A DIALOGUE ON DICTION
> three days later, safely at anchor in Poe Cove, Key Island
> Virginia
>
> SUSAN: *Blam!? Blooey!?*

FENWICK: Damn straight. That storm blew up like a sawn-off
simile. (*Sabbatical*, p. 11)

So Fenwick Scott Key tells his pregnant wife Susan Seckler at the launch
of Barth's postmodern panto. That storm-fraught tale itself, subtitled "A
Romance," blew up in verse:

There was a story that began,
Said Fenwick Turner: *Susie and Fenn*—

Oh, tell that story! Tell it again!
Wept Susan Seckler . . . (ibid, p. 9)

Barth is as consciously self-reflexive a writer as American postmodernism has produced and perhaps the most delectable to read. *Blam! Blooey!*
go Barth's stories, in wonderful narrative gusts. They are becalmed, picking their own sores until you could scream. Away again, then, diving
like dolphins into myth and folktale, from Homer and Scheherazade
(who are on-stage characters in Barth) to dark tales of CIA-trained Chi-
lean state terrorists drowning dissenters in their own diarrhea. And all
of this in one vast, gong-tormented Ocean of Story.

"One should, if it's worthwhile, repeat the tale," mused Barth's story
"Echo," in his minimalist collection *Lost In The Funhouse* ([1968], 1980,
p. 97). Nobody had cause to be surprised, then, when *The Tidewater Tales:
A Novel* ([1987], 1988) began

Tell me a story of women and men
Like us . . .
    Their Houses's
Increase is the tale I wish you'd tell. (P. 21)

And *BLAM! BLOOEY!* (p. 23), there are those twin storms again, on 15
June 1980 and 29 June 1980 in Chesapeake Bay, Maryland, a sail-dotted
stretch of water for which, like the state itself, Barth is poet laureate.
Twins wait to be born (they are everywhere in Barth) while their parents
Peter Sagamore and Katherine Sherritt, aboard their sloop *Story*, tell
them amniotic tales in the moon-swayed fortnight tide that becomes, in
small, all of human life: egg loosed on its Night-Sea Journey toward
upward-swimming sperm, *Wham! Bam!*

Is this kind of storytelling nothing better than a tedious, remorseless
jape, a puzzle for poststructuralists? By no means. Barth is singular in
his insistence that we must revive the art of the taleteller. His tutelary
muses are Homer and Scher (as he companionably dubs her), Cervantes
and Twain, and their plot-besotted creations. For refreshment in an ex-
haustion of well-wrought fictions, Barth revives again and again his cen-

tral narrative insight: that the Key to the Treasure *Is* the Treasure. Of course, this ingenious postmodernist is hardly in the moralizing or catchpenny tradition of (say) a middlebrow Herman Wouk or Morris West, let alone a lowbrow Jackie Collins. This teller's treasures are locked in twin boxes, each containing the key to the other.

"Another story about a writer writing a story!" complained the writer of "Life-Story," also in *Lost In The Funhouse*. "Another regressus in infinitum! Who doesn't prefer art that at least overtly imitates something other than its own processes?" (p. 114). Barth knows too much to surrender to his own readerly hungers (as his near-namesake Roland Barthes would have it), but happily he also knows enough to satisfy ours. On the one hand, *The Tidewater Tales* is an exhaustive return to *Sabbatical* and *Chimera* ([1972], 1977) and indeed all of Barth's ever more involuted and self-referring oeuvre. On the other, it is a compelling study of the creative and intelligent men and women, adrift off the poisoned capital of Western civilization in the late twentieth century, waiting for bomb and babies to drop, blocked in their love and their work by righteous knowledge and dread.

The frames of Barth's late novels are scant enough, but enough for the work they must do: birth, copulation and death, as Eliot told us, and stories about them. The tales, however, are extraordinary: where Odysseus went when the spark failed in his rekindled marriage to Penelope, why the Thousand Nights and One Night were that number and no other (explained with teasing brilliance in the tale of Scheherazade's first second menstruation, which a decent respect for the reader's pleasure prevents me from explicating here); what became of Don Quixote when he descended by rope into the cavern of Montesinos in the middle of his huge book, and how the tale of Fenn and Susie was really told by Franklin Key Talbot, who turns the same key within his name; how Peter Sagamore, sagaless blocked writer of fat novels and slender squibs like Barth's own, detoured by the aesthetic prescription "Less is More," finds the lead returned to his pencil; how Katherine Sherritt will "share it"— all the good things of the world—with blessed ease and grace, while her evil brother Willy shares herpes and toxins with the unsuspecting in the company of Kate's rapist first husband, "Poonie" Porter, Katherine-and-Porter having split up prior to a party honoring Katherine Anne Porter, author of *Ship of Fools* (1962), where K. met P. II. If those puns are not sufficiently outrageous, one might note that the eleventh-century Sanskrit compendium by Somadeva, "Ocean of Rivers of Stories," is preceded, as is *The Tidewater Tales*, by "the Story of the Story," which in Sanskrit is the *kathapitha*, the Kath-and-Peter.

All of this mingles in a vast interlocked river of stories that gives revived meaning to an outdated genre, the *roman-fleuve*. Barth's resuscitation of this mode, this "river novell" (far more negotiable than Joyce's own in *Finnegans Wake*), makes his fiction funhouse an exhilarating place to be lost: a place where the mirrors that always show you the same thing never show you the same thing twice.

Barth's mode is not at all surrealist; whether it is transrealist is moot. It forces one to reconsider the very endeavor of fiction. Telling stories for a living is surely one of the strangest of all jobs. It is a process of controlled madness, a learned practice of reporting in carefully duplicitous words one's impersonation of at least one other human being, and a nonexistent one at that, even if it is based upon oneself. What impulse drives this immersion into myth, tale, otherness? In John Updike's memoir *Self-Consciousness* ([1989], 1990) the consummate chronicler of American middle-class life reflects with a sort of desperation on the self's mystery: "Yet isn't it a miracle, the oddity of consciousness being placed in one body rather than another, in one place and not somewhere else, in one handful of decades rather than in ancient Egypt . . . ? Billions of consciousnesses silt history full, and every one of them the center of the universe. What can we do in the face of this unthinkable truth but scream or take refuge in God?" (p. 40).

As the premier storyteller of the postmodern dispensation, Barth knows better than to sink self's mystery and agonies in an absconded deity. For Simon William Behler in Barth's *The Last Voyage of Somebody the Sailor* (1991), the "once-sort-of-famous" (p. 5) New Journalist "Bill Baylor," bailing for his life is the fate foreordained in his name. In the literal and metaphorical torrents dragging him down in a Pincher Martin flood of narrative, self is the strung-out story Scheherazade tells for the thousand nights and one to forestall self's death.

Self, indeed, is the first and continuing invention of the storyteller: the stories Sindbad the legendary sailor tells his dinner guests, of voyages into Arabian nightmare, stories Baylor is obliged to filch, demystify, re-imagine. They are the silt of history panned for narrative gold. The silt (as always, one knows) is Barth's own life, which he has been trawling for our delectation and his own, its tide returning the same waves endlessly renewed, a veritable Ocean of Story in which he both waves and drowns.

For Simon Behler's first love Daisy, tough and father-molested, he is, 'Simmon or Persimmon, the sort of guarded jest or revelation that John Simmons Barth hides in his biography. It is, however, an anticlue, for in every important sense the reader need know nothing at all about Barth's life, although much is gained by immersion in the hall of mirrors, the funhouse of his many mutually imbricated books in which one becomes happily lost. Lost in time as well as text is the fate of Baylor, nine-tenths drowned off Sri Lanka during a comic and poignant reenactment of

Sindbad's final voyage, then fished up a thousand years earlier in Sindbad's very world. It is that sailor's exotic life that his own echoes and at last, in a triumph of transrealism, literally displaces.

Matching Sindbad's tales of epic voyage with naturalistic accounts of his own six several climacterics (to borrow a favorite Barthian archaism), Baylor appropriates Sindbad's seventh voyage to Serendip, a Ceylon as fabled in that medieval Baghdad as any utopia in Scheherazade's compendium of imagined landscapes. Or is that too-literalizing a reading? Is this, rather, a book of dreams, the wanderings of an unhinged contemporary mind? A brief, baffling frame-tale suggests as much, placing dying Behler in a mental hospital at the close of the twentieth century, speaking his figurative life to his own dead twin sister (a trope eerily reminiscent of Philip K. Dick, whose texts were suffused by his lost twin sister, dead shortly after birth). As I noted above, habitues of Barth await twins as they anticipate his inimitable blend of sweat-reeking realism and transreal fables high and low.

Or has Behler bailed out less than halfway through his tale, like Golding's Pincher Martin hallucinating a life even as the drowning waters rush into his mouth and lungs for the last choking gasp? *"Then he died!* (*The Last Voyage*, p. 233) declare the unequivocal italics, although we have 340 more rich, perplexing, delightful pages yet before the Destroyer of Delights returns, sleek-nyloned, auburn-haired, to take Somebody away and close the last page, shifting him into Paradise, perhaps, and us out of it.

"Somebody." It is an apt naming—the only possible naming, really—for a character who signifies in his utterly ordinary domestic life the mystery of identity and consciousness. Behler sheds fragments of his selfhood even as he finds and constructs himself, until at last (in our world) he is simply "Baylor"—which rhymes, perhaps not accidentally, with "Mailer"—an accidental tourist living the somewhat detached biography of a professional voyeur, a storyteller. In midlife crisis, with a lover astringent, tender and absolutely fated, this "Somebody" chooses the absurd adventure of retracing the last voyage of Sindbad in a 10-meter cutter. He is lost at sea in a storm. He fetches up, alone and desolate, at mythic Sindbad's table. He meets the master mariner's daughter Yasmin, and falls in love one final time, and . . .

Nothing is this determined, however, in Barthian transrealism. Despite the tropes of fable, Yasmin and Somebody have cause to know one another when they meet (apparently for the first time) at her father's opulent feast—as does every reader, meeting every set of characters in every new book. The knowledge Yasmin has of Somebody, who has raped her (though with mitigating circumstances) is hardly the sort one might expect to lead to passionate devotion; feminist readers can hardly relish every turn of his plot. In certain respects, subverter of convention though he is, Professor Barth—which rhymes, one might say, with "Mailer"—is a confirmed sexist to the very depths of his Y-chromosome. Barth knows this perfectly well. His transrealism documents the way men of his age (sixtyish, as he wrote those books, liberal academic) construed and constructed a contemporary world as convulsively strange as any island haunted by Roc, Djinn or cyclops.

So the Old Man of the Sea who clings to Sindbad's shoulders proves to be, inevitably, Sindbad himself, locked in oedipal collusion with his young victim. So too is Baylor locked with the legend of his own shipwrecked masculinity, poor Somebody clinging to the digital watch that is the sole evidence of his unbelievable tale, the single tawdry mechanism able to bring him back to the future (as time must, remorselessly, for each of us), back to the book's closing words (p. 573), back to his death:

Follow me, now:
Two. One.

MORE PICTURES AT AN EXHIBITION

For all their power, such imaginative and imaginary sites and actors fail to approach fully the condition of transrealism. For that, we need to examine a typical fantastic passage by, for example, Philip K. Dick, and contrast its striking textuality—blending zany dislocation with the hurtingly real—with exemplary citations from, say, Henry James, Harold Brodkey and Dick's own non-sf narrative methods. A convenient James fragment is from the opening page, lovingly nuanced in its observations and reflections, of *The Wings of a Dove* ([1902], 1972):

She waited, Kate Croy, for her father to come in, but he kept her unconscionably, and there were moments at which she showed herself, in the glass over the mantle, a face positively pale with the irritation that had brought her to the point of going away without sight of him. It was at this point, however, that she remained; changing her place, moving from the shabby sofa to the armchair upholstered in a glazed cloth that gave at once—she had tried it—the sense of the slippery and of the sticky. She had looked at the sallow prints on the walls and at the lonely magazines, a year old, that combined, with a small lamp in colored glass and a knitted white center-piece wanting in freshness, to enhance the effect of the purplish cloth on the principal table; she had above all, from time to time, taken a brief stand on the small balcony to which the pair of long windows gave access. The vulgar little street, in this view, offered scant relief from the vulgar little room; its main office was to suggest to her that the narrow black house-fronts, adjusted to a standard that would have been low even for backs, constituted quite the publicity implied by such privacies. (1972 ed., p. 5)

Seventy years later, the masterful short-story writer Harold Brodkey begins "Innocence" (1973) thus:

Orra Perkins was a senior. Her looks were like a force that struck you. Truly,
people on first meeting her often involuntarily lifted their arms as if about to
fend off the brightness of the apparition. She was a somewhat scrawny, tuliplike
girl of middling height. To see her in sunlight was to see Marxism die. I'm not
the only one who said that. It was because seeing someone in actuality who had
such a high immediate worth meant you had to decide whether such personal
distinction had a right to exist or if she belonged to the state and ought to be
shadowed in, reduced in scale, made lesser, laughed at.

   Also, it was the case that you had to be rich and famous to set your hands on
her; she could not fail to be a trophy, and the question was whether the trophy
had to be awarded on economic and political grounds or whether chance could
enter in.

   I was a senior, too, and ironic. I had no money. I was without lineage. It
seemed to me Orra was proof that life was a terrifying phenomenon of surface
immediacy. (Pp. 163–64)

Compare these citations with a characteristic passage from a "mainstream" (or non-science fictional) Philip K. Dick novel, *The Broken Bubble*,
published in 1989 after his death but written in 1956. Childless Patricia
Gray, divorced from sterile Jim Briskin but trapped in a mutually mas-
ochistic bond with him, makes love to his protégé Art Emmanual, a
stammering youth ten years her junior, himself the husband of pregnant
Rachael, with whom Jim is sexually and emotionally involved.

"Jim shaves twice a day," she said, teasing [Art], playing with him. She walked
nearer to him, and then all at once her delight vanished. In its place was lust,
and she put her arms around his bare waist and clutched him as lightly as she
could; she prevented herself from laying hold of him with her real devotion.

   "Watch it," he said, a little apprehensively. And then she thought, with clarity,
that her ambition had been opened to him at last. At once she released him;
flustered and embarrassed, she retreated.

   My child, she thought. Now he put his shirt back on and began to button it.
A sullen boy, she thought, controlling her hunger, permitting the mere dreams,
the desire and hallucinations, to gallop through her mind. The scenes fled past
and she reviewed them; she identified them as old fantasies that had always
been with her but could never be acted out. She waited and remained placid
until they subsided. But they were not gone. They would never be gone. . . . She
wanted to dress him and comb his hair, but she kept her hands away from him.
A great expanding bloom of love and weakness loosed itself inside her; it detached itself from her and rose up. It hovered within her throat, and then it came
forth in a muffled shriek; she walked hurriedly away from him, not wanting him
to hear. But he was aware, in some dull fashion, so it made no difference. She

could not conceal it from him, and anyhow, she thought, he did not care. (Pp. 164–65)

Are James's Kate, Brodkey's Orra and Dick's Pat simply the same American princess separated by three generations and a certain emerging democratization of voice? Intriguingly, this is unlikely to be true of Philip K. Dick's monstrous Kathy Sweetscent, whose absent presence in the opening stanza of a transrealist sf novel—*Now Wait for Last Year* (1968)— is hardly less potent, poignant and considerably more hilarious:

The apteryx-shaped building, so familiar to him, gave off its usual smoky gray light as Eric Sweetscent collapsed his wheel and managed to park in the tiny stall allocated to him. Eight o'clock in the morning, he thought drearily. And already his employer Mr. Virgil L. Ackerman had opened TF&D Corporation's offices for business. Imagine a man whose mind is most sharp at eight a.m., Dr. Sweetscent mused. It runs against God's clear command. A fine world they're doling out to us; the war excuses any human aberration, even the old man's.

Nonetheless he started toward the in-track—only to be halting by the calling of his name. "Say, Mr. Sweetscent! Just a moment, sir!" The twangy—and highly repellent—voice of a robant; Eric stopped reluctantly, and now the thing coasted up to him, all arms and legs flapping energetically. "Mr. Sweetscent of Tijuana Fur & Dye Corporation?"

The slight got across to him. "Dr. Sweetscent. Please."

"I have a bill, doctor." It whipped a folded white slip from its metal pouch. "Your wife Mrs. Katherine Sweetscent charged this three months ago on her Dreamland Happy Times For All account. Sixty-five dollars plus sixteen per cent charges. And the law, now; you understand. I regret delaying you, but it is, ahem, illegal." It eyed him alertly as he, with massive reluctance, fished out his checkbook. . . . Well, he reflected grimly, Kathy is off again. The creative urge, which can only find an outlet in spending. (Pp. 9–10)

One notes superficial contrasts between this and the first three ("realist") citations: a certain increased laxity in Dick's later syntax, above and beyond the informality of free indirect discourse; a measure of inartistic "infodumping" in Sweetscent's half-conscious reportage of what is, for him, self-evident, such as his boss's name and station; the delightful novelty of his extrapolated future world. All four passages notate common itchy human experiences (however culture-bound and ideologically restricted these might be, judged under the aspect of eternity), and do so by similar formal means. Still, one sees in the Sweetscent passage sundry striking deviations from normative fiction-making, starting with that jolting adjective "apteryx-shaped." It instantly constitutes a kind of whimsical signification vortex, which for the knowing reader gathers together connotations—all at once and unconsciously—from a number of incongruous directions.

As a distinctly unusual word—"apteryx" is a technical term for "kiwi," the New Zealand flightless bird—it evokes expertise. But one assumes that this expertise, rather like Henry James's reference to vulgar little house-fronts and backs, is embedded in Sweetscent's ordinary fund of cultural capital. But what, at the literal level, can it denote? A workplace designed ludicrously in the form of a huge standing Kiwi, entered via an "in-track?" Or is this merely its floor plan, the shape it shows when seen from the air, perhaps suggesting a futuristic culture where "air-cars" as well as foldable "wheels" are in common usage? Perhaps, though, the term is a pun: the building is a blockhouse, "without wings"? If so, is this joke drawn from the intellectual small talk of Sweetscent's society, or is it a self-indulgence on Dick's part, a wry shrug at the crass ignorance of his genre readers? (Or, indeed, a charming instance of the fantast's "creative urge, which can only find an outlet in spending"?) Whatever is the case, the term certainly signifies *for us wingless readers* (on the fly, as it were) the alien, the dislocated, the unknown—and, in a simultaneous paradox, sf's typical domestication of strangeness. One might compare the inventiveness of this passage with the opening of a "classic" science fiction novel, Jack Williamson's *The Legion of Space* ([1935], 1980), a text as distant from either realism or transrealism as one could imagine:

John Star, lean and trim in his new Legion uniform, stood at attention before the desk where the stern, white-haired officer sat toying with the silver model of a space cruiser. He felt the major's merciless eyes come up from the tiny ship to search out every detail of his small-boned, hard physique. Taut and almost quivering, he endured that probing gaze, burningly anxious to know his first assignment. (P. 13)

Remarkably, this volume is still in print in paperback release. Like the equally "classic" E. E. "Doc" Smith series (set in the "Skylark" and "Lensman" universes), Williamson's books retain a marketable appeal—presumably in the main for small-boned, quivering boys—which few works of the period, let alone potboilers, can boast. One is reminded, after all, of the staying power of myth even in execrable recensions.

Unlike John Star, lean and trim in his new Legion uniform, Eric Sweetscent swiftly persuades us of his grubby humanity. And this despite the pleasures and obscurities of neologism and artful bafflement—the Dickian wise-cracking robant bill-server, the puzzling purchases of ancient trivia. Sweetscent is a transrealist creation, if an early and transitional one. "In a Transrealist novel," Rucker tells us, "the author usually appears as an actual character, or his or her personality is divided up among several characters. . . . The Transrealist protagonist is just as neurotic and ineffectual as we each know ourselves to be" (Rucker, *Transreal!*,

p. 436). Nor is this motivation from life an accidental feature of Rucker's analysis, for he coined the term *transreal* "after seeing the phrase 'transcendental autobiography' in a blurb on the cover of Philip K. Dick's *A Scanner Darkly*" (p. 529).

Even as Dick's genre-marketed texts hover at the edge of glib stereotype, sexist and distasteful by standards prevalent a third of a century on, we do not doubt the authentic human pain and confusions enacted by his characters. There is no question that Eric Sweetscent's muddled relationship with his beautiful, drug-altered, estranged wife reflects Dick's own autobiography, to our advantage (Sutin, *Divine Invasions*).

Someday the hardness, the inflexibility, would pervade her; the anatomical bounty would calcify. And then what? Already her voice contained it, different now from what he remembered of a few years back, even a few months. Poor Kathy, he thought. Because when the death-dealing powers of ice and cold reach your loins, your breasts and hips and buttocks as well as your heart—it was already deep in her heart, surely—then there will be no more woman. And you won't survive that. No matter what I or any man chooses to do.

"You were excluded," he said carefully, "because you're a pest." (Dick, *Now Wait for Last Year*, p. 59)

This withering misogyny reflects its time, and Dick's own troubles with his several wives and lovers, adding a powerful dimension to his paranoid fantastic imagination—a realistic density that supports Rucker's most audacious claim: "*Transrealism is a revolutionary art-form. A major tool in mass thought-control is the myth of consensus reality.* . . . Actual people are weird and unpredictable; this is why it is so important to use them as characters instead of the impossibly good and bad paper-dolls of mass-culture" (Rucker, *Transreal!*, p. 437, italics in original). The transrealist manifesto is, finally, an insistence that empathy, or a suffering awareness of its absence, must suffuse the fantastic, supplanting rote formula or egotistic wish fulfillment.

"You would have made love to me just now, if that was why you were leaving." She rebuttoned her dress. "You don't care about me." Her voice held certitude; he recognized the drab, thin tone. Always this barrier, this impossibility of getting through. This time he did not waste his time trying; he simply went on stroking her, thinking, It'll be on my conscience, whatever happens to her. And she knows it, too. So she's absolved of the burden of responsibility, and that, for her, is the worst thing possible.

Too bad, he thought, I wasn't able to make love to her.

"My dinner's ready," he said, rising.

She sat up. "Eric, I'm going to pay you back for leaving me." She smoothed her dress. "You understand?"

"Yes," he said, and walked into the kitchen.

"I'll devote my life to it," Kathy said. . . .

"Lots of luck," he said.

"Luck? I don't need luck; I need skill, and I think I have skill. . . . I wish I could tell you what it is; it's an incredible drug, Eric—it changes your entire perception of the universe and especially of other people. You don't ever view them the same again. You ought to try it. It would help you."

"Nothing," he said, "would help me." (Dick, *Now Wait for Last Year*, pp. 62–63).

The drug JJ-180 that has changed Kathy Sweetscent's life, perfect fictive analogue of the act of fiction itself, switches its user back and forth in time, and across into alternative histories where one might track the consequences of acting otherwise. On the face of it, this sf trope betrays beyond question the generic frailty of the text, its rootedness in wishful, power-mad escape fantasy. But Dick's phantasmagoria eludes this stricture, to the extent that it does, by returning us to confusion, plurality, indecent motive, vulnerability. Genre fiction in the age of science, and under its shadow, will tend inevitably to the low pleasures of escape. "But," as Rucker asserts, "there is no reason to let this severely limited and reactionary mode condition all of our writing. Transrealism is the path to a truly artistic SF" (Rucker, *Transreal!*, p. 437).

That is because it goes beyond stipulating cosy formulae about our world (traditional naturalist realism) or even asking how it is we know that world (the modernist, epistemological project). Situated in the complexity, the psychic and social density, of observed life, transrealism can take an extra step into systematic, exploratory doubt—the step intrinsic to postmodern science—and confront the experiential varieties of all possible worlds: the liberating project of fiction raising radically *ontological* issues—fiction that questions the very nature of our shared reality. There are two paths leading toward such profound topics. One is transrealism itself, exemplified by Philip K. Dick and Rudy Rucker. There is, and always has been, another: a fiction of extreme technological or psychic dislocation.

THE LANDSCAPE OF LACK

As with all marginal, suspect forms of writing, science fiction's humus yields strange bright blooms that rarely thrive within the cropped borders of literature's own canonical garden beds. Jacques Lacan rewrote Freud as the geographer of lack. "When, in love, I solicit a look," he somewhere observed, "what is profoundly unsatisfying and always missing is that—*You never look at me from the place from which I see you.*" The best science fiction of the 1950s and early 1960s teased unconscious material into startling, vivid imagery. Science fiction's canon is drenched with preposterous wish fulfillments of exactly that poignant Lacanian absence: mind readers, shape-shifters, paranormal *gestalt* superhumans built up—organ by organ, as it were—out of maimed, bitterly lonely individuals. Perfect embodiments of that last conceit were Theodore Sturgeon's *More Than Human* ([1953], 1986) and *The Cosmic Rape* ([1958], 1977). In the supposed sf Golden Age of the 1940s, science fiction sounded like this (again I cite Jack Williamson): "his puttylike face held a moronic stare," or "Karen looked hopefully at the door, presenting a breathtaking profile."[10] A decade later, Sturgeon's modernist pen excised the twaddle at a stroke:

The idiot lived in a black and white world. . . . His clothes were old and many-windowed. Here peeped a shin-bone, sharp as a cold chisel, and there in the torn coat were ribs like the fingers of a fist. (Sturgeon, *More Than Human*, p. 3)

The idiot is Lone, retarded brain of a new life-form, *Homo gestalt*. So he is not the book's hero, merely a dazed part of it. If Sturgeon speaks of the monstrous, it is, after all, us: isolate, yearning, severed (like Lacan's lovers) behind the glass of a mirror.

Thirty years on from Sturgeon's masterpiece, Greg Bear's *Blood Music* ([1985], 1986) turned the tropes of surreal transformation into a cunningly paced melodrama at the margins of transrealism. Vergil Ulam, a self-centered, heedless biotech cowboy, brews the world's first intelligent microbes and lets them loose in his own bloodstream. Is this a ridiculous premise, less transreal or even surreal than simply fatuous? It seems less so with each year. Serious mathematical work has been published by reputable scientists (the late Richard Feynman, for one) on the prospects of a forthcoming nanotechnology revolution, using programmable machines smaller than blood cells (Drexler, *The Engines of Creation*, 1986; Broderick, *The Spike*, 1997). This fact, though, is perhaps irrelevant. Bear's premise may be construed entirely as metaphor. In swift order the world's population is melting down, each mind and soul absorbed into its own endless fecund angelic orders of smart tissue. Lacan's lovers are lost in endless narcissism, then set free into microbial quantum heaven. The novel can be indicted as corny and faked, but there are moments of visionary power that exceed the boundaries of conventional fictive modes: "With her last strength she came to him and they lay in each other's arms, drenched in sweat. . . . With each pulse of blood, a kind of sound welled up within him as if an orchestra were performing thousands strong. . . . Edward and Gail grew together on the bed, substance passing through clothes, skin joining where they embraced and lips where they touched" (Bear, *Blood Music*, p. 109). But is Bear's ferocious apocalypse an instance of transrealism, or are its generic limitations located exactly in the doubtful realism of its characters? The critic John

Foyster complained: "Vergil Ulam . . . is only half-constructed as a character [yet] the nature of the universal alien who dominates the second half of the book is surely determined by the nature of the onlie begetter. The failure to create in Ulam an adequate Everyman leads to the failure of the novel" ("The Long View," p. 27). (One might wonder, of course, whether it is possible to have a fully constructed Everyman.)

We return now one final time to a species of science fiction, emblematized perhaps in the texts of Greg Egan, that moves in exactly the opposite direction from transrealism: into a fiction of the almost inconceivable.

NOTES

1. This is Justina Robson's slightly modified formulation; she adds that "slipstream strives to duplicate the complexities of actual experiences by allowing experience to be paramount and letting everything else serve that purpose" (personal communication, 23 June 1999), a position close to Rucker's. Information about the anthology is posted on Robson's Web site: http://www.westroyd. demon.co.uk/

2. David G. Hartwell, "Slipstream Slip Sliding," *The New York Review of Science Fiction*, issue 122, vol. 11, no. 2 (October 1998): 24.

3. Bruce Sterling, "Catscan 5," *Science Fiction Eye* 1, no. 5 (July 1989), here cited from his unpaginated freeware text files; I am grateful to Mr. Sterling for making this material available to me.

4. Edward Whittemore, *The Sinai Tapestry* (1977; London: Magnum, 1979), *Jerusalem Poker* (1978; London: Magnum, 1980), *Nile Shadows* (New York: Holt, Rinehart and Winston, 1983) and *Jericho Mosaic* (New York: Norton, 1987). Whittemore died in 1995.

5. Personal communication, 29 October, 1998.

6. Stanislaw Lem, "Reflections on My Life," in *Microworlds: Writings on Science Fiction and Fantasy* (London: Secker & Warburg, 1985) p. 12.

7. George Slusser, "The Frankenstein Barrier," in George Slusser and Tom Shippey, eds., *Fiction 2000: Cyberpunk and the Future of Narrative* (Athens: University of Georgia Press, 1992), p. 46.

8. John Baxter, personal communication.

9. Cited in Christopher Priest, "Landscape Artist: The Fiction of J. G. Ballard," in *The Stellar Gauge*, ed. M. J. Tolley and K. Singhe (Melbourne: Norstrilia, 1980), p. 194.

10. Cited in John Foyster, "The Long View," *Australian Science Fiction Review* (March 1986): 10.

6

Terrible Angels: Science Fiction and the Singularity

What is it about technology and science—or rather, the politicized rhetoric of contemporary technology and science—that allows us to menace our entire planet with dangerous, brittle technologies, and yet accept this action as something wise and plausible and somehow good for us? . . . It's done because of the culturally unquestionable sublimity of the technological imperative.

Science fiction is an aspect of this phenomenon. Only a culture crazily enamored of any kind of knowledge and furiously hungry for any kind of power could create a literature like science fiction.
—Bruce Sterling, "About 'Our Neural Chernobyl' " (p. 237)

Ever since the momentous innovations of the first industrial revolution the mind has sought with an ever-increasing sense of urgency to anticipate all the consequences of the perpetual flux by creating patterns of expectation. There is no end to the modelling of possible future worlds.
—I. F. Clarke, *The Pattern of Expectation: 1644–2001* (p. 303)

Here, around the start of the twenty-first century, we are ghosts haunting the futurist dream nearly a century old. Reminded of the brash functionalist lines of "tomorrow's city," the clean Mondrian Formica kitchen surfaces, the sparkling electric railways, we find that we have accelerated by mistake into Gothic mode: the broken apartments of Lebanon and

Kosovo, the desolation of much of Africa, gutted South Bronx at the edge of the world capital of capital, jittery crack zombies in the skyscrapers' shadows.

Writers of speculative fiction, the transrealists especially, have known all along that we might wake to this nightmare. *What if* (the basic science fictional opening move) there'll be *no* human history, no ensemble of possible histories to be modeled by humanist fiction or futurism? What if the start of the third millennium sees a phase change into some altogether unprecedented state of being, neither Apocalypse nor Parousia but some secular mix of both? What if, as Vernor Vinge and a few other extravagant sf writers have proposed, exponentially accelerating science and technology are rushing us into a Singularity (Vinge, *Marooned in Realtime*; VISION-21 Symposium), or what I call the Spike (Broderick, *The Spike*)? Then there's no pattern of reasoned expectation to be mapped, no knowable Chernobyls to deplore in advance. Merely— opacity.

But sf writers are rarely silenced by this futurological abyss. At the very least, there are tales to be told of the runaway ride up the slope of the Spike. By reaching into myth and the most expansive vistas of advanced physics, neuroscience, biology and even cosmology, perhaps we can guess at some of the immense prospects that loom beyond the veil.

Runaway change can be represented as a singularity because it is a spike on the graph not just of human progress but of human reality in its entirety. The strangest feature of such a graph, taken literally—and Vinge, a mathematician, does look at it in his fiction with the straightest of faces—is that the higher you rise on its curve, the faster it climbs ahead of you. The slope is worse than Sisyphean, because we can't even get to the top and then slide despairingly back to the base. "As we move closer to this point, it will loom vaster and vaster over human affairs till the notion becomes a commonplace," Vinge points out. "Yet when it finally happens it may still be a great surprise and a greater unknown."[1]

In that sense, which I find persuasive, sf's enterprise is both quixotic and impossible. It is—to fall into the inevitable religious comparisons I'd rather skirt—akin to the futility of a theologian or a physicist attempting to understand "the Mind of God" (as atheist Stephen Hawking rhetorically and misleadingly dubbed his own scientific efforts). Such utter dislocation of knowledge and feeling alike is the traditional literary figure for the incomprehensibly sublime. Perhaps a less odious comparison, to both believers and nonbelievers (although regrettably bearing its own kitsch New Age freight) is a Rilkean Angel. Rainer Maria Rilke, in the *Duino Elegies*, makes our blood shudder with his vision of the beings (although he did not know this) that, in all truth, might stand beyond the veil of the Singularity. Pressed to the heart of such a being, its beauty inseparable from the terror it instils in us, we would simply perish, for, in Rilke's great and tolling words, "Every Angel is terrible."[2]

The singularity, for Vinge, Michael Swanwick, Iain M. Banks and a few other sf pioneers, usually begins with artificial intelligence: rogue, benign or simply—*there*. Evolution takes such a *long*, agonizing time to ratchet itself up a notch. Break free from that mindless process, via machine self-programming or genetic engineering or both, and everything changes *fast*.

How fast? Vinge, in nonfiction mode, is uncompromising: "The precipitating event will likely be unexpected—perhaps even to the researchers involved. ('But all our previous models were catatonic! We were just tweaking some parameters . . .') If networking is widespread enough (into ubiquitous embedded systems), it may seem as if our artefacts as a whole had suddenly wakened" (Vinge, VISION-21 Symposium).

After that, after the first machines have awoken? Nobody knows. "For all my rampant technological optimism," Vinge himself states, "sometimes I think I'd be more comfortable if I were regarding these transcendental events from one thousand years remove . . . instead of twenty" (Vinge, VISION-21 Symposium). While it's a millennium too late for that, in his influential novel *Marooned in Realtime*[3] Vinge placed his characters at a 50 million year remove—in the remote future, after a Spike had passed across the world, leaving only traces of vast, unintelligible engineering works and decaying cities. How these inadvertent survivors managed their delayed second chance, and what became of them, makes an intriguing tale. But what's truly arresting is the dark place at the center of that imagined history. You wake up to find that the Parousia has come and gone, Gabriel's Trump has blasted its brazen song and you *missed* it.

The Spike will be a sort of immanent transcendence, an accelerating dash into incomprehensible glory—or ugliness, always a possibility: feral nanotechnological grey goo, turning everything on the planet into sludge, or viral green goo, or a thousand varieties of unbalanced superminds let loose in the playground of the solar system. Here and there in Vinge's novel are hints of what might have occurred when humanity vanished clean away while the reader's back was turned. " 'Mankind simply graduated, and you and I and the rest missed graduation night,' " one character tells another. "Just talking about superhuman intelligence gets us into something like religion . . ." (Vinge, *Marooned*, p. 111). One need not be earnest about this prospect. Iain M. Banks's Culture novels are peopled by posthumans rewired to "gland" hormones by choice, whose postscarcity anarcho-communist polity is mostly located on starships and Orbitals run by AI Minds who seem to keep their organic partners around as pets.[4] Colossal artifacts with facetious names like the

Very Little Gravitas Indeed roar across the galaxy, while enhanced humans and snide machines frolic within their protective fields. Here's a happy moment, exactly catching Banks's way of taking sf's gewgaws and doing rude things with them:

"To the Culture," he said, raising his glass to the alien. It matched his gesture. "To its total lack of respect for all things majestic."[5]

THE RUSH INTO POSTHISTORY

How fast could such chiliastic changes really happen? A marooned Vinge character muses doubtfully that even in a swiftly changing world, "there had been limits on how fast the marketplace could absorb new developments . . . what about the installed base of older equipment? What about compatibility with devices not yet upgraded? How could the world of real products be turned inside out in such a short time?" (*Marooned*, p. 172). Vinge seems here to start interrogating his own cool idea only to back away hurriedly. It is a piece of narrative flimflam in the guise of rhetorical questioning.

Yet some of the steps that make this headlong alteration thinkable, if not altogether feasible, are sketched in Vernor Vinge's seminal novel. "High-tech" people from close to the Singularity wear headbands that augment their native abilities, computer patches to the raw stuff of evolved brains with their limited memories and even more limited attention windows. More up-to-date scenarios by Greg Bear and Greg Egan expect such chips to be surgically implanted deep in the brain, or perhaps grown there using engineered cells or nanoconstuctors, or just bypassed when humans upload entirely into computer substrates. In a way, it's evidence of Vinge's own case that only a decade or two after his proposition was announced, we already find many of his once-wild projections rather tame and unadventurous.

Today, even the smartest of us can hardly retain a conceptual grasp on more than seven different items at once, and five is the usual mental handful. So we live in a cognitive universe dimly glimpsed through the narrowest of cracks, and the width of that aperture is set by our inherited neural hardware. Boost it, link our augmented minds together, and who knows what wonders of awareness might burst open into consciousness?

"Humankind and its machines became something better," speculates the most advanced of Vinge's pretranscension high-techs, "something . . . unknowable" (*Marooned*, p. 176). Yet that character's own experience at the opening of the twenty-third century is almost incomprehensible to us a mere two hundred years earlier at the turn of the millennium. With his seven colleagues, he was engaged in mining the sun for antimatter, "distilling one hundred thousand *tonnes* of matter and antimatter every *second*. That was enough to dim the sun, though we arranged things so the effect wasn't perceptible from the ecliptic"—the orbital region around the sun that contains the earth and other planets and most asteroids. Working so far from home, he and his companions were brutally severed from the real action, "hundreds of light-seconds away" (p. 173; italics in original).

You may pause to smile at this fancy. Pause a little longer, though, to reflect on what such a world might be like if it truly existed. Two hundred years ago, Europeans explored and conquered large parts of a single world many months distant from their political and mercantile masters at home. Today, by contrast, nobody with access to a phone is more than fractions of a minute from anywhere else on the globe. Computer networks, swapping information and financial transactions, blur into a haze of virtual instantaneity. Imagine the rapidity of a world where people exiled halfway across the solar system are unalterably amputated from the current action, because the speed of light is an intractable barrier to faster communication.

On Earth, large corporations with better computers merge their staff into linkages of thousands. Is this a horrible prospect of soul-death, extermination of the self? One might expect such an interpretation from a libertarian like Vinge, but in fact he suggests otherwise: "There was power and knowledge and joy in those companies . . ." As the Vingean Singularity approaches, the mind-to-mind linkages and augmentations become extreme, a form of group mind: "By the beginning of the twenty-third, there were three *billion* people in the Earth/Luna volume. Three billion people and corresponding processing power—all less than three light-seconds apart." Inevitably, transhuman plans turn to cosmic engineering, the creation of black hole star-gates, the implosion of entire stars. Might this explain the Extinction? "We'd been 'uppity cockroaches'—and the real owners finally stepped on us . . ." (p. 177).

ZONES AND POWERS

Vinge's next novel, *A Fire Upon the Deep* (1991) and its belated prequel *A Deepness in the Sky* (1999), ornate, multileveled machines of tales within tales, offered a series of complex analogies for the states of mind and body and existence that might prevail beyond any immediate Spike. They propose as metaphor a galaxy partitioned like some Dantean cosmology, from a bleak Inferno of the Unthinking Depths, where matter dominates and light-speed is the final limit, through a Purgatorio of the Slow Zone flaring outward from the galaxy's spinning wheel, and farther yet into the Beyond, where minds are vast and instantaneous: Powers, "gods" in the ancient sense.

Certainly some form of tiered analysis is needed if we are to build models of enhanced intelligence. It is not that human mental life is different in kind from the progressively more limited kinds found in dogs and cats and parrots and goldfish and slugs and sunflowers and bacteria. Of course, many people argue that our minds *are* exactly differentiated from those of "lesser creatures" in some mystical, unapproachable way. Even supposing that it turns out to be true—that people have an extra gadget—let's call them *souls*—that provide our self-awareness and radical creativity—that conclusion would need to be attained by long, scrupulous investigation. It would be, in a sense, a negative hypothesis: something we would be forced to entertain solely because of the failure of more rational models compatible with everything else we know about the physical universe. (And we now know a *colossal* amount, most of it tied together into patterns not easily edited or expanded without shredding the lot.) Posit, then, that human minds are not *mysterious things* but are rather *very complicated processes* going on inside living brains connected by senses to the outside world. Is it reasonable to guess that doubling the power of a laptop computer, and doubling it again, and redoubling for another fifteen or thirty years, will automatically produce a smart machine, then an intelligent machine, and finally—*a hyperintelligent machine?*

Vinge poses this rather neatly: "Imagine running a dog mind at very high speed. Would a thousand years of doggy living add up to any human insight? (Now if the dog mind were cleverly rewired and *then* run at high speed, we might see something different . . ." (Vinge VISION-21 Symposium). No computer is currently anywhere near the doggy level of cleverness, of course, but some of them approach the simplest insects. Might running an insect brain very, very fast turn it into someone you'd like to discuss politics or art with? It seems obvious that the answer is no, but what if that insect brain joins a swarm of its fellows, and they learn (or are taught) the trick of specialization, so that one bunch of insect brains swaps information about how stuff *looks* today, from a number of strategic angles, and another lot focuses on *sound vibrations,* while other bunches of ant-brains store these impression and disgorge them on command from yet other groups. This is the principle of the hive. In many ways the hive is much cannier than any of the dumb modules with legs and wings that comprise it. It also looks something like a complex brain—a *human* brain, in fact. Each of our neurons is a little like an insect (simpler, in fact, and much smaller), but it has better lines of communication than any single ant. Take a hundred thousand million of *them* and let them cross-wire to each other in some kind of self-organizing hierarchy, and you do indeed get—*us.*

Which does not answer the original question about speeding up a doggy brain. No, even if you added in a big pack of extra memory, a dog's brain lacks the architecture to think like a person. What about an immortal and massively augmented dog, genetically engineered to grow as many cortical neurons as a human, but arrayed as they would otherwise be in a normal dog. In his near-Spike novel *Holy Fire* (1996) Bruce Sterling has one of these wonderful beasts, a poignantly articulate talk-show host which/who, due to neurological deficits, can't read. I suppose it is remotely possible that such a dog might, perhaps with great inner agony, teach itself the tricks of self-consciousness. It would need access to a brainy culture, clearly enough, and right now we are the only one available. So a true hyperdog would require eyes capable of reading, and paws dexterous enough to handle pages or keyboard, and a jaw and larynx rewired for speech—a big job. Almost certainly no such wonder could emerge from a single, extreme mutation that just pumped up the puppy's brain capacity in utero (the conceit in Olaf Stapledon's superb *Sirius* [1944, 1979].)

It is much easier to reallocate uses to machine memory, to rewrite code and try it out and discard it when it fails, and try again, and keep trying until you get it right. That is presumably true even if the machine is boot-strapping its own abilities, driven away from stolid stable inner states by random changes somewhere in its operating system, in the software that makes it a process rather than just a lump of expensive silicon. This is the evolutionary model of teaching a machine to be a person. In a sense, we know that this has to work, because on a geological timescale it is what produced us. Mutation, contest and cooperation, differential survival of genetic patterns according to the success of the bodies they built: natural selection, in a word.

That is the path of AI or artificial intelligence. Vinge observes that there is a quite different method of attaining advanced cognitive abilities: a switch in emphasis that is captured deftly by a switch in the name— IA, or *intelligence amplification*. Now it's the human brain that is being boosted, or linked to others of its kind (as the near-singularity companies in his novel were composed of group minds). Again, this is eerily familiar, precisely because it is a definition of a society or a culture. Already our brains store much of their knowledge outside the skull, in books and film and magnetic tape, in the huge hard structures of cities and aqueducts and farms, in the facts and opinions we share by talking to each other. Vinge sees the path from this existing state of affairs to enhanced intelligence as rather easier than the AI route, because we have done it a number of times without quite realizing it. Currently, access to the Internet through a fast workstation is a genuine augmentation of a researcher's capacity: In effect you can now think faster, put information together more swiftly, send your results out without delay, gain the reciprocal benefit from others cruising the network. Once improved methods are devised for getting information out of a database and shaping knowledge without the need for writing or keyboarding or even talking—and yes, I do mean something like the cyberpunk dream of "jacking in to cyberspace"—it will be a whole new kind of life. One small step for the individual cybersurfer, one mighty swarming leap toward the Spike.

EXPLORERS OF THE SPIKE

Vernor Vinge has not been alone among imaginative writers in trying his hand at portraying what is strictly inconceivable, a world on the far side of the Spike. William Gibson, coiner and explorer of cyberspace in novels such as *Neuromancer* (1984), is only the best known. A brilliant stylist, Michael Swanwick, has done so several times, most notably in the novels *Vacuum Flowers* (1988) and *Stations of the Tide* (1991). In the former, revived suicide Rebel Elizabeth Mudlark proves to be a kind of antidote to a postmodern, poststructuralist affliction: the dispersion of the self in a culture where personalities are optional plug-ins, bought off the shelf as we buy or hire videotapes. Rebel's capital importance is her possession of—indeed, her constitution in—the rare and perhaps trans-realist trick of assuring her own hyperstable self-presence. All around her, post-Singularity space habitats are gladly giving in to centripetal attractions. Earth's home population has already merged into a multibillion-headed colony organism, a sort of slime mold or coral comprised of former individuals. Indeed, this new entity calls itself the Comprise.

Rebel's partial solution to this encroaching monolith is to disperse the microworlds as seed pods among the stars—a scattering that enacts on a literal level the dispersion of selfhood that the late twentieth century agonizingly diagnosed as our epoch's characteristic feature. When Swanwick names the armless girl who speaks for the colony mind—"the focus. . . . of perhaps a billion Comprise, as massive a point source of attention as Earth ever needed to assemble"[6]—he calls her "Snow." The name reflects what every child learns at an early age: that every single snowflake is identically simple, with its sixfold symmetry, yet utterly unique in the details of its shape. Swanwick's 1987 naming recalls, in turn, an earlier fictional group mind, in a 1959 novel, *Wolfbane*, by Frederik Pohl and Cyril Kornbluth: the Snowflake. Apparently these apprehensions have been curdling through the discursive unconscious of Western culture. It is Vinge's special genius to understand that they might become *literally* true.

And if they do? Swanwick is not reassuring. Starting from primitive AIs and rudimentary brain-computer interfaces, he posits a seed of "thirty-two outlaw programmers" about whom the Comprise, a massively parallel human-machine hybrid, starts to crystallize. Born in glory, power and understanding, the new entity reaches to others in the net willing to join it, rewriting its own structure as it goes, deepening its algorithms. "Within three minutes everyone on the net was ours. We controlled everything that touched upon the net—governments, military forces from the strategic level down. . . . With a fraction of our attention, we designed the transceivers, retooled the factories to make them, and reorganized the hospitals to perform the implants. . . . We ate the Earth" (Swanwick, *Vacuum Flowers*, p. 224). It is a totalitarian longing and one that today's culture fears desperately even as we yearn for the balm of that sweet joining. "We reached out and out," the Comprise tells Rebel, "expanding toward Godhood." It adds at once, candidly, "We had ambition, and ascended into Hell" (p. 224).

. If this is a disturbing prophecy of a hungry post-Spike consciousness, Swanwick was more terrifying still in *Stations of the Tide*, where nothing holds still for long. People split their minds into agents able to impersonate them, act on their behalf, report back and extinguish themselves. They move their point of awareness into surrogate bodies, the very reverse of Rebel's armored solidity of selfhood. When an agent of colony-mind Earth is met, it is something out of Milton and Swift, an authentically monstrous manifestation in virtual reality. If you wonder what a post-Spike world might contain, regard this Brobdingnagian figure:

The encounter space was enormously out of scale, a duplicate of those sheds where airships were built, structures so large that water vapor periodically formed clouds near the top and filled the interior with rain. It was taken up by a single naked giant.
Earth.
She crouched on all fours, more animal than human, huge, brutish, and filled with power. . . . Her limbs were shackled and chained, crude vizualisations of the more subtle restraints and safeguards that kept her forever on the fringes of the system.[7]

This vast, sweat-stinking, musky monster is, one sees, a figure familiar from psychoanalysis: the archaic Mother, a sort of feral female phallic force, more mythic than misogynistic in Swanwick's making. And like that clammy image from post-Freudian analysis, complete with vagina dentata, it invites Swanwick's bureaucrat into its mouth. In the overwhelming presence of an Earth utterly overborne by technology out of control, he asks the agent:

"What do you want from us?"
In that same lifeless tone she replied, "What does any mother want from her daughters? I want to help you. I want to give you advice. I want to reshape you into my own image. I want to lead your lives, eat your flesh, grind your corpses, and gnaw the bones." (Swanwick, *Stations of the Tide*, p. 147)

One sees why the augmented humans of that future must keep their ancient parent shackled, but hardly powerless. It is Hansel and Gretel for true. And we, here and now, can readily fall in with Swanwick's forebodings, considering the prospects of a world that is perhaps only a generation away from birthing nanotechnology and artificial intelligence and machine interfaces and human intelligence amplification.

It need not be that way, of course. One might wonder if it is even remotely plausible. Grimm's fairy tales, after all, caught the rural voices of the nineteenth century and earlier, perhaps not altogether salient to a world remade by science. Yet we carry our history with us, tucked away inside our narratives and nightmares, ready to be snatched up in the slipstream of science.

Will we, preserved by the wiles of that science into the Singularity (or, if not us, then our transhuman children or great-grandchildren) any longer be "human?" Perhaps not, or not for long. Maybe we will live almost infinitely accelerated lives within a virtual computer in a grain of sand at the edge of the world's last drained sea. Maybe we will be quantum states of a cosmically dispersed, radio-linked hypermind. Maybe we will be, well, quite literally *gods*, inflating fresh universes out of the quantum foam and placing our impress upon everything that forms there. Or maybe we'll all stay at home and watch the ultimate television channel, forever.

COMEDY OR TRAGEDY?

Must the Spike, the Singularity, the amplification of human intelligence, or its replacement by hypermachines, be seen as either a farce or a horror story? No doubt this is the way it will be portrayed by Hollywood, embodying the usual false binary opposition. Mind versus Passion! Love throttled by Rationality! In *Charly* (1968), based on Daniel Keyes's heartbreaking story "Flowers for Algernon," surgically enhanced intelligence lifts a sweet moron to the heights of sensitive genius before smashing into Nature's Revenge, dashing the tragic hero back into stupidity and early death. In the fifties' cult movie *Forbidden Planet* (1956) a device for increasing IQ and linking minds into a planetary gestalt frees the Monster from the Id, those vile forces boiling destructively in the unconscious (in pop Freudianism), and kills an entire world. Star Trek's Mr. Spock and Lt. Commander Data did a little better, but paid for their cleverness in the inevitable coin: They were forbidden human depth and feeling.

This is a very strange cliché, standing as a polar contrary to transrealism. Its supposed truth is denied by the slightest contact with real, passionate, sometimes frenzied human scientists and technologists. But perhaps this is what *really* frightens us: when strong feelings, devotion and hatred and prejudice, are joined powerfully with effective strategies for influencing the world. Then we get holocausts, the risk of global nuclear war that could serve nobody's purposes, mad cults with real weapons.

Is the Spike likely to bring just such unholy conjunctions to a new pitch of fearful strength? We have evolved in hundreds of millions of years of sluggish tribal life, dealing with each other face to face, vulnerable to the fists and scorn of others, sensitive to their smiles and touch. What happens when we allow ourselves to deal with others wholly through a monitor's window? Anyone who has watched, or taken part in, a "flame war" on the Internet knows how these exchanges escalate into brutal rudeness and sarcasm, the kind of thing that leads on the highway to "road rage" murders. It is a stroke of luck that we cannot yet easily kill our foes through the screen. But perhaps an enhanced human, locked into symbiosis with potent programs running on computers all around the world, would indeed learn how to smite enemies in world-shaking tantrums.

With luck, this interregnum would be brief. By and large, people are not mad dogs. It is already possible, and has been for decades, to make lethal bombs from common agricultural substances, or gun down children in a playground, yet when this is done by a few crazies the rest of us are genuinely grief-stricken, if only for a brief time before our own concerns drift back to the surface. The transition from intelligence amplification (IA) to the Spike, when enormous numbers of changes happen with immense swiftness, will probably not occur as an all-at-once crystallization—or at least we must hope not. Even so, in John Barnes's *Mother of Storms*,[8] Singularity occurs when Louie Tynan (one of the first humans on Mars, now in Earth orbit) and Carla Tynan (on her submersible yacht *MyBoat*) quite plausibly get absorbed into the net in 2028, after a global catastrophe, then spread between orbit and the Moon and eventually into a comet from the Kuiper belt. Such transition into superintelligence should bring with it the solutions to most of our traditional woes: hunger, thirst, nakedness to the elements—scarcity, in a word. The means to those solutions might not even be glimpsable yet, but the likely paths are obvious: nanotechnology, direct AI-interfaces, genome control and repair, massively extended lifespan, and so forth.

"Suppose we could tailor the Singularity," Vinge proposes. "Suppose we could attain our most extravagant hopes. What then would we ask for: that humans themselves would become their own successors, that whatever injustice occurs would be tempered by our knowledge of our roots" (Vinge, VISION-21 Symposium). In this authentic golden age, immortality would no longer be a fantasy of consolation in the imagined world beyond death, but a literal indefinite extension of life in a utopian world without want. But somehow that tale chills us and with good reason. We are aware of our limitations, the weaknesses of brains and bodies built by blind Darwinian selection. Each of us expires a few decades at most after a fertile span of some thirty or forty years. We are put together as disposable gene-carriers. Our beautiful minds rot with our fallible, corruptible brains and are gone forever. What would happen with such temporary mechanisms if they were repaired again and again, held safe from the corrosion of time? Nightmare, perhaps. "A mind that stays at the same capacity cannot live forever," Vinge notes; "after a few thousand years it would look more like a repeating tape loop than a person" (Vinge, VISION-21 Symposium). So extended life must also be enhanced life. For immortality we would need to be smarter, even if we didn't already need amplified gifts to attain immortality. (In fact, we might not, as medical consequences of the Human Genome Project show the way to endless cellular repair.)

More to the point, what is the "we," the "I," that is going to survive into the post-Spike utopia? This is a crux for any transrealist writing, one that Rudy Rucker himself has tended to answer in novels *outside* his transrealist oeuvre, as we shall see in chapter 8. If poststructural theory tells us that the self is always-already a construct, an illusion, that improbable perspective will be even harder to dispute in a world where we can send out "partials" or "agents" from ourselves into the global net. Already, our brains are composed of dedicated, somewhat partitioned modules resembling the "faculties" of an older philosophy. Of course these specialized components tend to work together, creating (most of the time) a sense of unified consciousness. Once we learn to split off fractions of our selves—or, rather, duplicate and amplify and elaborate those fractions, as in the Swanwick novels—we will no longer be strictly human. Vinge notes: "These are essential features of strong superhumanity and the Singularity. Thinking about them, one begins to feel how essentially strange and different the Post-Human era will be— *no matter how cleverly and benignly it is brought to be*" (Vinge, VISION-21 Symposium, italics in original).

An audacious Marxist (or perhaps post-Marxist) version of a world going through, recovering from and absorbing a Singularity has been sketched by Ken MacLeod, like Iain M. Banks a Scots writer with affinities to the anarchist left. These novels began with *The Star Fraction* (1995), which nearly won the Arthur C. Clarke award, a kind of frenzied Trotskyist vision of a world convulsed by political fractions—unlike the more intimate kind mentioned above—and manipulated by an emergent AI weapons system. Subsequent volumes explore a variety of future cultures that might emerge from this abrupt discontinuity. *The Sky Road* (1999) actually revises the future history of the other three, ensuring that a menacing Spike does *not* occur, or at least is delayed. *The Stone Canal* (1996) and its sequel *The Cassini Division* (1998) portray with high, sly humor and impressive technical and political insight two contesting utopias, one a Banksian anarchosocialist Union on a damaged Earth, the other an anarchocapitalist libertarian world on the far side of a wormhole, 10,000 light years from Earth and in its future. Both alternative regimes (or antiregimes) are thus at arm's-length yet able to communicate and even visit. Jupiter, meanwhile, has been redesigned by posthuman entities, the "fast folk," that blend organic roots and AI enhancements. Are they dreadfully dangerous—trapped in psychotic virtual realities, but likely to emerge at any moment—or should they be welcomed as our successors? MacLeod is superbly sardonic in setting all these groups at each other's throats and minds. His vision of a Singularity is distinctly unnerving, and his several contrasted utopias are no less troubling even as they seduce us in succession.

THE ROAD TO XANADU

Earlier imaginative writers staked out this territory before Vinge got there. Perhaps the most notable was the late Theodore Sturgeon, a poet, dreamer and storyteller currently somewhat in eclipse. In the 1950s, his short fiction returned again and again to territory we now see as the boundaries of the Spike, while drawing much of its power from his transrealist immersion in fallible characters carefully observed. Often— strangely enough, for an American writing at the height of McCarthyite Red Menace hysteria—his wistful parables told of maimed, lonely, isolated men and women finding one another in the company of a greater unity, a colony mind, a hive, *homo gestalt*. Yet Sturgeon did not abdicate from the precise, piercing joys of quirky individuality, or the prickly demands of freedom. His fiction may yet prove to come closest to one tendency in the posthuman condition.

In "The Skills of Xanadu" (1956), a primitive world is found by a high-tech militarist. The naked savages wear a curious belt but little else, and inexplicably their disorganized play fetches them everything they require in life. This harmony, maddening to the rigid newcomer, proves to be a by-product of their single crucial item of technology: the belt, which links all brains into a shared knowledge base. Faced with a problem, you simply *understand* the answer. The skill of the best practitioner of any craft is instantly available to you. When the warmonger leaves, taking a belt, he hopes to use it to transform his rigid society into a perfect dictatorship. Instead, the belts convert his world into a harmonious network of free individuals, each of them experts in the skills of "logic and love; sympathy, empathy, forbearance."[9] Years later, Sturgeon wrote wistfully: "I yearn to live on Xanadu, and wear their garment, and join with them in their marvellous life-style" (p. 228).

That ambiguous hunger for sharing, for life within a colony organism, was brought to a peak in "To Marry Medusa" (1958), a novella later expanded slightly under the unpleasant title *The Cosmic Rape*, which is exactly what it is not. Aliens invest the Earth, turning everyone into hapless members of a cosmic hive, the Medusa.

Full of wonder, the human hive contemplated itself and its works, its gains, its losses and its new nature.

First, there was the intercommunication—a thing so huge, so different, that few minds could previously have imagined it. . . . Though bound to the organism, Mankind, as never before, I am I as never before. . . . The things which disappeared now proved their unreality by the unruffled silence in which they disappeared. Money. The sense of property. Jingoistic patriotism, tariffs, taxes, boundaries and frontiers, profit and loss, and language itself (except as part of an art) with all the difficulties of communication between languages and within them.[10]

This rather conventional liberal wish list strikes us, half a century later, as curiously limp and plainly mistaken in places. An enhanced mind might improve its semiotics, its semantics, its syntactics, but it will hardly abolish language, which is the very mechanism of mind. But Sturgeon is not done. Unlike a *Star Trek* Borg—a voraciously assimilationist group-mind that exterminates the selves of its press-ganged components, giving rise to the neat term "borganism"—Hive Mankind reaches out to enliven the invading Medusa. For the Medusa, poor thing, was built out of interstellar termites, and the infusion of all these terrifically individuated humans gives it a fresh lease on life. Sturgeon hails his new Gestalt cosmos in an outburst of sticky sentimentality: "So ended mankind, to be born again as hive-humanity; so ended the hive of earth to become star-man, the immeasurable, the limitless, the growing; maker of music beyond music, poetry beyond words, and full of wonder, full of worship" (Sturgeon, *Cosmic Rape*, p. 155).

Gurlick, the cheap bum, the guttersnipe, who starts the transcendental ball rolling, reacts to Humanity with a premonitory parody of Arthur C. Clarke's great line about stars inside the black Monolith in *2001: A Space Odyssey*. "My God," he blurts, "it's full of people!" (p. 157). Just as you feared that saccharine uplift would unsettle your lunch, Sturgeon snatches you back from the brink with a brilliant stroke. This awful creature remains unchanged in his noxious humanity: " 'Bastits,' Gurlick would mutter in the dark, hating . . . happy: 'Lousy bastits' " (p. 160).

The grace to permit remnants of the old, unreconstructed humanity to live in peace may be the best we can hope for from augmented or borganized posthumans. Well, one happier option is conceivable, for those open to the charms of self-deceptions: Our successors might choose to disguise themselves as our servants. Vinge hints at "benign treatment (perhaps even giving the stay-behinds the appearance of being masters of godlike slaves)" (VISION-21 Symposium). Unaltered humans would be the metaphysical equivalents of the Amish, serene agricultural throwbacks in our mechanized, electronic world. That appears to be a difficult way of life to sustain, even to negotiate, and its future version would surely be harder still to endure without soul-wrenching episodes of blatant bad faith, lack of resolution when times grew tough and one's body aged while everyone else remained healthy and young, backsliding by the next generation.

Eugene Leitl, a brilliant young Russian-German transhumanist with a powerful Internet presence, perceives a range of cautionary possibilities when the first Spike consciousness awakens and looks around itself. It might not be a safe time to be alive; it might be the end of all histories that concern us.

Here's an ethical question: you need the Earth for resources, but there are some guys living down there still. You have basically three alternatives:

1) Let them live. Life is sacred, etc., etc. A bummer.

2) Upload them by force, delete all memories, make them unaware of a discontinuity. Alternatively, give them the illusion that they have died and live in a Heaven of their particular religion. Dunno what's better.

3) Life? Which life? Life's solid-state. This surface is contaminated by primitive life precursors. Ablate the atmosphere by antiparticle beam, we will need the vacuum for disassembly. FFFFFFFFFFFFFFFFFt. Operation completed, cooldown countdown started. Units 43. 4534.3345.745 to 55.353.455.454 state 433.43 ready for spindown. Stand by.[11]

Do the last two alternatives in this horror story explain the Great Silence in the skies, the mysterious absence of any radio or optical traffic between worlds out there in the galaxy and beyond? If the technology and culture of every civilization Spikes within a century or two of their discovering radio and space flight, they might all be tucked away into the folds of local space-time like the hidden, rolled-up dimensions of string theory. They might even be living *there*, colonizing those intricate, implicate spaces.

So what should be our attitude to these posthumans who seem likely to replace us, perhaps within a century or even sooner? Terror? Awed worship? Serene acceptance? The hope that we might join them in a *gestalt* superhuman Comprise? The paradox of wish met with despair is captured quite deliciously in a mocking poem by writer and systems scientist Mark Crosby, a sharp blasphemy—to traditionalists and transhumanists alike—on transcendental creeds:

A Protestation of Faith

We believe in the One Power
Who will make the great transform
transcending us all;
the best and brightest, eternally replicated,
through Whom all things are changed.

For us and for our salvation,
we must solve all the problems of the world
here and now.
We must disdain any link with
suboptimal subsystems of the past.
We must be the future, now.

For our sake we will be frozen and adamant,
insisting on only the best from this world,
the fluid ease of evolution resisted.
In any case, we shall come again,
always judging both the living and the dead,
in a kingdom that will have no end.

We believe in the Singularity Allmighty,
which will transport us to infinity and beyond,
to all that is now uncountable and inconceivable
(transforming the KnownNet overnight).

With the Powers and Omega,
the Singularity is expected and glorified.
The spirit of the Web speaks through
the invisible hand of the market,
and we are transfixed.

We acknowledge commitment to
endless expansion,
wait for the insurrection of uploads,
with atom-by-atom Nanotech control
of the life of the world to come.

Amen (and on to Alef-one!)[12]

GEOGRAPHIES OF THE INCONCEIVABLE

Many alternative paths lead from where we now stand into the transhuman and the posthuman futures of the Spike. As we have seen already, Greg Egan is exemplary in his development of this intuition. It is not at all clear that there's any role at all for us mere humans on the far side of the Spike's looming wall. It will be uncomfortably interesting to learn how sf writers in the twenty-first century meet this extreme narrative challenge—and how everyone else deals with the history-breaching reality following hot on the heels of the fiction. Meanwhile, we must continue to tell tales of the barely conceivable by anchoring them in our own limited yet intimately complex experience—the basis of the transrealist project.

NOTES

1. Talk given at the VISION-21 Symposium sponsored by NASA Lewis Research Center and the Ohio Aerospace Institute, 30–31 March 1993. This fecund discussion of the Singularity posit is available at several sites on the World Wide Web, for example: http://www-rohan.sdsu.edu/faculty/vinge/misc/singularity.html

2. Rainer Maria Rilke, *Duino Elegies*, trans. Stephen Cohn (Manchester: Carcanet, 1989).

3. Vernor Vinge, *Marooned in Realtime* (London: Pan, 1987).

4. See especially the feuding Minds in Iain M. Banks, *Excession* (London: Orbit, 1996).

5. Iain M. Banks, *Use of Weapons* (London: Orbit, 1990), p. 259. Oddly, Banks is inconsistent with his hypertechnologies. In a culture where major surgery is performed routinely in preparing for parties, an older man chooses to wear glasses: "old-fashioned enough to wear his age rather than disguise it" (p. 216).

6. Michael Swanwick, *Vacuum Flowers* (New York: Ace, 1988), p. 222.

7. Michael Swanwick, *Stations of the Tide* (New York: Ace, 1991), p. 146.

8. John Barnes, *Mother of Storms* (London: Millennium, 1994).

9. Theodore Sturgeon, "The Skills of Xanadu," *The Golden Helix* (New York: Dell, 1979), p. 259.

10. Theodore Sturgeon, *The Cosmic Rape* (New York: Dell, 1977), p. 143.

11. Internet posting, cited with permission.

12. Internet posting, cited with permission.

Transreality: Living
What You Write

Often I feel that the relationship between my experience and my
writing is that I rehash my experiences again and again and can
never figure out why things happened, what for, and what they signified, if anything. And then if I cast them into a novel, especially
s-f, I can coerce them by the artistic creative process into making
sense . . . There is no reason for writing an s-f novel if you believe
what you're writing is true, because then the s-f form is a sort of
code, a device to say "what you can't say and get away with it really," and that isn't so, you can say anything short of libel . . . I had
no preconception, nothing to sell people on, to preach to them, to
convince them of . . . merely . . . a making use of what I went through
and saw to feed back into my life as a writer, so that it was not
wasted in that respect.
　　　　　　—Philip K. Dick, *The Dark-Haired Girl* (pp. 183–85)

Is the transrealist project—its program, indeed, its recommendation—
finally nothing more than the most banal of writing workshop advice?
Write what you know. That admonition has always seemed to me death
to imagination, or at least to that species of imagination on the wild side
that sf and the fantastic require. At its most generous, its counsel takes
the form offered by George Turner as "one of the great truths about
imaginative fiction: some of the most striking effects are obtained by the
revelation of strangeness in *familiar* things." He added that "most of the
really memorable science fiction has succeeded not in flights of fantasy

but in casual distortion, subtle re-aligning or outright upsetting of our comfortable scenes of everyday."[1] This might have been Turner's own estimate and practice, but it is of doubtful validity—are the diabolical serpents of the planet Lithia in Blish's *A Case of Conscience*, let alone the posthumans of Greg Egan's work, merely a subtle adjustment of life in the suburbs? Turner's prescription sounds more like a formula for creating the oeuvre of Stephen King, replete as it is with recognizable brand names, homey East Coast American geography and small-town settings, uncanny twists on the *Twilight Zone* unease of daily life, or the earlier British equivalent in John Wyndham's cozy catastrophes.

Sf, almost by definition, is usually fiction detached from the known, aslant to it (and often askance, sidelong, questioning and questionable). Still, it is perhaps no accident that those writers most readily identified with transrealist fiction—one thinks primarily of Philip K. Dick, some of his epigones, and Rudy Rucker who coined the term—do indeed write what they know, because the world(s) they inhabit are skewed and subverted in advance. Dick especially was a man plagued by the unreality of the visible, pestered and perhaps nearly broken by intimations of psychosis, which he managed miraculously, most of the time, to translate into dazzling art, even as he transformed the kitsch of his Californian world. John Clute catches his achievement:

when he found the tale within his grasp, he was brilliantly inventive, gaining access to imaginative realms which no other writer of sf had reached. His sympathy for the plight of his characters—often far from heroic, small, ordinary people trapped in difficult existential circumstances—was unfailing, and his work has a human interest absent from that of writers engaged by complexity and convolutions for their own sake.[2]

This might seem ingenuous, since so much of Dick's fiction is patently generated by the machinery of pulp sf, with its recomplications, comic-strip political reversals, and what Clute himself accurately dubs "ideative mazes" (Clute, "Dick, Philip K.," p. 329). Still, the key to Dick's contribution is also caught by Clute: "he was astonishingly intimate, self-exposed, and very dangerous. He was the funniest sf writer of his time, and perhaps the most terrifying. His dreads were our own, spoken as we could not have spoken them" (p. 330). This is the very ensign of transrealism, and perhaps the condition it notates, which we might term *transreality*. Perhaps that merely renames the condition of postmodernity (since, as I have argued, following Fredric Jameson and Brian McHale, Dick is the inevitable exemplar of postmodern ontological fiction), but again perhaps it opens a window on a fresh way to compose our experience in a time when human and machine, the known and the conjectured, the richly experienced and the coolly posited start to blur and flow together, like a policeman's tears.

THE AUTHOR IN THE TEXT

Sometimes, of course—perhaps increasingly, in and out of literary fiction, slipstream and sf alike—authors are introduced recursively into their own texts. We are no longer shocked by John Fowles's physical intrusion into the plot of *The French Lieutenant's Woman,* or even his rescinding of its course, as he steps into his character Charles's railway coach:

But at the very last moment, a massively bearded face appeared at his window. . . . The latecomer muttered a "Pardon me, sir" and made his way to the far end of the compartment. He sat, a man of forty or so, his top hat firmly square, his hands on his knees, regaining his breath. There was something rather aggressively secure about him; he was perhaps not quite a gentleman. . . . [3]

The transition, which uncannily we might find ourselves expecting, comes via the voice of the novel itself, as it were, addressing us as readers: "In my experience there is only one profession that gives that particular look, with its bizarre blend of the inquisitive and the magistral; of the ironic and the soliciting" (Fowles, *French Lieutenant's Woman,* p. 348). And then the hand of the god-author is shown explicitly: "So I continue to stare at Charles and see no reason this time for fixing the fight upon which he is about to engage . . . [The solution is] to show two versions of it. That leaves me with only one problem: I cannot give both versions at once, yet whichever is the second will seem, so strong is the tyranny of the last chapter, the final, the 'real' version" (p. 349).

Dick's very disturbing novel *Valis,* the imaginative transformation of a 1974 event he regarded as a kind of supernatural epiphany, indeed theophany, features several duplications of the author: as himself, "Philip K. Dick," and as Horselover Fat, a Greek-German transform of his name and a character embodying his wilder, more credulous avatar. (In a document published in 1981 in the fanzine *Niekas,* Dick reveals that the new savior, named Tagore, currently lives in Sri Lanka. An incarnation of the Logos, hideously burned and crippled, Tagore has taken upon his own body this torment that figures the "macrocrucifixion" of the world at the hands of pollutive and careless humans. The revelation is presented as by Horeslover Fat with Dick as his rather reluctant intermediary.)[4] Characters named "James Ballard" are not unknown in J. G. Ballard's own novels, especially in the pornographic non-sf novel *Crash* (1973). Kurt Vonnegut has visited his own novels in his own person, most explicitly in *Breakfast of Champions* ([1973] 1974): "I had come to the Arts Festival incognito, I was there to watch a confrontation between two human beings I had created: Dwayne Hoover and Kilgore

Trout. I was not eager to be recognized" (p. 179). Something of the same
intrusion, rationalized via zany meditations on infinitely dimensioned
Hilbert space, occurs in Rucker's *Master of Space and Time* ([1984], 1985),
which interestingly is not one of the novels he regards as transrealist.
The ontological glitch takes place in a chapter entitled, flagrantly, "Rudy
Rucker Is Watching You":

There was a man behind us, a run-down man with short hair and lambent eyes.
He had the taut features and heavy stubble of a drifter. His lips were slightly
parted to show his crooked teeth. Seeing me notice him, he gave the barest flicker
of response—a twinge of gloating, a pulse of lust. His cool, hungry stare filled
me with horror.[5]

   Yet this odd demonic figure—the gloating lust is a far cry from
Fowles's magisterial if not-quite-gentlemanly commanding vehicle, or
Vonnegut's discomfited discretion—is not the immediate creator of nar-
rator Joe Fletcher's world. That is Alwin Bitter, who is literally thinking
or wishing the cast of the novel into existence. (One of Rucker's own
names, we recall, is Bitter; moreover, he is the author's transrealist equivalent in *The Sex Sphere* [1983].) Still, "In my mind's eye," Fletch tells us,
"I kept seeing the terrible hungry face of the man who watched. Perhaps
Alwin had dreamed me, but that man had dreamed Alwin" (Rucker,
Master of Space and Time, p. 226). For a throwaway line, it is a wonderfully
terrifying moment.
   It is a postmodern commonplace to regard all as text, while disposing
of any authorial "authority" over words that have emerged out of the
author's fingers and brain, organs deemed to be instruments, above all,
of prevailing discursive formations. Dick and Rucker alike are haunted,
oddly enough, by just such apprehensions. A highly intelligent autodi-
dact, Dick built an explanatory system for himself from Kant, Gnosti-
cism, existential psychoanalysis and a melange of acid culture theories
of mind and reality. He wrote to Australian commentator Bruce Gillespie
(then a young teacher not long out of university studies in English): "for
each person there are two worlds, the *idios kosmos*, which is a *unique* private world, and the *koinos kosmos*, which literally means *shared* world. . . .
No person can tell which part of his total worldview is [which . . .] except
by the achievement of a strong empathetic rapport with other people."[6] In
most of his novels, Dick declared, the protagonist's *idios kosmos* is breaking
down, if not the reality substrate of the shared universe itself. It is a
theme manifest early: *The Cosmic Puppets* (1953), stages a small-town conflict between embodied Zoroastrian divinities Ahriman and Ormazd,
who transform daily reality into symbol. In *Eye in the Sky* (1957),

a particle accelerator accident disrupts the local reality of eight characters whose shared world fluxes as they struggle for dominance; Jack Hamilton, notes Douglas A. Mackey, "is forced to realize that people live in separate worlds inside their own minds, and that a powerful mind can pull others into its version of reality."[7] Alternatively, as a Dickian protagonist's personal construct of the world decays, the noumenon is revealed, often dreadfully.

It was an account that critic George Turner found unconvincing: "The metaphor fails because it cannot stand against the weight of reality as we know it." This sturdy declaration from the *koinos kosmos* located Dick's recurrent tropes—unhinged "reality," the dominance and manipulation of collective realities by a strong personality—in the writer's own instability: "What personal statements Dick has published tends to confirm the obsessional nature of his preoccupation and also suggest that, between the lines, some psychological reasons for it."[8] Such a blunt reading elides, of course, those very ideological dimensions manifested in Dick's work which make it the preeminent staging of postmodern tropes identified by Fredric Jameson: a certain flatness, a lack of mimetic or illusory "depth"; loss or attenuation of discrete subjectivity and memory, yielding an odd blend of flattened affect and a "peculiar kind of euphoria"; the abandonment by the artist of any pretense to a unique style localized in history, in favor of *pastiche*, jargon, and nostalgia; schizophrenic *ècriture*, especially jumbled *collage* and a radical breakdown in reality testing; the "hysterical sublime."[9]

HUMAN, ANTIHUMAN

Dick's own grasp on his transrealist methods was insecure. Despite his fondness for antihumanist and reality-disrupting literary mechanisms, he repeatedly made every effort to construct himself as a classic humanist. In 1970, writing to Gillespie's fanzine *SF Commentary*, he stated that:

The Universe disintegrates further and further in each of my novels, but the possibility of faith in one given human being or several . . . can be found—usually—in the novel somewhere, at the center of the stage or at the very edge. . . . Basically, he is found at the heart of human life itself. He is, in fact, the heart of human life. . . . Perhaps [some critics] are bothered by the fact that what I trust is so very small. They want something vaster. I have news for them: there is nothing vaster.[10]

It is strikingly revealing, then, that some four years later, following his delusional theophany, he began the ever-more-obsessional search for meaning traced hilariously in his immense million-word, 8,000-page *Ex-*

egesis notebooks, extracts from which are now in print. This hunt for the noumenon culminated, perhaps, in his parodically titled "The Ultra Hidden (Cryptic) Doctrine: The Secret Meaning of the Great System of Theosophy of the World, Openly Revealed for the First Time," of 2 March 1980.[11] There is nothing vaster? The eponymous *Valis*, first in his final bizarre thematic trilogy, stands for "Vast Artificial Living Intelligent System," the cosmic computer mentality or perhaps deity that Dick came to believe (at least some of the time) to be directing the course of his life.

Given this chimerical bent in Dick's private and public personae, how better to read his texts than as transrealism: fantastical transformations of his daily, if unusually eccentric, life-world. He was a writer drenched in sf imagery; even in his bleakest or most intensely lyrical moments (sometimes the same moments), he found the perfect correlative to his inner states in just that kind of fanciful mutation of external reality he and his colleagues had formulated as science fiction idioms, as diegetic counters in the mighty megatextual game. He wrote a typical inflated, subtly bullying yet surely suffering honest letter to his prospective lover Linda (one of the very young "foxy chicks" he found himself obsessively and mostly ruinously drawn to in later life):

The fear of losing you, the anguish, dreadful, haunting, bitter terror at suddenly finding you gone—this aches through our bones . . . [I]f something happened to you intrinsically . . . everyone would wither away at the heart and sicken and perish, varying from person to person, in different degrees and at different rates. My books would become more weird, more tired, more empty. . . . Like in Bester's *The Demolished Man* I would look up into the sky at night and see the stars flickering off one by one, and I'd fucking be indifferent. I'd walk through the side of a building and it'd collapse into dust. Wheels would fall off cars, like in an old W. C. Fields movie. Finally my foot would sink through the sidewalk. Do you see what you mean to us, Linda?[12]

W. C. Fields and Alfred Bester at play in the decaying kibble-landscapes of the Phildickian oeuvre! It is this interpenetration of suicidally sad reality and preposterously exuberant apocalyptic landscaping that is one hallmark of the transrealist.

Some critics, however, will resist this temptation to peer into biography, if only on the quite prudent grounds that usually we lack access to it, and that even when we do have access, it is never to be trusted, being no less a construction than the fictional texts themselves. Bruce Gillespie has commented of Dick's revealing posthumous publications that "on the one hand it was fascinating to learn how much of his novels, even and especially his SF novels, are based on autobiographical detail: but on the other hand, the books seem so much bigger than the man. As," he added, "do all the great books, I suppose."[13]

Yes and no. Phil, as his many admirers know him (most of whom never met him except in his writings), contained multitudes without ever quite moving sideways into psychosis. A great deal is now known about his sometimes bleak, much-married life. It does indeed call echoes from the refrains in his life's work: the doppelgangers, simulacra, apparent humans who turn out to be "electric ants," programmed constructs. Philip Kindred Dick (the middle name is his mother Dorothy's surname) was a twin born in Chicago on 16 December 1928. His sister Jane Charlotte died six weeks later; it might be that Phil never recovered from this loss or its consequences. When he was four his parents divorced after living in Berkeley, California, for two years, and in 1935 his mother took him to Washington, D.C., returning to Berkeley when he was 10. Evidently he was at popular at school, although his relationship with Dorothy swung between coldness and ardor. Attracted early to science fiction, at 14 he wrote a novel influenced by Swift, now lost, and between 1944 and 1946 had psychiatric and drug treatment for agoraphobia; this kind of marginalizing childhood is common among sf writers (perhaps all writers). In the California of his adulthood, it led almost inevitably into what Istvan Csicsery-Ronay Jr. aptly names "a therapy-universe,"[14] one he shared with many of his wives and lovers, co-extensive with the banality of daily life.

Unusually, he left his mother's custody before finishing high school, sharing digs with several gay poets, including Robert Duncan, then moved to an attic by himself. He'd once had an explicit dream of having sex with his mother, he declared to his third wife's astonishment (Anne Dick, *The Search for Philip K. Dick*, p. 17); at 18, Dorothy would visit him at work, and people took her for his girlfriend: "she had long dark hair, and was thin, and Garboesque" (p. 323). Physical complaints afflicted him, including tachycardia. A long dependency on various medications began. Working in the sort of small TV repair and record store that figures in many of his sf and mainstream books, he studied philosophy and German briefly at Berkeley, marrying and very quickly divorcing Jeanette Marlin, whom he met while serving in the shop, in 1948. A fellow Berkeley student, Kleo Apostolides, married Phil in June 1950. He was already writing without success and published his first short story, "Beyond Lies the Wub," in *Planet Stories* (July 1952), "the most lurid of all pulp magazines."[15] By 1958, he had sold more than eighty stories. In roughly the same decade or so, he also wrote eleven mainstream novels and failed to sell any; by a bitter irony, all were published after he had made his name as an extraordinary fantasist, mostly after his untimely death at 53.

The rest of his productive if largely unremunerative life is amply documented: the increasing, frenetic pace of sf novel production, fueled by scotch, amphetamines and industrial quantities of other uppers and downers, the domestic instability.[16] Moving with Kleo to Marin County, he met recently widowed Anne Williams Rubenstein, who already had three daughters, Hatte, Jayne and Tandy, and quickly divorced Kleo and remarried. In 1960, Anne and Phil had a daughter, Laura Archer, whom he regarded as a link with Jane, his dead twin (Jane was a lesbian, he solemnly told Anne). As the sixties began, Dick created astonishing if confused and often unfocused novels of psychic powers, machine doubles, conspiracy, cheeky robots and appliances, run-down interplanetary locales, at a dizzying rate, sixty pages a day, on the wings of amphetamines; not surprisingly, he had breakdowns. In 1963, his brilliance was recognized by a Hugo Award from the science fiction community for his superb, artistically successful novel *The Man in the High Castle*, portraying a counterfactual world where Germany and Japan had won the Second World War. By the following year, his marriage with Anne was in trouble, and his visions had begun with a glimpse of "the hollow eyeslot, the mechanical metal arm and hand, the stainless-steel teeth, which are the dread stigmata of evil . . . in the overhead sky at noon" in 1963.[17] That imagery would find its place in his well-regarded 1965 novel *Three Stigmata of Palmer Eldritch*, although a decade later he would reverse its sting, perhaps because he had come to see its origins in infant memories of his father donning a First World War gas mask: "under the anger, under the metal and helmet, there is . . . the face of a man. A kind and loving man." It is almost a prefiguration of the climax of George Lucas's *Star Wars* trilogy, with the sinister black-helmeted Darth Vader redeemed and curiously redemptive.

Dick, however, was not yet close to any kind of succor. The 36-year-old Phil turned to Nancy Hackett, a 21-year-old with psychiatric problems of her own. They married in 1966, and the following year had a daughter, Isolde. In 1970, after a bout of pancreatitis caused by adulterated street speed took Dick to hospital, Nancy left with baby Isa. Depressed, Phil sank further into abundant and inventive drug use, taking up with Kathy Demuelle, then 17 and still at high school, and hung out with dope dealers, addicts and small-time criminals. Phil was using a thousand methedrine "beans" a week, balanced by 40 mg of Stelazine a day plus other prescription tranquilizers. When his San Venetia residence was trashed on 17 November 1971, Phil blamed the CIA, and his paranoia increased. Perhaps he was a thermometer of the times. Christopher Palmer observes: "As Dick went zanier, so did the culture around him. In his reflections on the break-in he suffered, he makes himself a kind of node of all the craziness of the times—or a sump?—CIA, Black Panthers, Minute men, drug dealers."[18] Indeed, Istvan Csicsery-Ronay Jr. remarks: "One could use Dick as a pretext for a whole history of postwar America" ("The Wife's Story," p. 325). Yet, like that history, by no means all is hysteria, anxiety and excitement; Csicsery-Ronay also notes acutely the "fascinating banality" typical of his work (p. 325).

In 1972, invited to Vancouver, Canada, to give a speech (the notable "The Android and the Human"), he was deserted in turn by Kathy and tried to take his life, not for the first or last time. A ferocious Synanon-style rehabilitation program, X-Kalay, straightened him out, and after another hopeless affair with a young woman, Jamis, he returned to the United States, to Fullerton, at the invitation of an academic enthusiastic for his work. Now he met the Linda extolled in the passage quoted earlier, yet within months announced that she had treated him with "the most cruel contempt possible."[19] Luckily, he swiftly met Tessa (Leslie Busby), "the kindest girl in the world . . . the sort of girl who would take a cricket to the vet's to get it stitched back up so that it could go crick again" (Dick, *Dark-Haired Girl*, p. 197), marrying her on 18 April 1973. Their son Christopher was born that year. And then in February and March of 1974, Phil was visited by a series of shattering theophanies.

His work had fallen away during these bad years, but in 1975, *Flow My Tears* won a prestigious jury prize, the John W. Campbell Memorial Award. Those strange works of his last years, starting with *Valis* and concluding with *The Transmigration of Timothy Archer* (and the *Exegesis* itself, surely not meant for publication), are the plainest examples—although artistically compromised—of his transrealist methods in writing. Everything of his tormented, self-damaging life flooded through all his work: the wives, the ruinous and self-deluding, rather heartless, manipulative, pathetic affairs with "foxy young chicks" barely out of high school, the mystical visions, the zany humor, the transformations of dread and illumination into scatty tales built, as always, from the detritus of pulp sf and his own marginal, somewhat streetwise life.

Disclosures from the noumenon increasingly energized, distracted and goaded Phil, taking ambiguous expression in his late novels. One key event is allegorized, barely changed in detail, in *Valis*, where God "fired a beam of pink light directly at him [the Dick figure], at his head, his eyes . . . exactly what you get as a phosphene after-image when a flash-bulb has gone off in your face" (*Valis*, p. 12). Another appears in his 1977 novel *A Scanner Darkly*. After experiments with "disinhibiting substances affecting neural tissue," a Bell Labs tech named Powers experienced "a disastrous drop in the GABA fluid [the neurotransmitter Gamma aminobutyrate] of his brain") and

witnessed lurid phosphene activity projected on the far wall of his bedroom, a frantically progressing montage of what, at the time, he imagined to be modern-day abstract painting.

For about six hours, S. A. Powers had watched thousands of Picasso paintings replace one another at flash-cut speed, and then he had been treated to Paul Klees, more than the painter had painted during his entire lifetime.[20]

The sequence flees across his gaze, now Modiglianis, now Kandinskis. A typical Dickian phantasmagoria? In *Valis*, four years later, this event is ascribed to his alter ego Horselover Fat, not in a fascistic future but in March 1974. "The month before that, Fat had had an impacted wisdom tooth removed. For this the oral surgeon administered a hit of IV sodium pentothal" (*Valis*, p. 97). Again, everything blurs; ontology reels more than ordinarily. Like Powers, like Fat, like "Dick" in the late novels, the actual Phil experiences "vivid dreams" about mute, telepathic, clawed alien invaders with three eyes that "manifested themselves as cyborg entities: wrapped up in glass bubbles staggering under masses of technological gear" (p. 93). Perhaps these are minions or aspects of the supernal Zebra entity from the Sirius star-system, which (with astounding, risky bathos) "had overthrown the Nixon tyranny in August 1974, and would eventually set up a just and peaceful kingdom on Earth where there would be no sickness, no pain, no loneliness, and the animals would all dance with joy" (p. 91).

Why Zebra? "Because it blended. . . . What if a high form of sentient mimicry existed—such a high form that no human (or few humans) had detected it?' (p. 60). Except in a theophany of grace. That was Phil's best guess. Indeed, perhaps Zebra or Valis dwelt in the future, a kind of superior intelligence that repeatedly altered the events in its own history to bring closer to perfection the many superposed universes familiar from sf and Dick's loony cosmologies in particular. (Dick would come to see certain core volumes—usually ten in number, although the list was subject to change—in his corpus as comprising a vast coded testimony, mysteriously written in advance of his illumination, awaiting a suitable exegesis.) This notion of parallel or superposed realities is, too, a reputable image from the frontiers of quantum science and cosmology—developed subsequently, and with the greatest seriousness, by relativist Frank Tipler and quantum theorist David Deutsch—as well as a palpable figuration of each artist's own shaping work of memory regained, text within text upon text imbricated, prepared for readers who can never know for certain which universe is authentic and which is playful or bogus.

When he died in 1982 in the hospital of heart failure, some years after separating from his fifth wife and third child, needy affairs with several other women, and increasing reputation, he left an unfinished novel, *The Owl in Daylight*, and a growing semi-cult of personality. Had he lived, might he have become a full-blown mountebank? Could he have found wealth and followers by inventing his own exfoliating religion, as L. Ron Hubbard and Dick's early favorite, A. E. van Vogt had done with Dianetics and Scientology? Or convinced himself of an absurd transcendental reality, as "UFO abductee" Whitley Streiber seems to have done, to his great profit? Perhaps not. Phil's sense of the ridiculous always saved him, even as he plunged into despair and hallucination. Arguably it was exactly his mastery of transreality that spared him the final banal temptation of guruhood. Our world, Phil assured himself, was already a collage, a superposition, of all possible worlds, or perhaps a gradually revised, achingly redemptive sequence of histories, a recovery from the Black Iron Prison, the unended Roman Empire masked by our collective delusion of modernity, or the entropic Tomb World of his oracular revelations and minatory fiction.

THE NEUROLOGY OF THE NUMINOUS

What can be surmised, recovered, from this necessarily elided precis of a writer's life? Can we probe with any hope of insight into the causes of his fermenting imagination, his endlessly bungled personal life, his manipulations and culpable gullibility, above all his sense of the numinous *breaking through*, for good or ill? One approach, rather clinical, is to ask bluntly: What kind of mind generates such imagery, entertains such preposterous explanations of the world, suffers so much (while laughing so loudly and bringing others to tears of laughter in turn)? Conceivably, a mind running like a slightly damaged mechanism inside a brain with some of its wiring gone wrong: a kind of gifted neuroelectric ant.

The secondary literature on Philip K. Dick is not lacking in attempted explanations for his disarray, which he turned so uncannily into art, if a confused and confusing art. Laura Campbell documents the uses and abuses of the oracular *I Ching*, Jay Kinney compares and contrasts shamanistic trance and schizophrenia, Gregg Rickman speculates on childhood molestation at the hands of his grandfather, Evarestus Kindred.[21] As Rickman notes, despite Dick's own claims to schizophrenia and his muddled use of this diagnosis in various novels, "Other, better theories exist to explain his experiences; Post-traumatic stress disorder (PTSD), dissociative identity disorder (DID) (in earlier psychiatric literature, multiple personality disorder [MPD]), or temporal lobe epilepsy (TLE). He suffered none of the key symptoms of schizophrenia. . . ."[22]

Granted, the idioms of depersonalization are a characteristic trope of twentieth-century writing, no doubt reflecting a heightened agony of consciousness in its artists and a wider psychic malaise in anonymous, rootless communities impacted by the double blows of modernity and postmodernity. Seeking a single intrapsychic explanation for this widespread anxiety is an ideological gambit serving to distract attention from the genuine failings and oppressions of a world where people are often treated as cyphers and slowly perceive themselves as such. Even so, the degree to which Philip K. Dick figured his world as a treacherous site of masks, labels, imposters, simulacra and literally crumbling or dissolving realities goes far beyond existential nausea or "literary" hall-of-mirrors disorientation. I would like to suggest a neurological parallel, perhaps supplementing these cultural diagnoses, found in the work of Professor V. S. Ramachandran, who has worked with victims of several extraordinary diseases of the limbic and temporal systems of the brain.

In his *Phantoms in the Brain* (1998), Ramachandran details two somewhat related and extremely rare disorders that hint at something of Dick's inner condition (although he does not, of course, make any reference to Dick). One is Capgras's delusion: that those dearest to you have been replaced by identical imposters or even androids. One patient "was convinced that his stepfather was a robot, proceeded to decapitate him and opened his skull to look for microchips" (p. 166). This affliction sounds eerily and terrifyingly like the plots of so many Dick stories and novels. A striking instance afflicts Jack Bohlen, in *Martian Time-Slip* (1964):

He saw the personnel manager in a new light. The man was dead.
  He saw, through the man's skin, his skeleton. It had been wired together, the bones connected, with fine copper wire. The organs, which had withered away, were replaced by artificial components, kidney, heart, lungs—everything was made of plastic and stainless steel, all working in unison but entirely without authentic life. (P. 69)

Bohlen attributes this to a schizophrenic episode, yet the key identity disorder in the novel is autism, almost certainly a by-product of development damage. In any event, the explanation for such errors as Capgras's now seems likely to be neurological rather than psychiatric. Specialized face-recognition neural modules, located in the temporal lobes on both sides of the head, normally send messages to the limbic system deep in the center of the brain (specifically, to the amygdala), where processed data gets charged with emotional color, marking its salience. Ramachandran argues that this link is broken or impaired in victims of Capgras's, so that the customary "warm glow" we feel on seeing someone close to us (or perhaps "hateful glower" in the case of enemies) is not activated. So the patient sees an expected figure, but one without any hint of an answering emotional tone. Who else can it be but a fake? When we construct the world around us, we largely project outward the tags and mental categories we have imposed on its actors. Hence, the Capgras's victim (mis)reads this emotional absence as a failure on the part of the *other* person—even, I suspect, as active malevolence. I do not for a moment suggest that Philip K. Dick suffered from anything as severe as Capgras's; he had no obvious empathic defects, and Anne said of their early time together: "Phil was the perfect husband . . . a wonderful companion, lover . . . helped with the children and comforted them when they had problems . . . the most considerate, most lovable person I ever met" (Anne Dick, *The Search for Philip K. Dick*, pp. 38–39). But might it not be that his various illnesses and preposterous doses of drugs gradually interfered with his temporal-limbic circuits (a rather Dickian way of putting it, admittedly), so that he, like so many of his characters, sometimes experienced these profound confusions of identity and affect in those he loved best?

A related disorder of the temporal lobes, mentioned by Rickman, sounds even more like Dick's later life story: epileptiform seizures that trigger visual images of immense intensity, powerful feelings of awe and transcendence, a sense of unity with the All and even a conviction of direct communion with God. Phil fits this description closely—but not altogether, which might have been his partial saving (or might simply falsify my suggestion). Ramachandran notes that temporal lobe disorders are marked by heightened emotion, a tendency to see cosmic significance in the trivial, to be "humourless, full of self-importance, and to maintain elaborate diaries that record quotidian events in elaborate detail—a trait called hypergraphia. Patients have on occasion given me hundreds of pages of written text filled with mystical symbols and notations . . . and they are obsessively preoccupied with philosophical and theological issues" (Ramachandran and Blakeslee, *Phantoms in the Brain*, p. 180). Dick fits this profile with alarming neatness—except that his self-importance was usually well in hand, and he was the very opposite of humorless. Philip K. Dick, in his writing at least, and by repute in person, was quite remarkably amusing.

Below is an extended passage, later recycled very closely into his pre-*Valis* draft novel published posthumously as *Radio Free Albemuth*. It is necessary to give it at length, as Phil's anecdotal humor is quiet, insinuating; it builds, paying off not in a belly laugh (although that is always lurking in Dick's work and zany nomenclature) but in a warm, smiling sense of ditzy insight. As Michael Andre-Driussi notes, you can come away shaking your head, muttering for more reasons than one, "That Phil!"[23]

In 1968, Anthony Boucher (William Anthony Parker), the shy, literate editor of *The Magazine of Fantasy & Science Fiction*, where many of Dick's best early stories appeared, died at 57 of cancer. Boucher was a Catholic, devoted to opera, poker, sf and mystery fiction. Phil learned that Tony had survived death in an unusual form, especially for a Catholic:

My cat had begun to behave in an odd way, keeping watch over me in a quiet fashion, and I saw that he had changed. This was after he ran away and returned wild and dirty, crapping on the rug in fear; we took him to the vet and the vet calmed him down and healed him. After that, Pinky had what I call a spiritual quality, except that he wouldn't eat meat . . . he wouldn't do anything cruel. Yet I knew Pinky was afraid, because once I almost shut the refrigerator door on him and he did a three-cushion bank shot of himself off the walls to escape, and clocked a velocity unique for a pink sheeplike thing that usually just sat and gazed ahead . . . Pinky died of cancer suddenly; he was three years old, very young for a cat . . .

I hadn't realised Pinky was Tony Boucher, out of love served up by the universe again, until I had this dream about Tony the Tiger, the cereal box character who offers you Sugar Frosted Flakes. In my dream I stood at one end of a light-struck glade, and at the other end a great tiger came out slowly, with delight, and I knew we were together again. Tony the Tiger and me. My joy was unbounded. When I woke up I tried to think who I knew named Tony. I had other strange experiences after Pinky died . . .

Tony or Pinky, I guess names don't count, was a lousy hunter all his life. One time he caught a gopher and ran up our apartment stairs with it. He placed it in his dish, where he was fed, because that was orderly, and of course the gopher got up at once and ran off. Tony felt that things belonged in their places, being an obsessively tidy person, his enormous collection of books and records was arranged in the same way—each object in its proper place, and a proper place for each object. He should have tolerated more chaos in the universe. However, he caught the gopher and ate it all, except the teeth.[24]

When Dick became ill with pneumonia in 1972 and 1973, Pinky attended him in bed. "When the pain was really bad, Pinky used to lie on my body until I realised that he was trying to figure out which part of me was sick. He knew it was just one part, around the middle of my body. He did his best and I recovered but he did not. That was my friend" (Sutin, *Shifting Realities*, p. 27). Like Vonnegut's, this is humor so piercing that it can bring tears to the eyes. Around this time, Phil had a vision of death's arrival in his apartment that terrified him into repeated prayerful Latin ejaculations, to his wife Tessa's irritation. Of course death had not come for Phil, not that time. He transforms this recollection (if that is what it is; if he has not invented it wholesale), in chapter 26 of *Radio Free Albemuth*:

Lying in my place on the bed I realised that no one could see the pale light but me; Pinky dozed, Rachel dozed, Johnny snored in his sleep . . . it filled all spaces equally and made every object strikingly clear. What is this? I wondered, and a deep fear filled me. It was as if the presence of death had entered the room.

The light became so bright that I could make out every detail around me. The slumbering woman, the little boy, the sleeping cat—they seemed etched or painted, unable to move, pitilessly revealed by the light. And in addition something looked down at us as we lay as if on a purely two-dimensional surface; something which travelled and made use of three dimensions studied us creatures limited to two . . .

We were being judged, I realised.[25]

That perspectival shift, that top-down view of himself and his loved ones, is commonly reported in near-death experiences. Psychologists such as Susan Blackmore explain it as unusual access to a partial perceptual construct of self and surrounds, perhaps related to the celebrated two-and-a-half dimension model of vision proposed by cognitive scientist David Marr (*Vision*). We form, in inaccessible and hence normally unconscious parts of our visual imaging systems, a kind of wire-frame portrait or composition of our immediate universe, and orient ourselves in it by reference to other sensory inputs: the kinaesthetic cues from the muscles, the balance mechanism of the inner ear, the depth cues and inferences of the eyes, differential access to the sounds around us. Lying near sleep or dazed by injury, motionless, it is possible to become momentarily aware of this inner sketch, to find oneself decoupled from the constructed sense of immersion in solidity. The out-of-body illusion tells us we are gazing down from the ceiling or wafting about the room. In the absence of feedback from the empirical world, fantasy and confabulation start to create their illusive narratives. For a mind primed for Gnostic wonders and terrors, it is not altogether surprising, perhaps, to see death enter the room, or perhaps even an eye-slotted, steel-toothed visage glaring from the heavens.

Most interesting to us as readers of fiction, of course, is what Philip K. Dick did with these perceptual aberrations. Their causation is intriguing, and the more we know about it the better placed we are to evaluate their oracular significance (unless mystical truth is delivered from a higher power via a malfunctioning temporal lobe), but finally what is important, as always, is the text, the writing, the reading and re-reading. Phil Dick had privileged access to the transreal condition, probably due to a damaged but brilliantly inventive and comic brain; it is through his imaginary worlds, and the often charmingly winsome words he used to notate them for us—flapples, police occifers, apteryx-shaped buildings—that we can recover what is most valuable in his work: its transrealist transform of his pain, his witty strange running commentary on experience quotidian and bizarre, his *heart*. Which failed him in so many ways and finally killed him.

EASY TRAVEL TO OTHER PLANETS

It might seem that choosing two god-dazzled crypto theologians, Dick and Rucker, as the prime exemplars of transrealism is simply shooting fish in a barrel. On the one hand, both Dick and Rucker are patently writers with unusual access to the inner cartoons and constructional apparatus of the mind, so their quotidian routine, transcribed, already possesses a joltingly odd-ball character. On the other hand, both make no bones about drawing almost nakedly on their biographies.

Certainly in Dick's case, this becomes clearer with every memoir and published study of his half century of life. In *The Search for Philip K. Dick, 1928–1982,* Phil's third wife (who still calls herself Anne R. Dick) acknowledges her own astonishment when she grasped just how undisguised his fictional versions could be. "I re-read all his novels and stories through twice in chronological order—sometimes laughing out loud with delight as they took me back in time to the late fifties and early sixties. I realized those books were autobiographical—unbelievably revealing—and packed with the everyday detail of our lives." (p. 2). Nor were these moments of recognition found only in the mainstream novels; close and emotionally charged observation of his own life and that of the people he loved and hurt are exactly what energizes Phil Dick's imaginative trash-boilers, enabling them to speak to us as only transrealist writing can do.

Still, the question remains: Is this claim so startling? What else would you expect? Anne Dick's memoir is introduced by Benjamin Gross, M.D., a retired psychiatrist and Fromm Professor of Literature and Psychology at the University of San Francisco. He offers the rather tired observation that the people, places and incidents in Phil's life were "filtered through his creative imagination" to be transformed into fiction, unsurprisingly since "all fiction writing is, of course, autobiographic. It is simply a matter of how much disguise the author, consciously or otherwise, introduces into the work" (p. vii). Quite, but work produced within the straitjacket of commercial genre requirements needs no great effort of disguise; the pieces are at hand, the main features of the narrative landscape are laid out in advance; the game can proceed with no greater intimate revelation than a game of Monopoly—a trope borrowed ingeniously, but without great depth, in Dick's own 1962 novel *The Game Players of Titan.* Both Rucker and Dick break free of rote, to the extent that they do, exactly by insinuating the fractal chatter of Real Reality (TM), its skirmishing and inconsistencies and multiple self-similar levels, into the often constrained and formulaic inventions of their chosen mode.

Dick's use of his own life-world and its inhabitants, both faithfully transcribed and warped or shaped to his artistic purposes, has become increasingly and painfully clear with Anne Dick's interviews, conducted after Phil's death among his school friends, some of the *Scanner Darkly* survivors (including Kathy and Linda), other wives, former lovers, adult male friends. The parallels are abundant, and while allowance needs to be made for Anne's own grinding axes and defensiveness, the shadings are patently colored to Dick's advantage. Introducing the first of his mainstream novels to achieve publication, *Confessions of a Crap Artist,* Paul Williams observed: "The reality of Philip Dick's characters stems quite simply from the fact that they are real to him; he hears them talking, in his mind, and records their conversations and thought—his dialogue, in almost all his novels, is excellent."[26] And the reason they are real to him is that quite often they *are* real: Kleo readily identified in several novels people she and Phil had known, such as "Mary" in *The Broken Bubble*, who "really existed . . . she taught Philip about sex. Philip was in love with her for a short time" (Anne Dick, *Search*, p. 342), not a particular distinguishing feature. His boss Herb Hollis and work-mates at University Radio are represented in many of the sf novels, as is Anne's former father-in-law who appears as Leo Bulero (in *Palmer Eldritch*) and other confident businessmen and wheeler-dealers. Dick confirmed this in a *Science Fiction Review* interview. Asked if he allowed his characters to write their own stories, rather than controlling them, he stated:

I try to remember—I write dialogue and develop scenes—how my friends did talk, and what they did say, and how they did behave, and how they did interact with one another, and the jokes they played on each another, and the games they played with one another, and so on . . . The last thing I want to do is put my ideas into their mouths . . . [that would be] furthest from the authentic thing that I want to achieve. So, although I write idea novels, I'm concerned more with the person facing the idea . . . [27]

Still, what is it that motivates this transform into *science fiction* rather than some other ideative mode or mimetic realism *simpliciter*? It is insufficient to point to Dick's many failed efforts to gain mainstream publication and success. He himself knew the *sui generis* value for his work of sf. Toward the end of his truncated life, he wrote in a freeform and rather self-mythologizing introduction to a short-story collection, *The Golden Man* (1980), that his incentive might be rage against the heedless cruelty of a God that had permitted so many of his friends to die, and horribly:

I want to write about people I love, and put them in a fictional world spun out of my own mind, not the world we actually have because the world we actually have does not meet my standards. Okay, so I should revise my standards, I'm out of step. I should yield to reality. I have never yielded to reality. That's what SF is all about. If you wish to yield to reality, go read Philip Roth; read the New York literary establishment mainstream best-selling writers. But you are reading SF and I am writing it for you. I want to show you, in my writing, what I love (my friends) and what I savagely hate (what happens to them).[28]

More than personnel are lifted from reality; the drag of entropy that assails the typical Phildickian landscape tore repeatedly at his own domestic situation. (As it does, too, by the way, in Philip Roth's fiction; plainly it is uncharitable and perhaps imperceptive of Dick to deny Roth's work its powerful challenge to status quo reality.) When his marriage to Anne was in its final crisis, "everything in the house was breaking. The dishwasher broke, the oven broke, one of the burners on the range broke, the washer-drier broke (although it was always breaking), the couch springs suddenly sagged to the floor—the whole house was falling to pieces" (Anne Dick, *Search*, p. 126). The Tomb World was no longer just a category from Biswanger's existential psychiatry; it was the dismal tenor of their decaying lives. As his life deteriorated over the next decades, the disarray of his own sexual and emotional being took odd turns. Talking to Joan Simpson, a mid-30s psychiatric social worker he took up with in 1977, Phil remarked "that, of the older girls, he'd always loved Jayne the best. It was Jayne he should've married, not Hatte. When Joan told me this in 1983, "Anne noted, we both looked at each other with a kind of amazed horror" (p. 252). The unusual co-dependency relationships and loathingly endured marriages of his fiction are all too plainly reworkings and pleas for mitigation, or perhaps simply self-centered reconstructions, based quite closely on his complex lived reality. That provides the *realist* half of his transrealist project; it is his wry, endlessly playful and inventive imagination that does the work of fantastical *trans*formation, making his oeuvre very much than a coded case history.

It also provides the key to the obverse side of transrealism, the need for, and preeminent value of, just those gaudy, trashy science fictional tropes and gadgets, all the narrative devices and opportunities of the sf megatext that are excluded from mundane fiction. Dick is the classic instance demonstrating how denuded his textuality became—however gratifying, in its own terms, it remains—when he attempted traditional or literary forms. His numerous mainstream novels, almost all of them now in print, possess a *reduced* reality, oddly enough. Mackey comments:

His style is still economical and distinctive, and his characters are beset by the same kinds of unhappy marriages and restless questing for meaning ... we find in his science fiction. . . . His characteristic humor and irony remain, if in somewhat muted form, but one has the feeling he has had to rein in his normally uninhibited and outrageous imagination in order to adapt his vision to the mainstream's conception of ordinary reality. (*Philip K. Dick*, p. 31)

Perhaps Dick had been spoiled (in both senses) by his early free access to the demented and excessive stage sets and narrative toolbox of sf. Other, later writers—Vonnegut, Pynchon, Barth, all the slipstreamers—found ways to enrich their literary heritage without falling headlong into the genre's candied phantasmagoria. Those writers with the sheer ability to move and release sophisticated readers beyond sf's inevitably somewhat childish half-world, wordsmiths as talented as Theodore Sturgeon, Damon Knight, Algis Budrys, Dick himself, seem to have found themselves trapped (to borrow a metaphor from current evolutionary theory) on a suboptimal peak in the fitness landscape of narrative space. Species often evolve certain adaptations that cannot be abandoned without cost, blocking superior moves in a kind of notional "fitness space": insects, for instance, cannot grow very large without throttling themselves, such is their basic design. Stuart A. Kauffman, investigating the origins of order and novelty in evolution, makes the very general point that "Boolean network space is full of local optima which trap adaptive walks. . . . Adaptation via fitter variants in network space becomes grossly hindered by the rugged structure of the landscape. Walks become frozen into small regions of the space."[29] Perhaps sf writers tend to doom themselves to a kind of pinched-off narrative spacetime, almost by definition unavailable to most readers who fear its singularity and isolation. It is a rather Dickian conceit.

Bruce Gillespie, one of the first commentators to understand the richness and value of Philip K. Dick's fiction, finds his non-sf at once thinner and too painful. Discussing *The Man Whose Teeth Were All Exactly Alike*, Gillespie remarks that without sf's metaphors to transform its "intensely detailed account of the battle between two families" it seems "too painful to read. One feels that there should be a filter between such emotional reportage and the reader . . . no general truth can be derived from such painful separate truths."[30] Still, of *Mary and the Giant*, Gillespie asserts: "Even Flaubert could not give a more accurate portrait of small-time people trying to be big-time. . . . Phil Dick committed himself to putting on paper the life of his own time—and nobody wanted to publish him" "The Non-Science Fiction Novels of Philip K. Dick," p. 4). He was a dirty realist *avant le lettre*, although lacking, as Gillespie notes, the lyrical gifts of an Anne Tyler or Raymond Carver.

The merit of Dick's non-sf, then, is that all action springs from character, rather than from externalized menace (precognitive doom, robotic simulacra, slime molds from outer space, the crushing pressure of entropy itself). Against Kim Stanley Robinson's claim that the non-sf novels lack Dick's saving and wonderful humor, Gillespie asserts the contrary: this is "the humour of incongruity" which "springs from the inconsistency between the way people see themselves and the way they seem to other people and, of course, the much-amused author"(p. 5). One might add that Dick's special gift is a portrayal of transactional lapse, the sort of effect that made Harold Pinter's name around the same time: the syncopes, gaps, evasions between uttered sentences, the decisions taken after agonies of doubt only to be rescinded in an instant, to a background dirge of shruggingly humorous despair.

Yet, as Gillespie notes acutely, drawing upon biographical detail in Sutin, the deep, strange truth of Dick's perception of the world is better located in his apparently fanciful sf than in the meticulous mimetic renderings of his small-town or suburban non-sf. "Behind ordinary life in an ordinary American town lies something else altogether. . . . What we

find in *Time Out of Joint* is that the bits and pieces of a science fiction su-
perstructure, which gradually invade Ragle Gumm's consciousness, are
actually more autobiographical, more real to the author than the accurately drawn worlds he presents in the non-sf novels" ("The Non-Science
Fiction Novels of Philip K. Dick," p. 8). This is precisely the effect of
transrealism and perhaps implies why it is not the narrative tool for all
writers. A certain dislocation from consensus reality in the originating
experience is needed, a detachment and even a somewhat delirious reworking that cannot be willed but needs to be known autonomously,
from within. Transrealism is, after all, as Rucker suggests, a species of
transcendental biography.

How can this recipe be distinguished from surrealism, or from the random or archetypal world-rewritings of the drug addicted and the insane?
By its ironic and playful devotion to the consensus (if glacially or catastrophically mutable) realities of science. Again, we face a kind of paradox. Why did Dick's mainstream novels fail to sell, let alone make his
literary name? Because, Gillespie claims, "in them Dick was constantly
pulling back from what he really wanted to say. This constraint improved his formal style, and the non-sf novels have little of the melodramatic flourished that threaten to destroy so many of the sf novels. But
having learned his craft, of showing the underlying reality of things
through surface appearances, Dick had trained himself to write the sf
novels, in which he could tell his own truth" ("The Non-Science Fiction
Novels of Philip K. Dick," p. 9). The downside, the failure, of Dick's own
oeuvre is perhaps that in the end he lost touch with any respect for the
consensus world beyond his own idiosyncratic truth, which after all is
not true—there is no cosmic artificial intelligence governing our lives, the
Roman Empire actually *has* ended (even if new perfidies have replaced
it), the antic novelties of a mind under extreme stress—exactly the material of the surrealists—do not best account for the profound machineries of the world.

NOTES

1. George Turner, ed., *The View from the Edge: A Workshop of Science Fiction
Stories with Vonda McIntyre and Christopher Priest* (Melbourne: Norstrilia Press,
1977), p. 7.

2. John Clute, "Dick, Philip K.," in *The Encyclopedia of Science Fiction*, ed. John
Clute and Peter Nicholls (London: Orbit, 1993), pp. 329–30.

3. John Fowles, *The French Lieutenant's Woman* (London: Granada 1971),
p. 346.

4. Philip K. Dick, "The Tagore Letter," in *The Shifting Realities of Philip K.
Dick: Selected Literary and Philosophical Writings*, ed. Lawrence Sutin (New York:
Vintage, 1995), pp. 314–15.

5. Rudy Rucker, *Master of Space and Time* (1984; New York: Baen Books, 1985), pp. 224–25.

6. Dick in Bruce Gillespie, ed., *Philip K. Dick: Electric Shepherd* (Melbourne: Norstrilia Press, 1975), pp. 31–32.

7. Douglas A. Mackey, *Philip K. Dick* (Boston: Twayne, 1988), p. 23.

8. George Turner in Gillespie, *Philip K. Dick*, p. 48.

9. See my entry "Postmodernism and SF" in *The Encyclopedia of Science Fiction*, ed. John Clute and Peter Nicholls (London: Orbit, 1993), p. 950, and the more extensive discussion, with notes and sources, in my *Reading by Starlight* (London: Routledge, 1995).

10. Dick in Gillespie, p. 45.

11. Sutin, *Shifting Realities*, pp. 337–50.

12. Philip K. Dick, *The Dark-Haired Girl*, ed. Paul Williams (Willimantic, CT: Mark V. Ziesing, 1988), pp. 60–61. This posthumous work is an ensemble of letters and dreams by Dick from about 1972, plus two lengthy speeches he prepared on the topics of androids versus humans and the problem of authenticity.

13. Gillespie, personal communication, 26 January 1999.

14. Istvan Csicsery-Ronay Jr., "The Wife's Story," *Science Fiction Studies* 24, Part 2 (July 1997): p. 330.

15. Philip Dick, "Notes," in *Beyond Lies the Wub*, Vol. 1 (London: Gollancz, 1988), p. 403.

16. See, for example, the several volumes by or edited by Lawrence Sutin devoted to Dick's life and work, especially his *Divine Invasions: A Life of Philip K. Dick* (New York: Harmony Books, 1989); *In Pursuit of Valis: Selections from the Exegesis* (Novato, CA: Underwood-Miller, 1991); and *Shifting Realities* (1995), and the other biographical material by other hands such as Dick's sometime literary executor Paul Williams (*Selected Letters of Philip K. Dick*, 5 vols. (Novato, CA: Underwood-Miller, 1991—), Gregg Rickman (*To the High Castle: Philip K. Dick: A Life 1928–1962* (London Beach, CA: Fragments West/The Valentine Press, 1989), etc., cited in those volumes.

17. In his 1976 speech "Man, Android, and Machine," in Sutin, *Shifting Realities*, p. 213.

18. Personal communication, 5 February 1999.

19. Dick, *The Dark-Haired Girl*, p. 197.

20. Philip K. Dick, *A Scanner Darkly* (New York: Ballantine, 1977), p. 20.

21. Rickman, *To the High Castle*, pp. 58–59.

22. Gregg Rickman, "*What Is This Sickness?*, Schizophrenia and *We Can Build You*," in *Philip K. Dick: Contemporary Critical Interpretations*, ed. Samuel J. Umland (Westport, CT: Greenwood Press, 1995), p. 146.

23. Personal communication.

24. "Memories Found in a Bill from a Small Animal Vet" (1976), in Sutin, *Shifting Realities*, 26–27.

25. Philip K. Dick, *Radio Free Albemuth* (1985; New York: Avon, 1987), pp. 177–78.

26. Philip K. Dick, *Confessions of a Crap Artist* (New York: Entwhistle Press, 1975), p. x.

27. Daniel DePrez, "An Interview with Philip K. Dick," *Science Fiction Review* (September 1976): 9.

28. Introduction to *The Golden Man*, reprinted in Sutin, *Shifting Realities*, p. 86.

29. Stuart A. Kauffman, *The Origins of Order: Self-Organization of Selection in Evolution* (Oxford: Oxford University Press, 1993), p. 214.

30. Bruce Gillespie, "The Non-Science Fiction Novels of Philip K. Dick," p. 9.

Rudy Rucker and the Future of Transrealism

[T]here are so many phenomena, even in physics, that are imperfectly understood, at least for the time being, that there is no reason to try to imitate the natural sciences when dealing with complex human problems. It is perfectly legitimate to turn to intuition or literature in order to obtain some kind of non-scientific understanding of those aspects of human experience that cannot, at least at present, be tackled more rigorously.
—Alan Sokal and Jean Bricmont, *Intellectual Impostures* (p. 178)

Rudy Rucker's fiction, especially the thematically linked narratives he identifies explicitly as transrealist, bears comparison to many of Phil Dick's novels and stories. A more obvious echo is from Robert Sheckley (and even the best of that high-production, unjustly neglected entertainer Keith Laumer, before his tragic decline). Simon Ings, discussing the retrospective short-story collection *Transreal!*, notes the risk run by his distinctive method: "Rucker finds his formula early, conveying mathematical extrapolation as American collegiate farce. . . . The breezy, dirty form he has developed could only handle a handful of core concepts."[1] Harsh as it is, there is some truth in this dismissive estimate.

Felix Rayman, the Rucker look-alike in his first published novel *White Light* (1980), spends much of his time out-of-body, whizzing around his tiresomely provincial upstate New York town but more significantly racing through the afterlife in search of the Absolute. What he finds is an endless comic strip, resembling the Donald Duck and Unca Scrooge adventures that one episode turns into, or the consumer landscape gone feral that Dick evokes in work like *The Ganymede Takeover* (co-written with Ray Nelson):

A dayglow orange unicorn reared up with seven soldiers impaled on his horn like so many unpaid bills, and a man-eating plant with an Oxford accent sucked dry one spinal column after another with a sound like a rude boy trying to suck up the last drop of a milkshake. . . . A brave band of lawnmowers and growling laundromat machines executed a brilliant flanking movement and attacked from the rear.[2]

Perhaps that indifferently written surreal battle scene owes something, as well, to William Burroughs, or even Henry Miller. Here is Rucker's version, tea on the infinite lawn of the transfinite Hilbert Hotel, where creatures from all possible universes gather for refreshment and conversation:

There was a table of rubbery carrots eating a rabbit stew. Then a whole group of liquid creatures in buckets connected by soda-straws . . . I saw two toads who took turns swallowing each other whole . . . At the table next to us a party of red-orange lawn-mowers were roaring their choppers around as the waiter set down a square yard of trembling purple sod and a quart of motor oil. (Rucker, *White Light*, pp. 92, 98)

Dick and Nelson normalize their phantasmagoria, since their scene is part of an hallucinogenic battlefield experience. Rucker carries the conceit a step further, for his events must be taken at face value (unless Felix is having a breakdown, or restlessly sleeping off a drunk, or smoking weed). These Escher fancies and Lewis Carroll pranks are literally *how it is* in the larger world beyond our limited space-time continuum. In the protocyberpunk sequence begun by *Software*, hallucinated perceptual and cognitive warpage is augmented by an increasingly fluid cast of biological robots, culminating in "moldies" who are artificial intelligences coded into alga-doped plastics, remarkably metamorphic, at once comic and sexually perverse. The most extreme manifestation of ontological fluidity in this series of novels is Shimmer, the physical manifestation of an extragalactic entity whose customary *Weltbild* has two time dimensions. This enhanced spacetime continuum allows the freeware alien and her kind a genuine extension of consciousness and choice, moment by moment, across all possibilities "from maybe to what-if" (*Freeware*, p. 261).

Astute as always, John Clute observes that for Rucker, despite being hailed as a cyberpunk pioneer, "the experience of living in a game-like world was much less important than the exercise of understanding its nature" (Clute, "Rucker, Rudy," p. 1033). The obvious sources of his effervescent narrative knickknacks are Carroll, Edwin A. Abbot's *Flatland*, Charles H. Hinton's researches into the fourth dimension, the mathematical conundrums of set theory (Rucker's first professional field) especially as explored by Gregor Cantor and Kurt Gödel. Cantor makes a personal appearance in *White Light*, which carries the subtitle—rather startlingly, in a pulp adventure format—*What is Cantor's Continuum Problem?* (The novel's imprint page notes that it "was written at the Mathematics Institute of the University of Heidelberg, with the financial support of the Alexander von Humboldt Foundation," where Rucker, his wife and three children lived for two years—funded by the German government, perhaps to its surprise.) Gödel is figured as the "moldie" genius Gurdle (and his lineage through to Gurdle-7), inventors of the Gurdle Decryption that permits aliens encoded into cosmic rays to be unpacked out of "Hilbert space prisms with gigaplex nontrivial axes" (*Freeware*, p. 247), a trope elaborated in *Saucer Wisdom*.

For Felix Rayman, too, the Cantorian quest for the highest infinity is no abstraction, fit for a dissertation or paper. Out-of-body, sent to a transcendental realm called Cimön in a kind of Dantean quest by the Devil and Jesus (perhaps in a rerun of Job's torments, construed as a Quixotic adventure penned by Franz Kafka on a happy day), Rayman voyages up the transfinitely endless slopes of Mount On. "In set theory," Rucker says, ' "On' is the name of the class of all ordinal numbers. Technically 'On' itself can also be thought of as a number, the largest possible infinity."[3] Its immense peak—and the vast Dreamland glacier where mortal souls romp or cringe in sleep, the spherical sea at the base of this inconceivably vast thermometer, and the infernal flames roaring below it—is topped by a white inferno, at once Absolute Infinity and Absolute Zero. Rene Daumal's unfinished 1944 story "Mount Analogue: A Novel of Symbolically Authentic Non-Euclidean Adventures in Mountain Climbing" is an acknowledged influence, but whereas Daumal's story breaks off at the start of the ascent, Rayman's seems likely never to end. He visits both ultimate Infinity and Zero, taking in the loathsome trash dump community Truckee along the way, accompanied by the floridly articulate beetle Franx (from whose crippled back he kindly scoops a rotting apple) and Kathy, a discorporate soul entrusted to his care by Jesus, whom he fails, and who finally infests his own earthly body, with disastrous consequences.

It sounds like the stuff of a medieval morality play, or perhaps a radio serial by Douglas Adams; in fact, tropes can be found here, as in Sheckley and Dick, that many years later wildly enriched more than one media success (perhaps by independent rediscovery). The closing chapters of *White Light* resemble a rather cleverer and much better informed version of the lively movie *Ghostbusters*. Rayman and his jaded small college scientist buddies inveigle "bloogs" or wandering aether creatures (their name, tellingly, is borrowed from Dr. Seuss) into a kind of ghost-trap, squeezing them into miraculous hypermatter spheres that can be sectioned endlessly into identical copies of themselves, since they have aleph-one components (an order of infinity greater than the kind you get by counting forever). In a movie, this would be just a zany invention— a kind of "flubber," say. For Rucker the mathematician, it is an artful application of the 1924 theorem of Banach and Tarski (*White Light* could as easily be titled *Gödel, Escher, Banach*), refined in 1947 by Raphael Robinson. This is the science part of a science fiction novel, and like the brilliant meditations of Douglas Hofstadter it informs while amusing.[4]

What made Rucker's novel startlingly fresh, in 1980, was the tincture of domestic *angst* it unobtrusively added to the standard slick Sheckleyan blend. Like Kafka's Gregor Samsa who classically metamorphoses into a beetle (it is perhaps no accident that FeliX mirrors FranX), Rayman is part of a family, albeit one under considerable stress. Repeatedly, if somewhat superficially, we share the domestic tensions between Felix and his long-suffering, irritated, sexy wife April, and his sentimental but palpable and convincing love for his baby daughter Iris.

Notoriously, science fiction novels have been "peopled" by characters without convincing homes, without much in the way of childhood, work history, emotional entanglements, certainly without children of their own. This thinness has been remedied in the last couple of decades, but sf's brutal generic abolition of personal histories from most of its figuration has been a distressing absence at the heart of the mode's slow accretion. It is a hole in the megatext you could drive a literary revolution through; many newer writers are doing just that. We need to recall how matters stood in the 1960s and 1970s to understand how eye-opening, how liberating, were these early transrealist bids by writers such as Dick and Rucker, for all the indifferent quality of their writing (much of the time), their ad hoc characterization, still trapped by Carrollian or van Vogtian allegory, or routine misogyny, or sheer untutored inability to break completely the boundaries of the field's dehumanized conventions.

LIFE AS A FRACTAL IN HILBERT SPACE

Like Philip K. Dick, Rucker is exercised by mystical apprehensions. The notable American mathematician and systems analysis theoretician John L. Casti, who lives in Vienna (but makes a point of noting that he has never met Rucker), declares: "When it comes to the matter of machines, minds, and souls, Rucker is a mystic of the first rank."[5] In part this is surely constitutional, in part a side effect of his occasional sampling of mind-and mood-altering substances (until he turned 50 he was a heavy drinker, and like Rayman a pot-smoking head), in part perhaps simply an outcome of his mathematical concerns. In *Mind Tools: The Five Levels of Mathematical Reality* (1987), which its jacket blurb modishly calls the "first popular book about postmodern mathematics," Rucker takes a stand that resembles his program for fiction: "Simple models are useful, but in the long run, mathematicians find it too galling to settle for approximations to reality. The ultimate dream . . . is to find a wholly abstract model for reality in all its richness. Whether or not they realize it, most mathematicians subscribe to Plato's notion that the physical world is but the shadow of the pure world of ideas" (Rucker, *Mind Tools*, p. 156). Rucker the Platonist takes our observable universe to be a low-dimensional projection or shadow of an Ur-reality of higher dimensionality—perhaps of transfinite dimension, like the complex-number Hilbert space used by physicists to analyze quantum theory. Mount On is a cartoonish projection in the contrary direction, a simplified model, in an amusing picaresque sf novel, of the infinitely vast fractal reality of the inaccessible noumenon that so frightened and exhilarated Phil Dick. Fractals, or noninteger dimensions such as 1.80372 rather than the customary 1, 2, 3, or 4, measure shapes that fold into indefinitely complex structures, forms that are self-similar at greater and lesser degrees of magnification. So a coastline twists and kinks when seen from the air, just as its beaches and cliffs do at ground level, as does the smallest bumpy edge of water-eroded rock at the shore. Rucker once envisaged a fractal biography, a new kind of text made possible by the inhumanly accurate memory storage of computers. In *Saucer Wisdom* he calls it a lifebox: "your recollections aren't linear; they're a tangle banyan of branches that split and merge. The lifebox uses hypertext links to hook together everything you tell it. Then your eventual audience can interact with your stories, interrupting and asking questions. The lifebox is almost like a simulation of you" (*Saucer Wisdom*, p. 56).

This fantasy proposes a machine-readable archive of endlessly embedded descriptions, footnotes within footnotes all the way down. It is a conceit found earlier in John Barth's slipstream novel *Giles Goat-Boy* (1966), where a parodic version of a formal university lecture is repeatedly annotated in just this way, using Hold and Gloss buttons (pp. 400–409). A textualized fractal life would resemble a garden of search trees, each trunk searchable for data and connections at the level of branch, subbranch, twig, forever. Later, when he moved into programming, Rucker revised this model to include *cellular automata* or CAs, "a kind of multidimensional grid of little cells that carry out interacting computations in parallel. Of course there's no grid in the real world, so the definition of a CA would have to be changed to make it more like a coral reef," cells connected to their neighbors; one thinks, inevitably, of the neural net of a human brain.[6] This view of the world as a giant automata calculation in Hilbert space, a Platonic world of Forms that ontologically precedes appearances in our experience, clearly lends itself to the mystical. That does not imply an evasion of the flesh and its urgencies, its joys and terrors and sorrows, a common and ignorant dismissal of mysticism (and cyberpunk). Rucker notes:

I think that any view of reality should include the mental element as well as physical space and time. And there's a real sense in which our minds inhabit a world of inconceivably many dimensions. But all the science can easily miss the immediacy of how the world feels. At an immediate level, reality is very gnarly and very novelistic. It's a supreme work of art, inconceivably rich. And we'll never know any final answers. ("37 Questions")

The fruitful equivocation between life, science and art is expressed by Alwin Bitter, a demiurge figure, in *Master of Space and Time*, who provides as well an intriguing link between a decentered pandemonium model of the self and the necessary plurivalence and openness of enduring art: "An individual is a bundle of conflicting desires, a society in microcosm. Even if some limited individual were seemingly to take control of our universe, the world would remain as confusing as ever. If *I* were to create a world, for instance, I doubt it would be any different from the one in which we find ourselves" (p. 40). This proves to be so in that novel, as it is in every narrative that escapes the subrealist or even the algorithmically realist algorithms ordained by strict genres (Derrida might argue: *indeed* in every narrative, *tout court*).

NOT EVERYTHING IS TRANSREALIST

Rucker's fiction, avowedly, does not all have this "transcendental autobiographical" character. His fictional work to date comprises several sets, two of which are not transrealist by intention. The *'Ware* tetralogy, *Software, Wetware, Freeware* and *Realware*[7] is the most notable of these: the first two early volumes are fairly described as protocyberpunk. The tetralogy's narrative arc concerns the emergence of early, self-reproducing robot intelligence on the Moon, the uploading of human consciousness into robot bodies or their storage in S-cubes and the revenge of various orders of artificial intelligence. *Master of Space and Time* and *The Hollow Earth* are independent novels. The table below provides a key to those of central interest, the avowedly transrealist books:

Transreal Series	Rucker Figure	Period of His life
The Secret of Life	Conrad Bunger	1963–67
Spacetime Donuts	Vernor Maxwell	1967–72
White Light	Felix Rayman	1972–78

Transreal Series	Rucker Figure	Period of His life
The Sex Sphere	Alwin Bitter	1978–80
The Hacker and the Ants	Jerzy Rugby	1986–92
Saucer Wisdom	Rudy Rucker	1992–97

To these might be added an explicitly autobiographical novel of the 1960s, *All the Visions*, indebted explicitly and formally to Jack Kerouac's stylistics and concerns, and very heavily harvested for narrative material in *The Secret of Life*, where the usual alienated Rucker figure proves to be literally a UFO construction built from the flesh of a slaughtered pig. And a version of Alwin Bitter, as noted previously, is also a figure in *Master of Space and Time*, so perhaps that also deserves to be included in the canon, if only marginally. But then so, too, perhaps, do the *'Ware* frolics, since crazed stoner Sta-Hi (later *noir*ish detective Stahn and later again Senator Mooney) "is based on a guy I used to hang out with, my own personal Neal Cassady."[8] Strictly, his "truly transreal books are only the books in which the main character is modelled on me" (Personal communication, 19 April 1995). This might be an unnecessarily restrictive proviso, as arbitrary and limiting as insisting upon first person narration or present continuous tense. Certainly, transrealist elements can be detected in most of Rucker's fiction.

SELF-FASHIONING

Rudolph von Bitter Rucker, apparently a great-great-great-grandson of Hegel, was born in Louisville, Kentucky, on 22 March 1946, a second son. His father Embry, for whom his 5-year-older brother is named, ran a small furniture-making business, later training for the Episcopalian clergy, taking orders when Rudy was in high school, and subsequently a parish priest. His mother Marianne, born in Germany, was an amateur artist. In 1963–67, Rucker majored in mathematics at Swarthmore College—*The Secret of Life* is a *bildungsroman* of those years, retrofitted from an early draft of *All the Visions* into a UFO story that only part way through proves to be science fictional when its protagonist learns to fly—and in 1967–72 took his Master's and Ph.D. at Rutgers University, New Brunswick, New Jersey, specializing in mathematical logic, with a thesis on Transfinite Set Theory. These topics would remain at the heart of his early professional life, as instructor, science popularizer, belated hipster mystic, and sf writer. He married Sylvia Bogsch at 21; between 1969 and 1974 they had three children (Georgia, Rudy Jr., and Isabel). For so unconventional a writer, this is a strikingly domestic record. Consider by contrast Philip K. Dick's rather shambolic multiple marriages and belated parenthood.

Rucker taught mathematics, including a Higher Geometry course, at the State University College at rainy, dull Geneseo, New York, memorialized unflatteringly as SUCAS in *White Light*. His serialized novel *Spacetime Donuts* (playing off the Rutgers years) started to appear in a semiprofessional sf magazine which died midstream, something of a harbinger. For 1978–80, the family moved to Heidelberg, where he wrote *Infinity and the Mind*, *White Light* and *Software*. (Both *Software* and a sequel, *Wetware*, won the Philip K. Dick Award for year's best paperback sf novel, and are accepted by some as early cyberpunk novels.) Back in the states, he found a post at Randolph–Macon Woman's College, in Lynchburg, Virginia (ironically the home seat of the Rev. Jerry Falwell), resigning in 1982 to try full-time writing. Despite a certain *succès d'estime* for his sf and popular science books, he moved the family to California and took a position at the San José State University (whose web site proudly declares it the Metropolitan University of Silicon Valley), where he started programming cellular automata (CAs). He became involved with R. U. Sirius and the other cyberenthusiasts at *Mondo 2000*, editing a book with them.

In 1988–92, his interest in CAs and a-life (genetic algorithms that mimic Darwinian processes in cyberspace) took him to John Walker's Autodesk in Sausalito, California, experience reflected in *The Hacker and the Ants*. Much of his recent professional work has involved software engineering, writing C++ code and other computer arcana, and documenting it, but his latest text is the distinctly transrealist *Saucer Wisdom* (1999). Not quite published as fiction (it is marketed as popular Science and Technology), it recounts his alleged experiences with UFO abductee Frank Shook. Beings literally coded into light, a variety of saucer aliens show Shook aspects of the world's and humanity's metamorphic future from the late 1980s to 4004 (mirror image, of course, of the fundamentalist Christian dating by Bishop Ussher for the creation of the universe). In this respect, Rucker says, it is "a Millennial work of future extrapolation." Many of its themes and much of its inventive and zany gadgetry had already appeared in *Freeware*, but perhaps this ambiguous text—the jacket also calls *Saucer Wisdom* a "nonfiction novel"—is Rucker's attempt to reach a mass audience unready for his wild and often transgressive fiction.

Perhaps most startlingly to those steeped in his tormented transrealist novels, Rudy and Sylvia are still married, a third of a century on, and despite his own gnostic and substance-assisted visionary bent, Rudy has evaded the threats to his sanity that snared Dick. " 'Not ending up like Phil,' " Rudy commented, "has always been one of my goals."[9]

The Hacker and the Ants (1994) parallels Rucker's move to California and his involvement with Autodesk, the ultimately failed enterprise founded by legendary programmer and polymath John Walker, who is parodied rather cruelly as Roger Coolidge, "a genius-level computer hacker, somewhat eccentric, and imbued with the self-confidence that came from having founded a Silicon Valley startup that had mush-roomed to a billion dollars in revenue in six short years. It was an honor for me to get to work so closely with him. Sometimes it was also a pain in the neck" (*Hacker*, p. 16). The nervy in-your-face candor of these nov-els, explicitly indebted to the fifties' Beats whom Rucker was half a gen-eration too young to join (Kerouac, Burroughs, Ginsberg), is no less confronting than Dick's bleeding if manipulatory reportage in *The Dark-Haired Girl* and *Valis*. Jerzy Rugby opens his tale with a burst of detes-tation for the Realtor (a sarcastic pun here, no doubt) trying to throw him out of the decaying home he now shares only with his protorobot Studly—a sentiment "of such intensity that had it been love, I would have proposed to marry her . . . it was my fervent wish . . . to crush her like a bug" (*Hacker*, p. 2). This is in some measure a displaced emotion, as we learn immediately: "Actually, I'd been feeling that way about lots of people lately. My wife Carol had left me two months ago, the bitch, and I was having trouble adjusting to life alone. One of our teenagers was at college, and the other two had gone with Carol, who was living with her boyfriend in a cheesy condo on the east side of the Valley" (*Hacker*, p. 2).

All writers are cannibals, this much is widely acknowledged; still, to be Rudy Rucker's spouse can never have been a comfortable assignment. The wife in *All the Visions, The Secret of Life* and *Saucer Wisdom* (where the protagonist steps forward under Rucker's own name) is "Audrey." In a footnote, Rucker tells us: "so as not to cause my wife unnecessary discomfort, I'm using a pseudonym for the first name of the *Saucer Wis-dom* character who (inadequately) represents her" (*Saucer Wisdom*, p. 22). Nor should *Hacker*'s transrealist divorce be read as a literal depiction with only the names barely changed. "Actually we never even came all *that* close to divorce," Rucker has commented, "though this was a period when we were fighting a lot." Rather, fiction provided a vicarious taste of freedom, "much as I've SFictionally tasted of things like superpow-ers."[10] Some reviewers protested his imaginary infidelity. "It's just words on paper, folks," Rucker retorts somewhat scornfully to such boorish literal-mindedness—but this is, for all that, a professional hazard of those drawing so visibly on the pulsing fluids in their own arteries. "Maybe by simulating it and doing a virtual walk-through in *The Hacker and the Ants*, I made it easier for me to stick it out till it got better again." That, of course, is another well-tested benefit of fictional transformation, for author and reader alike.

Still, much of the wounded detail of the hacker's anxious professional life is all-too-obviously a reworking of Rucker's time as an Autodesk programmer. Not only is proprietor Roger Coolidge an explicit rendering of his former employer, but Walker has amusingly published a further "chapter" of the novel on his web site www.fourmilab, in which Roger's pratfall death is rescinded and he is revealed as the novel's secret hero. Walker's house in Switzerland is the setting for Rucker's own closing scenes, sketched in accurate detail. Jerzy's "redeployment" letter from rival firm West West—following an earlier dismissal by GoMotion Incorporated for accidentally infecting the DTV fiberoptic television cable system with virus-like artificial life "ants"—directly copies the one Rucker got when he was sacked from Autodesk (*Hacker*, p. 194). Despite this tense background, he remains on good terms with Walker, who vets his books for scientific and technological accuracy, keeping his transrealism directed into the slipstream of science.[11]

IF YOU ASK, GOD WILL HELP YOU

John L. Casti's diagnosis of Rucker as "a mystic of the first rank" is one key to the disruptive impact of his fiction, especially when the headlong narrative rush is spliced to the dirty socks and dirty secrets and habits of its ruthlessly observed characters. A recurrent device is the throw-away epiphany or theophany. "It took almost an hour to ride the trip out. Towards the middle Stahn saw God. God was about the same as usual—a little more burnt, maybe. He wanted love as bad as Stahn did."[12] A "synchronicity drug" is "almost like being dead, but better" (*Wetware*, p. 85), a piercingly funny line that could perhaps only be uttered in a sf novel where uploading is a pragmatic choice. Even robots experience the Void. Ralph Numbers, the first AI to throw off the human constraints mockingly dubbed "asimov circuits," perishes repeatedly and is rebooted from his stored memories (which, inevitably, omit any recall of events later than the back-up). Shortly before one death, "a question came, and with it an answer ... an answer Ralph had found and lost thirty-six times before.

> *"What is this that is I?*
> *"The light is everywhere."* (*Software*, p. 29, ellipses and italics in original.)

Speaking in his own fictionalized persona in *Saucer Wisdom*, Rucker declares: "In my twenties and early thirties, I'd become interested in mysticism. I adopted the notion of a supernal yet immediate One Mind, a cosmic white light that shines through ordinary objects like sunlight through stained-glass windows." By his forties "my theories about mysticism had come to seem like a dry, academic game ... I was haunted by one of the last things my father had said to me before his stroke crippled him: 'Rudy, all I know about life is this: *you get old and you die*' " (*Saucer Wisdom*, p. 26, ellipses added). That opening chapter ends:

"finally, for the first time in years, I let myself pray. *Dear God, please be with me. Protect me and let me do your will*" (p. 26). Heartbreakingly, the final chapter gives Rudy a wish. "If I were going to lie to you, I'd claim that I wished I could see the aliens. But in fact I wished for something that lies deeper and closer to my heart: I wished to remain sober" (p. 274). The book ends in a curiously antique, prescientific affirmation, perhaps a desperate one:

"God is everywhere, and if you ask, God will help you.

"Wisdom enough." (p. 277)

A necessary wisdom, perhaps, even if delusional, for one in the life-long agony of a twelve-step recovery program (p. 193). Had Phil Dick followed his own theophanies into sobriety, perhaps some sequel to *Valis* might have ended with the same plea, the same expression of hope in external salvation—but of course for the mystic such salvation is always-already immanent as well as transcendent, since God is the white light illuminating our murky glass.

Some will find these intimations at once banal and dangerous, as ul-tratechnologies really do begin to carry us pell-mell into a future where immense power will be in the hands of individuals, where consciousness can be tweaked, warped, accelerated, simulated and detached. If trans-realism is a critical category suffused with the transcendent, as Rucker's coining of the term implies, it might have limited value for artists who aim at clear-eyed and clear-headed transformations of the real into heightened text. Perhaps, though, transrealism can escape this vortex, this tug toward the White Light. In Rucker's own oeuvre, it has done so from time to time. "As I say, it all came clear to me in 1972, and I got my enlightenment," avers Conrad/Rudy in *All the Visions*. "And now? Am I still enlightened? . . . I mean, now, I hear 'enlightenment', I think *fine, I'll have some*, but also am still thinking about like how to make some money, and how to get along with my wife and children . . . And come back to the office and write some more, and come home and love my family, fuck my wife, play with my children, try not to get drunk too often, stretch it out, piece it together, keep life going that much longer, see God now and then, and postpone death. It's a life" (*All the Visions*, pp. 61, 64). It is; exactly. It's a life.

ON AN ENDLESS ROLL

Half memoir, half fabulation, that belatedly published book has just the edgy, streetwise surface Rucker plainly aims for in all his work but is perhaps denied, usually, by the constraints of genre packaging. A beat *hommage*, it echoes *On the Road* in more ways than one. With just three paragraphs in its 125 pages of free-form, associative, compulsively read-able text, it is flavored by self-mockery:

And right now I'm writing down a lot of memories on a continuous roll of copier paper that I got from Leech & Hicks Office Supplies just over the Killeville hill from my office here, its a brisk stoned walk through negro streets of dawn in search of an angry fix (Rucker, *All the Visions*, p. 120).

True to the original, the paper he types on is

in a giant roll like paper towels, like the paper for a teletype machine such as the divine Jack K. used for the initial mindblast sevenday draft of *On the Road*, you wave, exactly like that paper, and I've got it rigged here in back of my dear old axe IBM Selectric, the paper is wrapped around a stout cardboard tube, and there happens to be similar tubing lying about the ruined abandoned building I rent . . . and you were right, so right, dear Jack, the endless jazz choruses unbroken by subliminal beat of the turd-counting page break . . . (P. 121)

(Of course, an irony must occur to any turn-of-millennium reader: this formerly radical novelty is now precisely the everyday condition, like it or not, of anyone who inscribes the endlessly scrolling virtual page of a word processor.)

Later, when Rucker mined this all-but-unpublishable prose poem for a novel with the typically self-derisory title *The Secret of Life*, he might have been playing on a discovery announced plainly in the chrysalis: "There are no secrets to life, there's just good stories, patterns in the fog. Of course something must lie beyond it, and sometimes you can feel it, although it's hard to put into words" (p. 77). At once banal and poignant, this announcement declares a necessary metaphysical faith in the same moment it speaks the secret of art, if not life: yes, it's hard to find the right shape—for the words, or the paint, or the melodic vibrations, or the dozen other media for the good stories. Rucker's own work frequently betrays a struggle with his medium, ranging from the embarrassingly clunky and slapdash to the radiant, exuberant, joyful and cruelly fecund, often next to each other in the same text. Especially in the earlier books, but also cropping up as late as the unimpressive *Saucer Wisdom*, word clumps can seem thrown down, or perhaps eked out on the page, with the stammered desperation of a tyro. Phrases seldom seen outside of writing school submissions are not uncommon. "Just then the badness of the situation became acute" (*Spacetime Donuts*, p. 172). The strange and alien are too often conveyed in artless lists of jumbled attributes: "She has a flesh-colored rose attached to one shoulder, an extra tongue in the hollow of her neck, a pair of long, lobsterlike feelers growing out of the left side of her head, a stout penis dangling from one side of her bare midriff, and what looks like insect mandibles on the backs of some of her knuckles" (*Saucer Wisdom*, p. 246). This is surely attributable to haste, since an early passage in *Secret* shows strikingly evocative skill. A page and a half closes chapter 3, set in January 1963, with Conrad Bunger a smart, solitary kid catching the raucous school bus home:

But then the bus pulled up anyway and they all ran through the rain and Conrad stepped in a puddle on purpose, and all the other bus guys were hurrying to get good seats. Conrad sat in back by himself, he felt so cut off and who gave a damn listening to the bus guys all excited about parties or cigarettes or getting drunk. He felt like a cold hand was grabbing his guts and squeezing them. The bus started moving and all the bus guys were shouting, not out of joy, but to get everyone to look at them, but nobody really noticed each other, except some of the guys who were really bugged about not making the scene were laughing at all the right times. Then the bus was really going, and Conrad was sitting at the window looking at the road all black shiny wet and being amazed at how humans move by going past stationary objects and not hitting them. (*Secret*, p. 25)

Clearly, Conrad is a cold-eyed guy fated to develop a taste for Sartre's *La Nausée* and for the young women who admire those who like it too. Rucker's ability to recapture a moment many of his bookish, alienated readers will recognize at once is not the most striking aspect of this passage, which is its source: originally in first person, it is very slightly reworked from his second published piece, "Bus Ride—December 20, 1962," from his Chevalier high school literary club fraternity magazine, *The Pegasus*, in 1963.[13] Not especially distinguishable from a thousand other high school annotations of *angst*, nonetheless it seems to promise a talent far more concerned with the detail and pain of everyday life, however abstracted into meditations of the laws of inertia and relative motion, than with gaudy visions of a lunar landscape crawling with rebellious boppers and stenchy imipolex moldies, with cellular automata ants on the rampage and hyperdimensional objects of lust, with trips downward to atomic scales and beyond, back to the known, dirty-sock universe itself.

Yet Rucker has a genuine ability to convey rich, zestful imagery in diverse and appropriate voices. The hip lunar robot Emul courts his beloved Berenice, who has learned her English from Poe's writings: " 'Berenice, life's a deep gloom ocean and we're lit-up funfish of demential zaazz, we're flowers blooming out till the loudsun wither and the wind blows our dead husks away. . . . It's so wonder wacky that we're here at all, swimming and blooming in the long gutter of time. . . . Come on home with me and spread, wide-hipped goldie sweet toot pots. Today's the day for love to love' " (*Wetware*, p. 34). Berenice is having none of it. A prom-queen among robots, she cools her ardent swain without quite rejecting him (since she means to blend her program with his in some future conjugation to produce a new bopper child). " 'So rashly sched-

uled a consummation would be grossly precipitate, dear Emul.' Her radio voice had a rich, thrilling quality. 'I have been fond of you, and
admiring of your complex and multifarious nature. But you must not
dream that I could so entangle the substance of my soul!' " (p. 34).

These impersonations are charmingly wrought and bear just the
weight they are meant to carry, if no more. Rucker's Dantean brush-
stroke picture of the robot's lunar crater Nest is similarly effective:

Cup-shaped and buffed to a mirror sheen, Maskeleyne G glittered in the sun's
hard radiation. At the focus of the polished crater was a conical prism that,
fourteen days a month, fed a vast stick of light down into a kind of mine shaft.
In the shaft's great, vertical tunnel, bright beings darted through the hot light;
odd-shaped living machines that glowed with all the colors of the rainbow. . . .
Boppers danced in and out of the light, feeding on the energy. The petaflops had
to be careful not to let extraneous light into their bodies; they had mirrored
bodyshells beneath their flickercladding. Their thoughts were pure knots of light,
shunted and altered by tiny laser crystals. (Pp. 31–32)

Part of the pleasure here is Rucker's knowing play on tropes both from
within and without the sf megatext, reaching into the general corpus of
Western literature and simultaneously toward and beyond recent scientific advances. For full effect, the reader needs some familiarity with
Kerouac and Poe, with computer terminology (a petaflop is a machine
processing information at a thousand trillion operations a second), with
the iconography of demons in hell and angels in heaven's divine light.
The very souls of these new machines are not just symbolically woven
of light and New Age crystals, but literally so, using optical processors
that shunt photons through laser gates. Here is all the delicious density
of sophisticated sf textuality. It is not, however, transrealist writing.

WHERE TWO OR THREE ARE GATHERED

Inevitably, though, Rucker's bent toward transrealist methods infuses
at least parts of the other fictions. The 'Ware novels contain more than
one familial network recognizably derived from the writer's own domestic circumstances and enriched by it. Rucker has declared "a transreal
element" in the tetralogy, especially in the account of Cobb Anderson,
father of bopperkind and a transform of Embry Sr. "At the end of *Realware* I feel like I've finally come to terms with my father, and with our
interactions, and with his death from a stroke in 1994," Rucker has commented. "It's a liberating feeling . . ." ("37 Questions"). Cobb, born in
1950, is by 2020 a "pheezer," a new breed of retiree, a "freaky geezer":
"barrel-chest, erect posture, strong arms and legs covered with curly
hair, a round white beard" (*Software*, p. 4). His relationship with daugh-

ter Ilse might strike readers as less interesting, from the transrealist perspective, than that of Stanley Hilary Mooney, zany doper Sta-Hi, troubled but finally mellow Stahn, born 1995, and his repressive father Stan, Sr., born in 1960, a Gimme cop. Stahn's own kids, Saint and Babs, born of his loving liaison with a mindless clone with a borrowed moldie soul, reflect the knowingness of a fond but not entirely sentimental parent. In a restaurant,

The kids broke apart with a flurry of screeches and pokes, and then both of them sat there calmly with their hands folded.

"It's Da's fault," said Saint.

"Da did it," added Babs.

"Da's bad," said Saint.

"Da's lifted and drunk," said Babs.

"Da has a drug problem," said Saint.

Stahn got the waitress and ordered himself a brandy and an espresso. "Anyone else for coffee or a drink? Anything? Dessert, kids?" (*Freeware*, p. 196)

Very little in science fiction, outside Philip Dick and those influenced by him, has this engaging, inveigling quality of life observed, keenly but with a measure of placid acceptance, from the inside.

So too with the family complex of Tre Dietz and his wife Terri Percesepe and their young children Dolf and Baby Wren. Tre writes advanced code, providing the key Perplexing Poultry multidimensional algorithms that allow Earth and Moon to be invaded by decrypted cosmic ray aliens. "While at UCSC, Tre smoked out, sought the spore, and transynchronized the Great Fractal, as did all his circle of friends—but Tre also managed to get a good grounding in applied chaos and in piezoplastics" (*Freeware*, p. 55). Laid back as he is, Tre is passionate about his work. When Terri is swallowed and kidnapped by a live robot, then flung toward the Moon, she manages to get a call in to her frantic husband back on Earth. Luckily, the moldies are prepared to ransom her, and Tre's associate ex-Senator Stahn is by now well-placed to effect the exchange. "He owes me big time," Tre tells his abducted wife. "Oh, Terri. I'm sorry I haven't been nicer to you. I love you so much." Moments later he says, "I'll talk to Stahn right away. And then I'm gonna jam some math. This stuff Emperor Staghorn came up with is pretty exciting." Surprisingly contained, or perhaps used to it, as Rucker's wife is doubtless accustomed to his own attention swings, Terri tells him uncomplainingly, "Take good care of the kids. . . . The view from here is stunning. I'd like to show it to them" (p. 150). In a "Doc" Smith space opera, such skiddy affect transitions are justly taken by sophisticated readers as proof that both writer and fans badly needed to get a life. In Rucker's hands, the fractured tonality is altogether more persuasive. Yes, this *is* the hacker mind, this *is* the fractal attention span of a man like Tre, and perhaps of Rucker himself. There are droll hints, for the watchful, of identification in play; an artificial construct named Jenny tells his wife: "Your husband's a real cutie, by the way, Terri. I bet he's such a good fuck" (p. 256).

AT THE CORE

Rucker's work is notable for its grounding in genuine mathematics and its wild but plausible extrapolations of current science and technology. Philip K. Dick, by contrast, knew little real science, and so his fiction is replete with absurdities—spaceships like recreational vehicles that even hard-up families can own and use to fly to a Mars that is not utterly inhospitable. Ironically, the most preposterous of his playful contrivances, the small pestish AIs, computerized cabs, "homeopapes" (rewritable news media) and so forth, once apparently even more laughably impossible than his space craft, are the very products we see emerging from the exponential success of today's computer industry. Of course, it is easy with Dick's work to allow that his narrative furniture is metaphoric, or *Dada*, that its purpose is zany delight or plot convenience, while his genuine issues are to be found in the transrealism with which he organizes his rich characters and their political surrounds. Rucker does not disagree with this emphasis: "all the science can easily miss the immediacy of how the world feels. At an immediate level, reality is very gnarly and very novelistic. It's a supreme work of art, inconceivably rich. And we'll never know any final answers" ("37 Questions").

Rucker's formally transrealist novels, starting with the clumsy if ingenious *Spacetime Donuts* and concluding, to date, with the jangling rawness of *Saucer Wisdom*, push his enquiry into biographical resonances more immediately identifiable, and perhaps reverberant, than those encoded in the rest. It is easier to find common ground with Conrad Bunger than with robot Ralph Numbers on the Moon, or Mason Algiers Reynolds, Virginia gentleman and unreliable narrator in the mid–nineteenth century (*The Hollow Earth*). Conrad, like some of the older of Rucker's readers, is growing up smart and out of place in late 1950s, early 1960s Louisville. "Heavy trip this noon," writes the other version of Conrad, in *All the Visions*, to his buddy Ace, "on realizing that now is future's nostalgia time—and everything grew in size until the radiator was a factory and I (heaviest favorite fantasy) a galaxy" (p. 39).

For Vernor Maxwell in *Spacetime Donuts*, this fantasy is just mundane fact. Using "The Geometrodynamics of the Degenerate Tensor" rather than a mantra or spell, his mentor Professor Kurtowski shrinks Vernor and his lover Alice so far—to microscopic, then atomic, then subquark scales—that they close the cosmic circle and emerge into a hypersphere metacosmos where galaxies are themselves the constituents of atoms. Shrinking cosmologically, they find themselves even larger than Conrad's dream galaxy, then smaller, and finally their transparent scale-ship craft is visible like a vast but diminishing moon above an Earth that, this being a Rucker novel and not some rewrite of Ray Cumming's *The Girl in the Golden Atom* (1922), they literally "fuck . . . into this Universe" (*Spacetime Donuts*, p. 131). Viewed from outside, "one could make out a pair of gods, naked and in each other's arms. Many a User's cock stiffened at the sight of a cunt the size of the Gulf of Mexico. Many a young girl's eyes sparkled at the sight of a cock the size of Florida. And for the first time in many years, the Users felt awe" (p. 135). This is good clean fun, of course, but not quite the unprecedented artistic achievement that Rucker's transrealist manifesto aims at.

That is approached more adequately in scenes equally uncommon in sf: Conrad's grubby way of going through the pockets of overcoats on a dance coat-rack, stealing money, gulping pilfered bourbon, stealing communion wine from his father's church, until he pukes, inevitably all over his date, enraging his disgusted parents (*The Secret of Life*, pp. 3–8). The transition from such commonplace but nicely photorealist scenes to the more baroque incidents of the novel—his levitations, his discovery that his true essence is a bar of alien light he can draw from his pig-meat body, his morphed appropriation of a disliked professor's appearance and life, his final time-halting teensploitation-movie triumph over campus enemies and space-time itself at the close—are effectively redeemed and enhanced by their gritty, shamelessly recorded naturalistic context.

And like Phil Dick's transrealist texts, Rudy Rucker's are often very funny. His humor ranges from slapstick and parody to relaxed, sardonic portraiture of his academic and Silicon Valley colleagues. *Spacetime Donuts* introduces sexually omnivorous, pharmaceutically adventurous Mick Stones—Rucker does not shrink from spelling it out—even as the Rolling Stones's "Gimme Shelter" plays on the sound system. The fourth and higher dimensions, hallowed in the mythology of Theosophists and New Age mystics, will never be the same after the burlesque of Alwin Bitter's priapic hyperspatial pursuit of the eponymous pheromone-exuding Sex Sphere from Hilbert space. Jerzy Rugby's jaundiced, harried career creating artificial life in a milieu not altogether alien to the software pioneer company Autodesk has a persuasive charm not easily invented from whole cloth, for all its exaggerations. Conrad Bunger, Vernor Maxwell, Felix Rayman, Alwin Bitter, Jerzy Rugby and even "Rudy Rucker," are comic inventions of some stature in a mode that is better known for its power/knowledge gambits than for its humor. (Although it has its own fertile tradition, writers mostly unknown in the larger literary world: Eric Frank Russell's anarchic buffoonery, Robert Sheckley's facile pranksterism, the more seductive wit of John Sladek, Thomas M. Disch, Dick himself, Stanislaw Lem and Kurt Vonnegut.)

Can transrealism move beyond this boisterous, wacky box of tricks? Perhaps *Saucer Wisdom* is Rucker's attempt to treat his fictive analogue more soberly, even somberly, as "Rucker" plays the straight-man to shady UFO abductee, visionary and half-mad Frank Shook. Futuristic inventions from the third and fourth of the *'Ware* novels reappear, in particular the "uvvy," a universal communicator permitting shared or merged thoughts and experiences, and the "alla," an anything-box or instantaneous replicator that can build what you wish using its stored quantum dot power and stock of algorithms. These are given a kind of technological filiation, as Frank is taken on a cat's cradle odyssey through parallel time, allowing him oracular glimpses of humanity's (and post-humanity's) next two thousand years. Copiously illustrated by Rucker's own pen renderings (the jacket rather hopefully calls them "delightful cartoon sketches"), these minimally dramatized expository lumps are re-lieved by a thin tale of Rudy's efforts to come to terms with this outra-geous testimony and its paranoiac, vexatious envoy. As a figure for the inventive thinking that propels sf, even if that thinking is construed as rationalized dreams or musings straight from the unconscious, the re-sulting catalog is simply inadequate, indeed misleading. Rucker did *not* get his madcap ideas by plagiarizing some feckless abductee—he made them up, perhaps with some effort. Here is his own informal account of its genesis:

My friend Mark Frauenfelder, editor of a zine called *bOING bOING* for which I wrote a regular column, got a job as an editor at *Wired* magazine, and then they put him on the staff of their new line, Wired Books. They had a lot of money and I had the idea of pitching a nonfiction book to them. I wanted to write a book about fractals, chaos, artificial life, cellular automata—my gnarly computer science interests, in other words. But they thought this idea was too been-done.

In the meantime I'd written a column for *bOING bOING* #15 which had a paragraph about a futuristic mind-recording device called a lifebox. So Mark said, "Why don't you pitch us a Wired Book of future speculation about stuff like the lifebox?" And I was into that. The close of the millennium is clearly the time to publish a book of this type. And then the editors were like, "There should be a frame for the future speculation. I mean how do you *know* this is all going to happen. Should you go to the future in a time machine? And then I started thinking it would be nice to have a UFO taking someone into the future. I'd always wanted to write about UFOs, as I feel there isn't enough good SF about UFOs. And I had certainly noticed Whitley Strieber's commercial success with *Communion*. So it seemed like a good idea to write about abduction. But rather than having *me* claiming be the one abducted, it would be someone I knew.

Meanwhile my old friend and fellow author Greg Gibson (the "Ace Weston" of *Secret of Life*) came to town. And I had a pitch-meeting with *Wired* coming up. I got the idea that to really clinch the deal, Greg should *pose* as my UFO-abductee friend. I had already fixed on the last name of "Shook" for this character because when I almost got drafted in 1967 there had been a hapless fellow conscript called Shook, and that had stuck in my mind. And when I started talking to Greg about having him pose as Shook, he said something about becoming my Frankenstein's monster, so I knew the first name had to be Frank. And of course it makes a good sentence: "Frankly, I'm Shook."

So Greg and I went to the meeting. He has long hair and is a weathered-looking guy, like a Viet vet. He posed as a very nervous and tetchy Frank Shook. And the two young *Wired* editors totally bought into it. Midway through the meeting it "got to be too much" for Greg and he stalked out. And for a few minutes the editors really didn't know if my UFO abductee friend was real or not. And after a bit I let them off the hook, and said, no, it had been an act. But they were dazzled and gave me the biggest advance by far that I ever got for any of my books, fiction or nonfiction. We were going to get my friend the underground cartoonist Paul Mavrides to do the illos. I would do sketches of the illos and Paul would redraw them.

The Wired Books editors were leaning towards promoting *Saucer Wisdom* as really being true, running it as a media hoax. And then maybe in a year we'd reveal that it had been a hoax, and get another little bit of publicity. I got more and more uncomfortable with this notion. The idea of having to lie in interviews made me uneasy. Also I was having conflicts over whether I should give Greg a cut of the advance for having helped me close the deal (in the end I didn't). Greg was into the whole trip either way, and he left some messages on my answering machine pretending to be Frank Shook.

The book had a tight deadline and I started writing it in a state of real anxiety, in March 1997. I was a little frightened of the whole subject, and it was getting off to a really weird start. To help get a leg up on it, I spent some time with my science-writer friend Nick Herbert who lives near here. Nick lives to theorize about UFOs. He was my second Frank Shook inspiration. Nick and I talked about UFOs over lunch at a restaurant called Adelita's in Boulder Creek, and this lunch served as model for my lunch with Frank. Nick's house is not unlike Frank's, although Nick's house is nicer.

My third Frank Shook inspiration was my artist friend Dick Termes, not so much for the way he acts as for where he lives, which is in North Dakota. Dick lives in a dome-shaped house and paints on spheres, he's remarkable artist. In order to come up with a finale for the book, I flew out to visit Dick in North Dakota—something I'd never done before, but had always wanted to do—and while I was there I drove from his house to the Devil's Tower and spent a day there.

When I finished the first draft, in November '97, *Wired* suddenly folded their book division. I got to keep most of the advance. But now it was hard to find a publisher for this odd orphan book. Finally David Hartwell of Tor picked it up early in 1998 and I even got another (smaller) advance.

I'd done the rough drawings for the book. I used to draw underground cartoons for the Rutgers University newspaper in the early '70s, and have always felt that I can draw, even though some might argue that I can't. I do not *try* to draw like Thurber, by the way, it just happens to look that way. Hartwell said something like, "Why not save money on the project and use Rudy's drawings? They're lively and charming. They're like the drawings a professor might put on the blackboard in a lecture. And how technically proficient do they need to be, after all, if they're supposed to be drawn by a guy who says he gets abducted by flying saucers?' So I got some new pens and redid all the drawings pretty carefully. Hartwell and Kathryn Cramer did some good editing of the text, and I finishing the illos and edits by Fall '98.

I always send all my SF manuscripts to my friend John Walker (model for the Roger Coolidge of *The Hacker and the Ants*), as John is such a knowledgeable engineer that he can spot any technical howlers I might make. He said *Saucer Wisdom* was the ultimate flowering of my transreal style; he suggested that in the 21st Century, the critical editions of this volume might include transparent overlays to point out how the various trans pieces dovetail with my real life. You might consider this note a start towards such an overlay! (Personal communication, 13 June 1999)

Nonfiction novel or not, *Saucer Wisdom* is redeemed, in the end, by flashes of just that Kerouac-flavored empiricism, that attention to the observed Real, which makes *All the Visions* more gratifying and successful than *The Secret of Life*. Sometimes these fragments seem to be doodles, vamping at the keyboard until something new finally strikes the writer (a little like the cigarettes that used to be smoked in absurd numbers by characters whose authors were momentarily stuck for something to put on the page, and had paused for one of their own). Even so, they are serviceable, and embed the lunatic revelations in Californian reality: "The next car was a whipped-to-shit van—all that was visible inside was a big beard, a nose, the brim of a mesh back hat. A tough mountain hippie. Even tougher was a hugely mustached man in a green vintage car, a fixed-up, tricked-out classic with fender skirts. There's a lot of illegal methedrine labs in the mountains; I wondered if he was from one of them" (*Saucer Wisdom*, p. 28).

This *is* the quotidian.[14] So too, in its late twentieth-century way, is the *Mondo 2000* party "Rudy" and Audrey attend:

The Brazilian Room was deep in the park on Wildcat Canyon Road. . . . Wes, the titular editor of *Mondo*, was dressed as an Arab woman named Amara. The Casbah theme had been Wes's idea. He felt that we should think of the Web as an arabesque labyrinth. The *Mondo* editors were big on understanding technology as metaphors—instead of actually learning anything hard. *Mondo* owner and chief editor Queen Mu was holed up in the kitchen, inaccessible behind starry eyes and rictuslike smile, her voice breathy and brittle, *stay away*. (P. 177)

Here is art as new journalism, as the rest of the book is popular science speculation as scat anecdote, one little story after another featuring oddly named people talking quite inventive future jive about oddly designed Dali-floppy technologies, until finally the book ends with Rudy's heart-felt prayer for sobriety. It is hard not to conclude, though, that this entire journey would be better split in two, each path followed separately: one a lively popular science exposition, in clear, of the coming bio/genetic-fueled wonders Rucker foresees, the other a knowing scientifically in-formed novel of manners in the slipstream of, say, Robert Stone or Don DeLillo.

Does this mean transrealism is dead, or vitiated, even as it is an-nounced? Not at all. Few artistic programs are summarized conclusively in one lapse of delivery, and Rucker's own arc is far from complete.

WHY, AFTER ALL, TRANSREALISM?

Four hundred years ago, as pictorial art emerged from the throttling hand of formalisms and sacred iconographies, Floris van Dijck marveled at the fresh approach of Caravaggio, who worked directly and solely from life. Arguably, this tactic reflected a *Zeitgeist* finally ready to em-brace empirical reality with both outstretched arms, often arms quickly piled up with booty or trade goods gathered from around the newly broadened globe, using tools and weapons created by the new sciences and technologies. Artists had long been the advance brush-cutters in this march toward adequate representation of the empirical real. In two strik-ingly successful fourteenth-century images showing how artistic insight and experiment preceded science, Margaret Wertheim has deployed Dante's very physical medieval hell, purgatory and paradise, and Giotto's Arena Chapel in Padua.[15] Giotto's Annunciation is an early tri-umph of perspectival rendering, complete with *trompe-l'oeil* effects lend-ing a third dimension, the depth of scientific space. Yet facing the chapel's altar is a Giotto masterpiece in the older, Dantean style, enlarged Christ at center, angels against blue spiritual space, damned and saved humans crowding below.

Between Dante's world and our own, what changed? Wertheim's al-legory explains how we use, construct, travel through and transcend space itself. The medieval world was doubled, its earthly landscape a projection of timeless sacred space. The Renaissance shifted from spirit to flesh, the Enlightenment from divine authority to space and time as Absolutes. Our own century dethrones both with relativity, placing each observer within an idiosyncratic but valid frame of reference. As a par-able, this catches the postindustrial disintegration of community. Will cyberspace, with its instant connectivity across the globe, reinstate links between atomized, lonely people? Or will it make matters worse by split-ting mind from body in a malign perversion of sacred dualities? Aloft in cyberspace's window onto endless imaginary worlds, will we forget the real pain and joys of fleshy life? Rucker's answers are ambivalent. His willful robots and moldies lust after life, which has to be renewed frequently as their fallible substrates swiftly decay. His humans often languish in gloom or accidie, yet seem pleased enough to find themselves forcibly uploaded, their lives extended and amplified in ways that alter the very nature and quality of their experience as sensate beings. As well, both orders of consciousness are drawn repeatedly into mystical vision-ary moments of bliss. Can any writing grounded in ordinary life compete with these exotic narrative temptations? That is surely Rucker's dilemma in advocating transrealism's strategies even as he capers in cyberplu-rality and multiple, superposed time dimensions.

A clue to the mitigating merits of transrealism might be found in an accolade paid to one of the premier poetic sf dreamers of the forties and fifties, Ray Bradbury, by an even greater literary master. Introducing a Spanish translation of *The Martian Chronicles* in 1954, the immensely nu-anced, subtle fabulist Jorge Luis Borges asked mournfully: "After closing the pages of the book, I wonder what this man from Illinois has done for his episodes about the conquest of another planet to fill me with such terror and solitude. How can these fantasies touch me, and in such an intimate manner?" His suggested answer is at once patronizing and acute, alarming for its truth and revelatory, perhaps, of the impulse at the heart of successful transrealist writing:

All literature (I dare to say) is symbolic; there are only a few fundamental ex-periences and it makes no difference if a writer, to convey them, resorts to the "fantastic" or to the "real," to Macbeth or Raskolnikov, to the invasion of Belgium in August 1914 or an invasion of Mars. What is the importance of the science-fiction novel? In this phantasmagoric book Bradbury has invested his long empty Sundays, his American tedium, his solitude, as Sinclair Lewis did in *Main Street*.[16]

Not only the tedium; perhaps the despair, or at least the anguish, the spiritual hurt and longing of a denuded urban wasteland choked with whirling toys, noise, affronts to our inner voices, corporate violence, spir-itual suffocation, runaway appetitive cravings ceaselessly whipped up and unslakable. Bradbury made of tedium's transcendence into cool green boyhood nostalgia an art always teetering, even at its best, on the ridiculously self-satisfied and complacently conservative. Rucker's more radical challenge, and ours at this fast-accelerating cusp of the millen-nium, is not tedium relieved by dying falls or hallucinations of semirural childhood but the brain-squeezing agony of *too much*. Little wonder Rucker's characters "seek the gnarl," the sweet slick moment of timeless bliss when intellect spins noiselessly, body moves so magically it might be pure Zen instrumentality, and everything slides smoothly, beautifully, a white-out moment that cannot, of course, in this literally sublunary world, last. The Real is more than Platonic Information. If nothing else, it is also Run-Time, the processing sequence of experience. So entropy or Phil Dick's kipple, mess, waste heat, aggravation, miscommunication, conflict, worn bearings in the machinery of the world, are its cost, as Dick told us tirelessly.

SUMMING UP

"Transrealism," we recall from the outset, "means writing about your immediate perceptions in a fantastic way."[17] It can also mean writing the fantastic in a way thickened, enriched and interrogated by conscientious scrutiny of your own immediate experience. So the gravy of actuality really does flavor young Conrad Bunger's alienated self-discovery, even as he takes his beloved for an aerial spin around the Eiffel Tower. Without the painful and sore-picking disclosures of his grubby adolescence and young manhood, his tale would be just one more wish-fulfillment flight of fancy. Rucker has wrought something deeper and more biting than that, although perhaps only just. Without the qualms and located observations of "Rudy Rucker," writer, mathematician and reformed drinker, Frank Shook's disclosures from the UFO aliens would be nothing more than a warmed-over list of notes for the final *'Ware* novels and their antic inventions. Braced by the transformed realism of Rucker's own day job in Silicon Valley, the giddy adventures of Jerzy Rugby become a curiously authentic and morally engaging foray into parts of cyberspace that more stylish virtual reality fabulists like Neal Stephenson and William Gibson can't reach.

Still, at the end of our investigation into this fresh narrative methodology, certain nagging questions remain. A major problem with the very postulate of transrealism, from both writer's and readers' viewpoints, is its flirtation with biographical fallacies and opacities. You might decide to *write* transrealistically, infusing your fantasies with the juices of your life, but how can I, the reader, know that exoterically—even if you assure me that it is so? As it happens, we do know a great deal about Philip K. Dick's complex inner and outer life and how those were translated into fiction and theophanic exegesis. We even know a certain amount about Rudy Rucker, but perhaps not nearly so much as people probably assume (recall that his use of "drugs" has been, by his testimony, very much less in quantity and exoticism than some have inferred). So how do we, finally, *read* texts securely from a transrealist standpoint, especially without hints from the (always unreliable and usually absent) author?

Rucker agrees that his term leaves us on a slippery slope.

If everything becomes transrealism, then the word is useless. Certainly schlocky no-talent books can be about the author's life. That's a bad kind of writing you see in amateurs, who might write about themselves beating out their rivals in a completely unironic and unaware way. With no consciousness of the psychological deep structure of what they are about. One wants the "transrealism" label to apply not so readily to undigested diary-hea.[18]

The term "transrealism" is itself, like science fiction, a zeugma. The *trans* component, we recall, was initially defined by Rucker as derived from "transcendental." But what is transcendental about writing? It is always local, always steeped in agendas conscious and otherwise, inevitably partial and partisan. The *trans* part is better understood, he now argues, as "transmutation," although that process, too, retains a certain mystifying alchemical allure or mystique in his account. "The real life has been transmuted in some way by the fires of SF" (Personal communication, 15 February 1999). *Realism* provides a steadying substrate for the transformative and distinctive literary exercise made possible by science fictional imagination. Indeed, a sign of transrealism might be "the presence of many precise telling details of description in the environment and telling quirkiness and singularity in the speech of the characters. A higher fractal dimension of the text, if you will. Maybe it's useful here to think about different kinds of 'realistic' painters. Impressionism is one kind of realism, Photorealism is another, Bruegel yet another, Frida Kahlo still another" (Personal communication, 15 February 1999). Transrealism is plainly a strategy that does work in varying degrees of success for its inventor (or discoverer), as it worked triumphantly for Phil Dick and a few others, even if Rucker himself has yet to achieve its best possibilities.

What would those best possibilities be? Perhaps we must wait to see. Aesthetic prescriptions are notoriously deadly and tend to be disdained or simply ignored by those who make effective and enduring art. Copying Dick, Rucker, or any of the other writers I have drawn together under the transrealist aegis, would produce only one more sharecropping franchise, the current bane of commodity science fiction. But the strategy they have pioneered seems to me to be suffusing today's most rewarding imaginative fiction, writing that is truly inscribed in the slipstream of the scientific revolution remaking our world at an ever accelerating pace. That strategy seems to me implicit in the following rule agreed by some attendants at the 1994 Sycamore Hill writing workshop, an annual mutual-criticism gathering of some of the finest sf writers in the southeast United States:[19] "The unreal situation must have some real counterpart, the science must be functional. The unreality must do something you could not do in a realistic story, something more than eliciting an emotional response. It must have an intellectual reason for being."[20]

Remarkable, the reversal of emphasis that has occurred among sf writers in the last generation or so. Once, the intellectual *raison d'etre* of a sf story was altogether taken as a given, perhaps as the single requirement (the "thought variant," the "idea as hero"). "Fine" writing, or indeed any sense of stylistic sophistication or appropriateness, was rare, and hardly a necessity. Emotional impact was always present, of course, since these were fictions to be read by people not robots, but both the more nuanced and rawest emotions of characters and readers alike tended to be shielded or sentimentalized. The transrealist prescription, to the extent that there is one, is no simple reversal of narrative values. It is grounded in an acknowledgment that writing today can find new voice, appropriate voice, in speaking truly of a life radically saturated with the machineries and insights of scientific discovery (to say nothing of its technological spin-offs, for good and ill).

Here is probably the single best way to gain benefit from the risky advance explorations of the transrealists we have examined: Allow their lessons to sink down to the bone and then find refreshed utterance (bubbled up like a gift from the inner modules of the partitioned soul and reshaped in the hard toil required of any artist) informed by both authentic immediacy and fantastic ingenuity. And, who knows, perhaps even catching a glimpse or two of the White Light, or the pink light theophanies of *Valis*—bearing in mind, of course, the unavoidable gamble that Phil Dick caught with wry irony in the last words of his wonderful, preposterously titled *Galactic Pot-Healer* (pp. 143–44):

With an asbestos glove, he tremblingly reached into the still-hot kiln and brought out the tall, now blue-and-white pot. His first pot. Taking it to a table, under direct light, he set it down and took a good look at it. He professionally appraised its artistic worth. He appraised what he had done, and, within it, what he would do, what later pots would be like, the future of them lying before him. . . .

The pot was awful.

NOTES

1. Simon Ings review of *Transreal!*, in *Foundation: The Review of Science Fiction* 54 (spring 1992): 98.

2. Philip K. Dick and Ray Nelson, *Ganymede Takeover* (1967; London: Arrow, 1971), p. 123.

3. Personal communication, 1 February 1999, where the link to Daumal's story is also noted. Is Cimön a version of the Spanish "cima" (peak or summit)? No, says Rucker; it is an "odd word" he borrowed from a dream his wife had when he was starting the book.

4. The science is described lucidly and in much greater detail in Rucker's popular science books, such as *Infinity and the Mind* (Boston: Birkhäuser, 1982) and *Mind Tools: The Five Levels of Mathematical Reality* (New York: Houghton Mifflin, 1987).

5. John L. Casti, *Paradigms Lost: Images of Man in the Mirror of Science* (London: Cardinal, 1989), p. 329.

6. Rudy Rucker, "37 Questions."

7. *Realware* was forthcoming (2000) from Avon as I wrote. I am grateful to his publisher for the opportunity to see the book in manuscript.

8. Personal communication, 19 April 1995.

9. Personal communication, 25 January 1999.

10. Personal communication, 3 February 1999.

11. Personal communication, 3 February 1999.

12. Rudy Rucker, *Wetware* (New York: Avon, 1988), p. 10.

13. Personal communication.

14. Rucker offers an implicit comparison between this passage and the beat approach to writing: "when Jack Kerouac sketches his surroundings in a cafeteria it's not like getting a schoolgirl-style letter from your cousin Beth on her first trip to New York City. The experience is being crafted and poeticized. *Trans* is happening to it; even though Jack's not an SF writer he's transmuting or transforming what he sees, making it mythic or painterly or High Art" (personal communication, 15 February 1999). This account, of course, risks weakening the case for transrealism as a special way of writing, reducing it back to a value-laden synonym for "good" or "effective" notation.

15. Margaret Wertheim discusses these works in the opening chapters of her otherwise lackluster study *The Pearly Gates of Cyberspace* (New York: Doubleday, 1999).

16. Jorge Luis Borges, "Borges on Mars," *Abaddon* 1 (spring 1998): p. 31, translated by Andrés Vaccari. This introduction to the 1955 Argentinian edition of *The Martian Chronicles* has not previously appeared in English. (I have modified Vaccari's translation slightly.)

17. Rucker, interview with John Shirley, "Introduction," *White Light* (San Francisco: Hard Wired, 1997).

18. Personal communication, 15 February 1999.

19. Their numbers have included Michael Bishop, Carol Emshwiller, Karen Joy Fowler, Lisa Goldstein, John Kessel, Nancy Kress, Jonathan Lethem, Maureen F. McHugh, James Morrow, Bruce Sterling, Connie Willis.

20. John Kessel, Mark L. Van Name and Richard Butner, Introduction, "Fun in the Burn Ward," *Intersections: The Sycamore Hill Anthology* (New York: Tor, 1996), p. 20.

Bibliography

Aldiss, Brian W. *Bury My Heart at W. H. Smith's: A Writing Life*. London: Hodder & Stoughton, 1990.

———. *"The Atheist's Tragedy* Revisited." In *The Detached Retina: Aspects of SF and Fantasy*. Liverpool University Press, 1995.

———, with David Wingrove. *Trillion Year Spree: The History of Science Fiction*. London: Gollancz, 1986.

Amis, Kingsley. *New Maps of Hell*. 1961; London: Four Square, 1963.

———, ed. *The Golden Age of Science Fiction*. London: Gollancz, 1981.

Atheling, William, Jr. (James Blish). *More Issues at Hand*. Chicago: Advent: Publishers, 1970.

Auerbach, Erich. *Mimesis: The Representation of Reality in Western Literature*. Translated by William W. Trask. 1946; Princeton, NJ: Princeton University Press, 1953.

Bailey, J. O. *Pilgrims Through Space and Time: Trends and Patterns in Scientific and Utopian Fiction*. 1974; Westport, CT: Greenwood Press, 1972.

Ballard, J. G. *Crash*. London: Jonathan Cape, 1973.

———. *The Empire of the Sun*. London: Gollancz, 1984.

———. *The Day of Creation*. London: Gollancz, 1987.

Banks, Iain M. *Use of Weapons*. London: Orbit, 1990.

———. *Excession*. London: Orbit, 1996.

Barkow, Jerome H., Leda Cosmides and John Tooby, eds. *The Adapted Mind: Evolutionary Psychology and the Generation of Culture*. New York: Oxford University Press, 1992.

Barnes, John. *Mother of Storms*. London: Millennium, 1994.

Barth, John. *Giles Goat-Boy*. 1966; London: Secker & Warburg, 1967.

———. *Lost In the Funhouse*. 1968; New York: Signet, 1980.

————. *Chimera.* 1972; London: Quarter, 1977.

————. *Sabbatical.* New York: Putnam, 1982.

————. *The Tidewater Tales: A Novel.* 1987; London: Methuen, 1988.

————. *The Last Voyage of Somebody the Sailor.* London: Hodder & Stoughton, 1991.

Barthes, Roland. *S/Z.* New York: Hill & Wang, 1974.

Bate, Walter Jackson, ed. *Criticism: The Major Texts.* New York: Harcourt, Brace and World, 1952.

Bear, Greg. *Blood Music.* New York: Arbor House, 1985; London: Gollancz, 1986.

Belsey, Catherine. *Critical Practice.* London: Methuen, 1980.

Bester, Alfred. *Tiger! Tiger!* 1956; Wendover: Goodchild, 1984.

Blackmore, Susan. *The Meme Machine.* London: Oxford University Press, 1999.

Blish, James. *After Such Knowledge.* London: Legend, 1991.

————. "The Development of a Science Fiction Writer." In *The Profession of Science Fiction: Writers on Their Craft and Ideas.* Edited by Maxim Jakubowski and Edward James. London: Macmillan, 1992.

Borges, Jorge Luis. "Borges on Mars." Translated by Andrés Vaccari. *Abaddon* 1 (spring 1998).

Broderick, Damien. *The Dreaming Dragons: A Time Opera.* Melbourne: Norstrilia Press, 1980.

————. *The Judas Mandala.* New York: Pocket Books, 1982.

————. "The Magi." In *Centaurus: The Best of Australian Science Fiction.* Edited by David G. Hartwell and Damien Broderick. 1982; New York: Tor, 1999.

————. "Postmodernism and SF." In *The Encyclopedia of Science Fiction.* Edited by John Clute and Peter Nicholls. London: Orbit, 1993.

————. *The Architecture of Babel: Discourses of Literature and Science.* Melbourne: Melbourne University Press, 1994.

————. *Reading by Starlight: Postmodern Science Fiction.* London: Routledge, 1995.

————. *The Spike: Accelerating into the Unimaginable Future.* Sydney: Reed Books/ New Holland, 1997.

————. *Theory and Its Discontents.* Geelong, Australia: Deakin University Press, 1997.

————. *The Last Mortal Generation.* Sydney: New Holland Press, 1999.

Brodkey, Harold. "Innocence." In *The Abundant Dreamer.* London: Jonathan Cape, 1989.

Brooke-Rose, Christine. *A Rhetoric of the Unreal. Studies in Narrative and Structure, Especially of the Fantastic.* Cambridge: Cambridge University Press, 1981.

Brown, Donald E. *Human Universals.* New York: McGraw-Hill, 1991.

Budrys, Algis. "Galaxy Bookshelf." *Galaxy* 27, no. 6 (January 1969).

Carter, Rita. *Mapping the Mind.* London: Weidenfeld & Nicolson, 1998.

Casti, John L. *Paradigms Lost: Images of Man in the Mirror of Science.* London: Cardinal, 1989.

Clarke, I. F. *The Pattern of Expectation: 1644–2001.* London: Jonathan Cape, 1979.

Clute, John. "Dick, Philip K." In *The Encyclopedia of Science Fiction.* Edited by John Clute and Peter Nicholls. London: Orbit, 1993.

————. "Rucker, Rudy." In *The Encyclopedia of Science Fiction.* Edited by John Clute and Peter Nicholls. London: Orbit, 1993.

———. "Slipstream SF." In *The Encyclopedia of Science Fiction*. Edited by John Clute and Peter Nicholls. London: Orbit, 1993.

Clute, John, and Peter Nicholls, eds. *The Encyclopedia of Science Fiction*. London: Orbit, 1993.

Copleston, Frederick, SJ. "The Problem of Universals." In *The History of Philosophy, Vol. 2: Mediaeval Philosophy, Part 1*. New York: Image, 1962.

Csicsery-Ronay, Istvan, Jr. "The Wife's Story," *Science Fiction Studies* 24, Part 2 (July 1997).

Davis, Erik. "Technomancer," *Village Voice Literary Supplement* (August 1989).

Davis, Mark. *Gangland: Cultural Elites and the New Generation*. Sydney: Allen & Unwin, 1997.

DePrez, Daniel. "An Interview with Philip K. Dick," *Science Fiction Review* (September 1976).

Derrida, Jacques. *Of Grammatology*. Translated by Gayatri Spivak. Baltimore: Johns Hopkins University Press, 1974.

Dick, Anne. *The Search for Philip K. Dick, 1928–1982*. Lewiston, MA: Mellen Press, 1995.

Dick, Philip K. *Eye in the Sky*. New York: Ace, 1957.

———. *The Man in the High Castle*. 1962; Harmondsworth: Penguin, 1965.

———. *The Game-Players of Titan*. New York: Ace, 1963.

———. *Martian Time-Slip*. New York: Ballantine, 1964.

———. *Three Stigmata of Palmer Eldritch*. 1964; London: Jonathan Cape, 1966.

———. *Now Wait for Last Year*. New York: Macfadden, 1968.

———. *Galactic Pot-Healer*. New York: Berkley, 1969.

———. Letter to *SF Commentary*. Reprinted in *Philip K. Dick: Electric Shepherd*. Edited by Bruce Gillespie. Melbourne: Norstrilia Press, 1975.

———. *Confessions of a Crap Artist*. New York: Entwhistle Press, 1975.

———. *A Scanner Darkly*. New York: Ballantine, 1977.

———. *I Hope I Shall Arrive Soon*. 1978; London: Grafton, 1988.

———. *Valis*. New York: Bantam, 1981.

———. *The Transmigration of Timothy Archer*. New York: Timescape, 1982.

———. *Radio Free Albemuth*. 1985; New York: Avon, 1987.

———. *The Dark-Haired Girl*. Edited by Paul Williams. Willimantic, CT: Mark V. Ziesing, 1988.

———. "Notes." In *Beyond Lies the Wub*, Vol. 1. London: Gollancz, 1988.

———. *The Broken Bubble*. London: Gollancz, 1989.

———. Introduction to *The Golden Man*. In *The Shifting Realities of Philip K. Dick*. Edited by Lawrence Sutin. New York: Vintage, 1995.

———, and Ray Nelson. *The Ganymede Takeover*. 1967; London: Arrow, 1971.

Dickens, Charles. *Hard Times*. Harmondsworth: Penguin, 1969.

Disch, Thomas M. Letter to *SF Commentary*, 67 (January 1989).

Dodderidge, Esme. *The New Gulliver*. 1979; London: The Women's Press, 1988.

Drexler, K. Eric. *Engines of Creation: the Coming Era of Nanotechnology*. New York: Doubleday Anchor, 1986.

Eagleton, Terry. *Literary Theory: An Introduction*. London: Blackwell, 1983.

Edelman, Gerald. *Bright Air, Brilliant Fire: On the Matter of Mind*. London: Allen Lane, 1992.

Egan, Greg. *Axiomatic*. London: Millennium, 1995.

———. "Learning to be Me." In *Axiomatic*. London: Millennium, 1995.

———. *Diaspora*. London: Millennium, 1997.

———. "Chaff." In *Luminous*. London: Millennium, 1998.

———. "Cocoon." In *Luminous*. London: Millennium, 1998.

———. "Luminous." In *Luminous*. London: Millennium, 1998.

———. "Mister Volition." In *Luminous*. London: Millennium, 1998.

———. "Mitochondrial Eve." In *Luminous*. London: Millennium, 1998.

———. "The Planck Dive." In *Luminous*. London: Millennium, 1998.

———. "Reasons to be Cheerful." In *Luminous*. London: Millennium, 1998.

———. "Silver Fire." In *Luminous*. London: Millennium, 1998.

———. "Transition Dreams." In *Luminous*. London: Millennium, 1998.

———. *Teranesia*. London: Gollancz, 1999.

Emshwiller, Carol. *Carmen Dog*. London: The Women's Press, 1988.

Fish, Stanley. *Is There a Text in this Class? The Authority of Interpretive Communities*. Cambridge, MA: Harvard University Press, 1980.

Fowler, Karen Joy. *Sarah Canary*. New York: Holt, 1991.

———. *Black Glass*. New York: Henry Holt, 1998.

Fowles, John. *The French Lieutenant's Woman*. London: Granada, 1971.

Foyster, John. "The Long View," *Australian Science Fiction Review* (March 1986).

Gibson, William. *Neuromancer*. New York: Ace Special, 1984.

Gillespie, Bruce. "The Non-Science Fiction Novels of Philip K. Dick (1928–82)," **brg** 1 (October 1990). [A fanzine]

———, ed. *Philip K. Dick: Electric Shepherd*. Melbourne: Norstrilia Press, 1975.

Gilman, Charlotte Perkins. *Herland*. London: The Women's Press, 1979.

Goldstein, Lisa. *The Dream Years*. London: Unwin, 1986.

Grant, Damian. *Realism*. London: Methuen, 1970.

Grant, Richard. "Git Along, Little Robot." In *The Profession of Science Fiction: Writers on their Craft and Ideas*. Edited by Maxim Jakubowski and Edward James. London: Macmillan, 1992.

Greene, Brian. *The Elegant Universe: Superstrings, Hidden Dimensions, and the Quest for the Ultimate Theory*. London: Jonathan Cape, 1999.

Gross, Paul, and Norman Levitt. *Higher Superstitions: The Academic Left and its Quarrels with Science*. Baltimore: Johns Hopkins University Press, 1994.

Guare, John. *Six Degrees of Separation*. Xeroxed filmscript, copyright 1989.

Gunn, James, ed. *The Road to Science Fiction, Vol. 5: The British Way*. Clarkston, GA: White Wolf, 1998.

Hartwell, David G. "Who Killed Science Fiction," *The New York Review of Science Fiction*, issue 103, vol. 9, no. 7 (March 1997).

———. "Slipstream Slip Sliding," *The New York Review of Science Fiction* issue 122, vol. 11, no. 2 (October 1998).

———. "Reasons to be Cheerful," *The New York Review of Science Fiction*, issue 136, vol. 12, no. 4 (December 1999).

Hemingway, Ernest. *A Farewell to Arms*. 1929; Harmondsworth: Penguin, 1974.

Humphrey, Nicholas. *A History of the Mind*. London: Chatto & Windus, 1992.

Jakubowski, Maxim, and Edward James, eds. *The Profession of Science Fiction: Writers on Their Craft and Ideas*. London: Macmillan, 1992.

James, Henry. *The Wings of a Dove*. 1902; Harmondsworth: Penguin Modern Classics, 1972.

Ings, Simon. Review of *Transreal!* In *Foundation: The Review of Science Fiction* 54 (spring 1992).

Jameson, Fredric. "Change, SF, and Marxism: Open or Closed Universes." In *Science Fiction Studies*. Edited by R. D. Mullen and Darko Suvin. New York: Gregg Press, 1976.

———. *The Political Unconscious: Narrative as a Socially Symbolic Act*. London: Methuen, 1981.

———. *Postmodernism, or The Cultural Logic of Late Capitalism*. Durham, NC: Duke University Press/Verso, 1991.

Kauffman, Stuart A. *The Origins of Order: Self-Organization of Selection in Evolution*. Oxford: Oxford University Press, 1993.

Kelso, Sylvia. Personal communication, 15 November 1998.

Kenner, Hugh. *A Homemade World: The American Modernist Writers*. New York: William Morrow, 1975.

———. "Notes Toward an Anatomy of 'Modernism.' " In *A Starchamber Quiry: A James Joyce Centennial Volume 1882–1982*. Edited by E. L. Epstein. New York and London: Methuen, 1982.

Kessel, John, Mark L. Van Name and Richard Butner. *Intersections: The Sycamore Hill Anthology*. New York: Tor, 1996.

Knight, Damon. *In Search of Wonder. Essays on Modern Science Fiction*. 2nd ed. Chicago: Advent, 1967.

Le Guin, Ursula K. *The Left Hand of Darkness*. New York: Ace SF Special, 1969.

———. *The Dispossessed*. 1974; London: Granada, 1975.

———. *Always Coming Home*. 1985; London: Gollancz, 1986.

———. *A Fisherman of the Inland Sea*. New York: HarperPrism, 1994.

———. *Four Ways to Forgiveness*. New York: HarperPrism, 1995.

Lem, Stanislaw. *Microworlds: Writings on Science Fiction and Fantasy*. London: Secker & Warburg, 1985.

———. *Hospital of the Transfiguration*. [1955]. Translated by William Brand. 1987; London: Andre Deutch, 1989.

———. *Imaginary Magnitude*. 1981; London: Mandarin, 1991.

———. *One Human Minute*. 1986; London: Mandarin, 1991.

Lethem, Jonathan. "Why Can't We All Just Live Together? A Vision of Genre Paradise Lost," *The New York Review of Science Fiction*, issue 12, vol. 11, no. 1 (September 1998).

Littlejohn, David. "The Anti-realists," *Daedalus* (spring 1963).

Lukács, Georg. *Studies in European Realism*. Translated by E. Bone. London: Merlin Press, 1950.

McHale, Brian. *Postmodern Fiction*. London: Methuen, 1987.

Macherey, Pierre. *A Theory of Literary Production*. London: Routledge & Kegan Paul, 1978.

Mackey, Douglas A. *Philip K. Dick*. Boston: Twayne, 1988.

MacLeod, Ken. *The Star Fraction*. London: Legend, 1995.

———. *The Stone Canal*. London: Legend, 1996.

———. *The Cassini Division*. London: Orbit, 1998.

———. *The Sky Road*. London: Orbit, 1999.

Marr, David. *Vision: A Computational Investigation into the Human Representation and Processing of Visual Information*. San Francisco: W. H. Freeman, 1982.

Merril, Judith. *The Year's Best S-F: Fifth Annual Edition*. New York: Dell, 1960.

Nabokov, Vladimir. *Lolita*. London: Corgi, 1961.

Pinker, Steven. *The Language Instinct*. London: Allen Lane, 1994.

————. *How the Mind Works*. London: Allen Lane, 1997.

Priest, Christopher. "Landscape Artist: The Fiction of J. G. Ballard." In *The Stellar Gauge*. Edited by M. J. Tolley and K. Singhe. Melbourne: Norstrilia, 1980.

Ramachandran, V. S. and Sally Blakeslee. *Phantoms in the Brain*. London: Fourth Estate, 1998.

Rickman, Gregg. *To the High Castle: Philip K. Dick: A Life 1928–1962*. London Beach, CA: Fragments West/The Valentine Press, 1989.

————. *"What Is This Sickness?*, Schizophrenia and *We Can Build You*." In *Philip K. Dick: Contemporary Critical Interpretations*. Edited by Samuel J. Umland. Westport, CT: Greenwood Press, 1995.

Rilke, Rainer Maria. *Duino Elegies*. Translated by Stephen Cohn. Manchester: Carcanet, 1989.

Rimbaud, Arthur. *Complete Works*. Translated by Paul Schmidt. New York: HarperColophon, 1976.

Rimmon-Kenan, Shlomith. *A Glance Beyond Doubt: Narration, Representation, Subjectivity*. Columbus: Ohio State University Press, 1996.

Robbe-Grillet, Alain. *For a New Novel: Essays on Fiction*. Translated by Richard Howard. New York: Grove Press, 1965.

Robinson, Kim Stanley. *The Novels of Philip K. Dick*. Ann Arbor, MI: UMI Research Press, 1984.

Rossener, Michaela. "Family Values." In *Nebula Award 31*. Edited by Pamela Sargent. New York: Harcourt Brace and Co., 1997.

Rucker, Rudy. *White Light*. New York: Ace, 1980.

————. *Spacetime Donuts*. New York: Ace, 1981.

————. *Infinity and the Mind*. Boston: Birkhäuser, 1982.

————. *Software*. New York: Avon, 1982.

————. *The Sex Sphere*. New York: Ace, 1983.

————. *Master of Space and Time*. 1984; New York: Baen Books, 1985.

————. *The Secret of Life*. New York: Blue Jay, 1985.

————. *Software*. New York: Avon, 1982.

————. *Wetware*. New York: Avon, 1988.

————. *Mind Tools: The Five Levels of Mathematical Reality*. New York: Houghton Mifflin, 1987.

————. *The Hollow Earth*. New York: Avon, 1990.

————. *All the Visions*. Mountain View, CA: Ocean View Books, 1991.

————. *Transreal!* Englewood, Colo.: WCS Books, 1991.

————. "A Transrealist Manifesto." In *Transreal!*. Englewood, Colo.: WCS Books, 1991.

————. *The Hacker and the Ants*. New York: Avon, 1994.

————. *Freeware*. New York: Avon, 1997.

————. Interview with John Shirley. "Introduction." In *White Light*. San Francisco: HardWired, 1997.

————. "37 Questions." A consolidated electronic file of excerpts of responses to e-mail interviewers Nozomi Ohmori, Alia Skourtsi, Michiharu Sakurai,

John Shirley, Patrick Clark, Matthias Penzel and Koen Hendrickx, unpaginated, 1994–99.

———. *Saucer Wisdom*. New York: Tor, 1999.

———. *Realware*. New York: Avon, 2000.

Russ, Joanna. *Picnic on Paradise*. New York: Ace SF Special, 1968.

———. *The Female Man*. New York: Bantam, 1975.

———. *The Two of Them*. New York: Berkley, 1978.

———. *The Adventures of Alyx*. 1983; London: The Women's Press, 1985.

Russell, Mary Doria. *The Sparrow*. 1996; New York: Ballantine Books, 1997.

———. *Children of God*. New York: Villard, 1998.

Ryman, Geoff. *The Unconquered Country*. London: Allen & Unwin, 1986.

Sacks, Oliver. *Seeing Voices*. London: Picador, 1991.

Shepard, Lucius. *The Jaguar Hunter*. London: Paladin, 1988.

Silverberg, Robert. "Gresham's Law and Science Fiction." In *Nebula Awards 31*. Edited by Pamela Sargent. New York: Harcourt Brace, 1997.

Slusser, George. "The Frankenstein Barrier." In *Fiction 2000: Cyberpunk and the Future of Narrative*. Edited by George Slusser and Tom Shippey. Athens: University of Georgia Press, 1992.

Slusser, George, and Tom Shippey, eds. *Fiction 2000: Cyberpunk and the Future of Narrative*. Athens: University of Georgia Press, 1992.

Smith, Cordwainer. *Norstrilia*. New York: Ballantine, 1975.

Sokal, Alan, and Jean Bricmont. *Intellectual Impostures: Postmodern Philosophers' Abuse of Science*. London: Profile Books, 1998.

Stableford, Brian. "And He Not Busy Being Born," *Interzone* 16 (1986).

———. "How Should a Science Fiction Story End?" *The New York Review of Science Fiction*, issue 78, vol. 7, no. 6 (February 1995).

Stapledon, Olaf. *Star Maker*. 1937; Harmondsworth: Penguin, 1972.

———. *Sirius: A Fantasy of Love and Discord*. 1944; Harmondsworth: Penguin, 1979.

Sterling, Bruce. "Catscan 5,"*Science Fiction Eye* 1, no. 5 (July 1989).

———. "About 'Our Neural Chernobyl.' " In *Paragons: Twelve Master Science Fiction Writers Ply Their Craft*. Edited by Robin Wilson. New York: St. Martin's Press, 1996.

———. *Holy Fire*. London: Millennium, 1996.

Stevens, Wallace. *Opus Posthumous*. Edited by Samuel French Morse. New York: Knopf, 1957.

Sturgeon, Theodore. *More Than Human*. New York: Farrar Straus and Young/ Ballantine, 1953; London: Gollancz: 1986.

———. *The Cosmic Rape*. New York: Dell, 1958; New York: Pockt, 1977.

———. "The Skills of Xanadu." In *The Golden Helix*. New York: Dell, 1979.

Suppes, P., B. Han and Z. L. Lu. "Brain-wave Recognition of Sentences." *Proceedings of the National Academy of Sciences* 95, no. 26 (22 December 1998): 15861–66.

Sutin, Lawrence. *Divine Invasions: A Life of Philip K. Dick*. New York: Harmony Books, 1989.

———. *In Pursuit of Valis: Selections from the Exegesis*. Novato, CA: Underwood-Miller, 1991.

———. ed. *The Shifting Realities of Philip K. Dick: Selected Literary and Philosophical Writings*. New York: Vintage, 1995.

Swanwick, Michael. *Vacuum Flowers*. New York: Ace, 1988.

———. *Stations of the Tide*. New York: Ace, 1991.

Talbot, Norman. "The Maltreatment of Fantasy." *Australian Science Fiction Review* (March 1988).

Tipler, Frank. *The Physics of Immortality: Modern Cosmology, God and the Resurrection of the Dead*. London: Macmillan, 1995.

Tolley M. J., and K. Singhe, eds. *The Stellar Gauge*. Melbourne: Norstrilia, 1980.

Tolstoy, L. N. *Anna Karenin*. Translated by Rosemary Edmonds. Harmondsworth: Penguin, 1954.

Turner, George. *In the Heart or in the Head*. Melbourne: Norstrilia, 1984.

———. *The Sea and Summer*. London: Faber, 1987.

Turner, George, ed. *The View from the Edge: A Workshop of Science Fiction Stories with Vonda McIntyre and Christopher Priest*. Melbourne: Norstrilia Press, 1977.

Updike, John. *Self-Consciousness: Memoirs*. 1989; New York: Fawcett Crest, 1990.

———. *Toward the End of Time*. London: Hamish Hamilton, 1998.

Vinge, Vernor. *Marooned in Realtime*. London: Pan, 1987.

———. *A Fire Upon the Deep*. New York: Tor, 1991.

———. Talk given at VISION-21 Symposium sponsored by NASA Lewis Research Center and the Ohio Aerospace Institute, 30–31 March 1993.

———. *A Deepness in the Sky*. New York: Tor, 1999.

Vonnegut, Kurt. *The Sirens of Titan*. 1959; London: Gollancz, 1986.

———. *Cat's Cradle*. 1963; Harmondsworth: Penguin, 1965.

———. *Slaughterhouse-5*. 1969; London: Panther, 1972.

———. *Breakfast of Champions*. 1973; London: Panther, 1974.

———. *Galapagos*. London: Jonathan Cape, 1985.

Watts, Alan W. *Psychotherapy East and West*. 1961; New York: Mentor, 1963.

Wertheim, Margaret. *The Pearly Gates of Cyberspace*. New York: Doubleday, 1999.

Whittemore, Edward, *The Sinai Tapestry*. 1977; London: Magnum, 1979.

———. *Jerusalem Poker*. 1978; London: Magnum, 1980.

———. *Nile Shadows*. New York: Holt, Rinehart and Winston, 1983.

———. *Jericho Mosaic*. New York: Norton, 1987.

Williams, Paul. Introduction. In Philip K. Dick, *Confessions of a Crap Artist*. New York: Entwhistle Press, 1975.

———. *Selected Letters of Philip K. Dick*. 5 vols. Novato, CA: Underwood-Miller, 1991–.

Williamson, Jack. *The Legion of Space*. 1935; New York: Pocket Books, 1980.

Willis, Connie. *Lincoln's Dreams*. New York: Bantam, 1987.

———. "Even the Queen." In *The Year's Best Science Fiction: Tenth Annual Collection* (pp. 62–75). Edited by Gardner Dozois. New York: St. Martin's Press, 1993.

Wyndham, John. *The Day of the Triffids*. 1951; Harmondsworth: Penguin, 1954.

Index

About the Author

DAMIEN BRODERICK is a Fellow in the Department of English and Cultural Studies at the University of Melbourne. He is the author of several science fiction novels. In addition, he has published numerous articles and short stories, along with several scholarly books on science fiction.

ISBN 0-313-31121-8

HARDCOVER BAR CODE